DOWNERS GROVE PUBLIC LIBRARY

DOWNERS GROVE PUBLIC LIBRARY
3 1191 00288 9624

JUN 3 0 1988

S0-BCA-047

WITHDRAWN
DOWNERS GROVE PUBLIC LIBRARY

623.443 THO
Thompson, Leroy.
Great combat handguns

4/97
38

Keep 11-08

GREAT COMBAT HANDGUNS

GREAT COMBAT HANDGUNS

A guide to using, collecting and training with handguns

Leroy Thompson & René Smeets
edited by John Walter

BLANDFORD PRESS
POOLE · NEW YORK · SYDNEY

First published in the UK 1987 by Blandford Press
Link House, West Street, Poole, Dorset BH15 1LL

Copyright © Blandford Books Ltd, 1987

Distributed in the United States by
Sterling Publishing Co, Inc,
2 Park Avenue, New York, NY 10016

Distributed in Australia by
Capricorn Link (Australia) Pty Ltd
PO Box 665, Lane Cove, NSW 2066

ISBN 0-7137-144 4 4

British Library Cataloguing in Publication Data

Thompson, Leroy
    Great combat handguns : a guide to using,
    collecting and training with handguns.
    1. Pistols
    I. Title   II. Smeets, Rene
    683.4'32   TS537

All rights reserved. No part of this book may be
reproduced or transmitted in any form or by any
means, electronic or mechanical, including photocopying,
recording or any information storage and retrieval
system, without permission in writing from the Publisher.

Typeset by Furlongers, Bournemouth
Printed and bound in Great Britain by
Butler & Tanner Ltd, Frome and London

Note

Throughout this book, to prevent unnecessarily cluttering the text, only the principal dimensions have been given in dual metric/imperial terms. Most of the range tests and shooting results appear 'as measured', and all bullet weights are expressed in grains (abbreviated throughout as gn) rather than grams (gm). The majority of exploded diagrams are from manufacturers' material, and where possible these use the manufacturer's own number systems.

Useful conversion factors

To convert grains to ounces – multiply by 0.00229
To convert grains to grams – multiply by 0.0648
To convert inches to millimetres – multiply by 25.4
To convert ounces to grams – multiply by 28.35
To convert pounds to kilograms – multiply by 0.454
To convert feet to metres – multiply by 0.305
To convert yards to metres – multiply by 0.914
To convert ounces to grains – multiply by 437.5
To convert grams to grains – multiply by 15.43
To convert millimetres to inches – multiply by 0.0394
To convert grams to ounces – multiply by 0.0353
To convert kilograms to pounds – multiply by 2.205
To convert metres to feet – multiply by 3.281
To convert metres to yards – multiply by 1.0937

Contents

Preface

Testing and evaluation

Any book such as this is inevitably subjective and the thousands of miles separating the authors complicates selection. As the revolver is appreciably more important in the USA than Europe, the attention given to Charter Arms, Colt, Ruger and Smith & Wesson is necessarily more comprehensive than that given to the individual European gunmakers who, considered corporately, produce a far greater number of differing designs.

Though the US gun-market is vast in size and distribution, it operates within a single national border. Despite the occasional quirks of individual state legislation, American-made guns are readily obtainable for testing. In Europe, unfortunately, barriers of trade, language, law and politics often hinder the acquisition of 'foreign' pistols by private individuals.

Though John Browning was American, some of his finest designs were manufactured in Belgium. Browning excepted, virtually all the major pistol inventors have been European, largely because the indigenous American automatic has never attracted the attention paid to the revolvers of Colt and Smith & Wesson, or, latterly, modern companies such as Ruger and Charter Arms. As a result, the choice of a European-made combat automatic is particularly vast.

Few of the small automatic pistols made in Europe are considered as 'combat guns' in their countries of origin. Though they may interest American enthusiasts seeking 'back-up' weapons, their European distribution is greatly restricted by law. In France, for example, the standard five-year licence grants gun ownership and an annual allocation of 500 rounds; in Britain, the firearms licence is renewable annually; in other countries, uniformed policemen are not even allowed to carry a gun off duty. Consequently, these small pistols are not only difficult to obtain but also rarely used.

The guns evaluated for this book include some classics, dating back to the turn of the century, and many brand-new designs. Each has been chosen because it offers features making it specially attractive for combat use, or is so widely used by police, civilians and military agencies that it could not be overlooked. Guns that have yet to achieve full commercial production, such as the Bren Ten and the Smith & Wesson Model 645, have not been included. Some pistols have proved impossible to obtain, owing to manufacturers' understandable reluctance to release guns before the inevitable teething troubles have been eliminated: years may elapse between the announcement of a new design and the appearance of guns in the shops. Walther, for example, declined to submit a P88 and it took superhuman efforts to obtain the Heckler & Koch P7M13 and SIG P226.

Other highly specialized or rarely encountered guns have been omitted, like the German Korriphila pistol, together with military guns unobtainable commercially — including the French MAC 50 — and burst-fire 'machine pistols' such as the Heckler & Koch VP70, the Beretta 93R and the Russian Stechkin.

We believe we have selected many of the best and most widely available combat guns, plus some poorer performers whose inclusion is warranted by misleading advertising claims. No-one needs 25 handguns, yet there are appreciably more than 25 combat-worthy European automatic pistols alone. While using this book as a basis for choosing a combat gun, therefore, the evaluations should be read with particular attention to the situations in which the gun is likely to be used. In this way, a decision can be based on substance rather than mere theory. The more varied tasks a handgun must fulfil, however, the more difficult selection becomes; and the best combat handgun may well be whatever is one's hand when life is threatened. But it makes sense to stack the odds on survival by selecting as efficient a gun as possible. Even though the ultimate choice is yours, we hope we have provided some useful guidance.

LEROY THOMPSON
RENE SMEETS

Combat Handguns

I. Europe: the early days

Handgun combat shooting undoubtedly has its origins in Europe, with the invention of the wheel-lock cavalry pistol. Until the eighteenth century, the wheel-lock and its improved successors — the snaphaunce and the flintlock — remained exclusively martial, and confined largely to mounted units. Unlike a longarm, the pistol could be manipulated in one hand while holding the reins with the other. For much of the 'cavalry period' before the First World War, until the machine-gun destroyed the massed charge for ever, the pistol remained a primary weapon alongside the sabre and the carbine.

The cavalry pistols were originally carried as a pair, in large holsters affixed to the saddle, but little thought was given to sophisticated pistol fighting techniques — quite unlike the 'scientific' study of the lance or sabre. Most cavalrymen simply charged up to the enemy, fired both pistols as rapidly as possible from close range, and then retired smartly to reload.

During the eighteenth century, however, new uses were found for the pistol, by now a shorter, lightened flintlock. The reduction in size allowed guns to be carried for personal defence and — the inevitable corollary — personal aggression. Increasing numbers of private citizens carried one or more short pistols to fight off the bands of marauders that haunted many a dark city street. Firing was almost always point-blank, or at least at ultra-short range, with the only proviso that the gun should be pointed in the direction of the target. If the shot missed, and the gun was insufficiently sturdy to be used as a club, the firer was best advised to run. During this period, experiments were made to increase firepower: magazine and revolving pistols were tested, with-

out success, though guns such as the 'duck's foot', which fired a swathe of lead from its splayed multiple barrels, enjoyed brief popularity. Though poor contemporary technology hindered developments, the breech-loading 'turn off' pistol, particularly popular in Britain, undoubtedly improved accuracy.

One important role filled by the pistol, particularly during the eighteenth and early nineteenth centuries, was in settling the nobility's affairs of honour: the duel. The importance of a single well-aimed shot was such that many of the greatest gunmakers of their time — Manton and Mortimer in England, Boutet in Napoleonic France — produced splendid matched pairs of duelling pistols, works of art that incorporated refinements such as muzzle-heavy barrels, hair-triggers, roller-borne frizzens and proprietary designs of pan and butt. Even the perfection early in the nineteenth century of the first 'scent bottle' percussion lock by a Scottish clergyman, Alexander Forsyth, initially did little but improve the certainty of a dueller's ignition.

The importance of duelling, and its chivalric code, ensured that every gentleman worthy of name trained assiduously with pistol and sword. Against such a backcloth, it is scarcely surprising that attention was also paid to the stance as well as the tools of the trade. During this period, the classic standing position was evolved in an attempt to minimize the target offered by one shooter to his rival in the absence of cover. The current international rapid-fire and 50m Free Pistol courses still embody some of the traditional elements of the duellists' art.

The duel, the first codified combat shooting, seems irrational by modern standards — but it must be remembered that the goal was as much to uphold a code of honour as promote deadly shooting. The idea that one participant, having fired and missed, should not move until his opponent had his chance to kill him clearly belongs to another age. However, experienced duellists soon

The birth of combat handgunning: the wheel-lock pistol, a cavalry weapon fired at close range.

learned to fire directly on the umpire's signal to gain a definite advantage; not only did it facilitate the first hit, preventing the opponent firing back, but it was known that nervous men often fired back instinctively even in unfavourable conditions. The cunning exponent of the duel stood upwind and fired first, so that the drift of his powder smoke inhibited his opponent's aim. The discipline necessary to fire as fast as possible, by gradually clearing one's mind and honing one's reactions, bears some similarity to modern-day martial arts techniques whose values are often overlooked in combat shooting.

II. America: the dawn of the revolver

Some of the earliest combat handguns used in the United States of America were the large flintlock dragoon pistols, used by cavalrymen at short range, and the comparatively few Kentucky pistols. The US Army had the ·54-calibre Harper's Ferry pistol, adopted in 1805, and though many other guns were acquired early in the century, most were cumbersome coach or saddle pistols. Even the 'concealment arms' of the day were bulky by modern standards.

Perhaps the most important single event in the development of reliable combat handguns was the perfection of the self-contained percussion cap, generally credited to Joshua Shaw in about 1816 (though his researches probably commenced a little earlier). Though an American inventor, Elisha Collier, had produced a surprisingly good mechanically-operated flintlock revolver in this period, it was left to Samuel Colt to perfect the cap-lock repeater. Whether we

may believe Colt's celebrated explanation of his 'flash of genius', inspired by the spokes of a riverboat's wheel, or suspect he knew more of Collier's endeavours than he ever admitted, the fact remains that his initial patent was granted in 1835 and the first Paterson Colts appeared a short time later. The earliest Colt ventures failed, after only small numbers of revolvers and revolving rifles had been made, but the Walker Colt of 1847 and the Pocket Revolver of 1849 paved the way for the amazingly successful ·36 Navy Colt of 1851. A ·44 Army Revolver followed in 1860, setting the standards of the US Civil War's combat handguns. However, the 'Pocket Model' Colts were comparatively large even for the deep pockets of the day.

The early champion of concealability was the Philadelphia Deringer, attributed to the gunsmith/gun-dealer Henry Deringer. The name is usually corrupted to 'derringer', the spelling preferred here on the basis of common use. During the California Gold Rush of 1849, for example, the derringer was indispensable to miners, gamblers, saloon girls: in fact, to anyone needing handy protection. In the goldfields, that meant virtually everyone. Another popular small gun was the Pepperbox, a multi-barrel proto-revolver capable of delivering four, five, six or more rapid shots when the need arose. Though the origins of the Pepperbox lay in Europe, great numbers were sold in the Americas before the perfection and subsequent dispersal of the percussion revolver.

In 1857, Horace Smith and Daniel Wesson marketed an innovative revolver whose cylinder, with its bored-through chambers, accepted self-contained metal-case ammunition with priming compound in the prominent rim. Though the pioneering Model No.1 was only obtainable with the ineffectual ·22 Short Rimfire round, it heralded a great advance in combat handgun efficiency. During the US Civil War, many Union (Federal) officers carried a small Smith & Wesson revolver to guard against the failure or loss of the larger service-issue guns.

The Civil War required enormous quantities of handguns. The Union forces were primarily armed with Colts or Remingtons, but there were appreciable quantities of Starrs, Whitneys and other service-calibre revolvers. Though Colts were also popular in the Confederacy, such guns were in desperately short supply. As the Southern states had few manufacturing facilities, most Confederate revolvers were acquired in Europe despite the production of a few Colt or Whitney copies made by Griswold & Gunnison, Leech & Rigdon and Spiller & Burr. A particularly interesting import was the French-made Le Mat, whose ·65-calibre shot barrel doubled as the axis pin for the conventional revolver cylinder. The wielder of the Le Mat, therefore, had nine ·40-calibre shots plus a charge of shot for use at close-quarters. Though the Le Mat is not an American design, most of its combat use occurred in the Civil War and it played an important part in US combat handgun development.

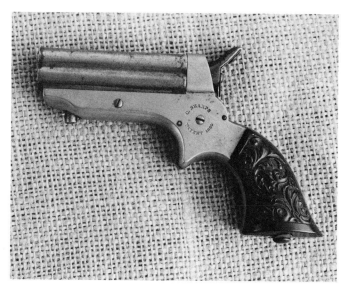

The Sharps four-barrelled derringer was a popular 'hide-out' gun in the late nineteenth century. (Courtesy of Bob Arganbright.)

The gambler's and dance-hall girl's favourite close-quarters gun: the Remington ·41 derringer.

One of the all-time classic combat handguns — The Colt Single Action Army Revolver of 1873. (Courtesy of Bob Arganbright.)

This Merwin-Hulbert ·44-40, an early full-bore pocket revolver, saw action on the Western frontier.

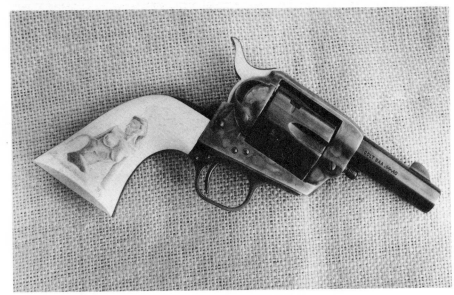

A short-barrelled ·44-40 Colt Single Action Army 'Sheriff's Model'. (Courtesy of Bob Arganbright.)

The Colt Lightning Revolver, in ·38 and ·41 calibres, was a popular combat gun from its introduction in 1877. Henry McCarty — alias William Bonney, or 'Billy the Kid' — was one of its principal advocates. (Courtesy of Bob Arganbright.)

The Colt Bisley revolver, specifically developed for target shooting. Note the flattened hammer spur compared with the standard Colt Single Action Army guns (see page 9), which improved the firer's view of the sights. (Courtesy of Bob Arganbright.)

Smith & Wesson's top-break Safety Hammerless Revolver, generally known as the 'Lemon Squeezer', was the most popular pocket revolver in the early years of the twentieth century.

The Borchardt pistol, patented in 1893, was the first commercially successful automatic. A little over three thousand were made in 1894-7. (Courtesy of John Walter.)

III. The late nineteenth century

Despite the exportation of French Le Mat revolvers during the US Civil War, together with the fragile Lefaucheux pinfires, the European combat handgun scene was in the doldrums during the middle of the nineteenth century. Most of the military authorities remained wedded to the concept of enormous single-shot percussion pistols, a tradition that was to persist well into the 1880s in some countries, while the commercial market was satisfied with a variety of pepperboxes and percussion revolvers, plus pinfire guns offering self-contained metallic cartridges at the expense of a dangerously exposed igniter pin.

Initially, the impact of the US-style percussion revolver in Europe was minimal, despite a particularly acrimonious campaign waged between Colt and the Englishman Robert Adams, whose large-calibre double-action revolver was preferred to the Navy Colt by many enthusiasts. The British, largely on account of widespread colonial experience, were particularly suspicious of guns with a calibre as small as ·36.

In the second half of the nineteenth century, the US market was completely dominated by the revolver, which answered needs ranging from short-range defence in the prospering towns of the eastern seaboard, gunfights in El Paso or Dodge City, to cattle-driving through the empty wastes of Kansas and Missouri. In 1870, Smith & Wesson introduced their No.3 single action ·44; three years later, sensing a loosening grip on the market, Colt replied with the Single Action Army Revolver (the 'Peacemaker'), destined to become the classic heavy combat revolver of the American West. The Smith & Wesson Schofield Model also entered production in 1873, while Remington produced a high quality holster revolver from 1875 until the 1890s. Though much less known, Merwin & Hulbert offered revolvers in ·44-40, some of which were sufficiently compact to be the large-bore 'snubs' of their day, along with some awesome Webley 'Bulldog' revolvers chambering cartridges as large as the ·476 Eley or ·577 Boxer.

The real pocket revolvers of the period, however, were the ·32 and ·38 top-break Smith & Wessons introduced in 1880, to be followed in 1886 by the classic S&W double action Safety Hammerless Model or 'Lemon Squeezer' — so called owing to its grip safety. Colt had introduced the 'Cloverleaf' and Pocket Model revolvers in 1871, and, in 1877, had added the Colt Lightning double-action revolver in ·38 and ·41-calibre. However, its much-admired novelty soon paled in the West once the delicacy of the. trigger system became obvious.

The readily concealable ·41 rimfire Remington 'over-and-under' two-barrel derringer, dating from 1866, was extremely popular with gamblers, lawmen and others who needed a hideout or back-up gun. Iver Johnson, Hopkins & Allen, Harrington & Richardson and others all specialized in small ·32 or ·38-calibre top-break revolvers during the last quarter of the the nineteenth century.

By the mid 1870s, greatly assisted by the efforts of inventors such as Adams, Tranter and Webley in Britain, and Chamelot & Delvigne or Nagant in Belgium, the revolver was also well established in Europe. The trend, however, was to smaller guns that could be supplied in presentation cases; combat shooting, in the manner practised in the American West, was all but unknown. During this period, the European revolver enthusiast favoured target shooting rather than combat training; and apart from the British Army, dispersed worldwide, few European armies used revolvers in anger. As the guns were largely issued to officers and senior NCOs, to be used only in emergencies, small size and comparatively small calibre were often desirable. The differing approaches may be seen by comparing the perfected Swiss service revolver of 1882 — an elegant gun firing an ineffectual 7.5mm cartridge — with the contemporary US Army revolver, the ·45 Colt M1873! Only the British were prepared to investigate combinations of power and efficacy, adopting, alone among the European powers, the efficient auto-extracting top-break Webley in the autumn of 1887. The slow-moving ·455 Webley bullet had great stopping power, and was destined to prove itself during the First World War. But the British Army was an exception; the attitude of Europe is better expressed by the

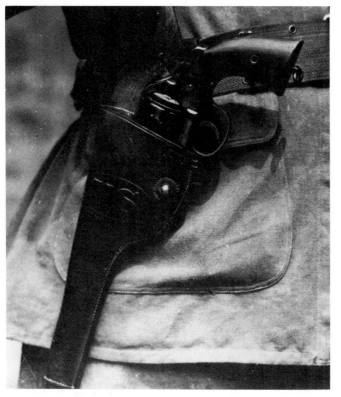

Colt's Model 1892 Army Revolver lacked stopping power. Experiences in the Philippine Islands convinced the US Army that something more powerful was needed, leading to the eventual introduction of the ·45 M1911 Colt-Browning. (US National Archives, photograph 165-WW-3872-2.)

Smith & Wesson's famed Model 10, still in production, is one of the most famous of all combat guns. This is the 'Victory Model', produced during the Second World War.

Germans, who rejected a break-action Mauser revolver in favour of the simplest of simple 10.6mm-calibre solid-frame guns in 1879. As the role of the NCOs was supervisory, the Germans decided, they should not be involved in combat; thus, the revolver had no extraction system, the ejector rod being carried separately atop the cartridge box.

Once double-action metallic-cartridge revolvers began to dominate the combat revolver markets, the only major innovation missing was rapid reloading, the ejector rod of guns such as the Colt being essentially cumbersome. Webley, the champion of top-break and auto-extraction, rapidly became the leader in European revolver design once Chamelot & Delvigne had been eclipsed and the impact of the Nagant brothers began to recede under the onslaught of the automatic pistol. In the USA, the solution proved to be the swing-out cylinder; companies such as Harrington & Richardson and Iver Johnson championed small-calibre top-break revolvers commercially, but the US Army was unimpressed. The first yoke-mounted swinging cylinder revolvers were the Colt Navy Model of 1889 and Army Model of 1892, both chambered for the ·38 Long Colt cartridge

that was to prove such an ineffectual manstopper in the Philippines that the ·45 ACP was ultimately substituted. Smith & Wesson produced its first swinging-cylinder revolver, the Hand Ejector Model, in 1896. These early yoked-cylinder Colts and Smith & Wessons were the prototypes of the principal US twentieth-century combat revolvers.

IV. The rise of the automatic pistol

While the revolver was attaining its majority, efforts were being made to develop smokeless propellant – experiments, indeed, that began in the 1830s but were doomed to failure until the stabilization of nitroglycerine, the perfection of guncotton and progress through cordite to the French Poudre B, adopted with the 8mm French Lebel rifle and cartridge in 1887. During this period, many inventors had been testing mechanically operated pistols, relying on systems of links and rods to transform a pull on the trigger or an accompanying lever into sufficient power to extract, eject and reload. These experiments were doomed to failure, but may be seen to have loosened something of the hold of the revolver on the Central European inventive mind.

Many of the earliest automatic pistols also failed. Almost all were clumsy, many were unreliable and some chambered badly designed cartridges. Only the Borchardt, introduced commercially in 1894, experienced much success among the earliest guns; its greatest legacy, however, is that the 7.65 and 9mm Parabellum cartridges were both based on it. In addition, owing to a complicated tangle of fortunes, the Loewe organisation allowed Mauser to take the Borchardt cartridge for the Mauser 'Broomhandle'. Where these guns led, many others followed. Initially, the work of inventors such as Georg Luger and John Browning had little impact on a market still obsessed with the revolver. By 1900, however, the perfected Borchardt-Luger pistol (the Parabellum, or 'Luger') and the first locked-breech double-link or 'parallel-motion' Colt-Brownings had paved the way towards military acceptance of the automatic pistol.

Soon, the commercial market was flooded with surprisingly effectual personal-defence pistols, inspired by the blowback Brownings made in Belgium by Fabrique Nationale and in the USA by Colt. Beginning in 1900, a million Mle 1900, Mle 1903, 1906 vintage 'Baby' and Mle 1910 FN-Browning pistols had sold by 1914, not even counting hundreds of thousands of Colt-made guns sold in the USA. Fortunes were to made by the great distributors such as Manufacture d'Armes et Cycles de Saint-Etienne and A.L.Frank ('ALFA') of Hamburg, whose catalogues clearly illustrate the profusion of small European-made pistols jockeying for supremacy with the cheap Continental revolvers (mostly Belgian), better products such as Webleys

and Nagants, and the more desirable American imports.

The decade preceding the First World War saw a scramble to adopt the new self-loaders, or 'automatics' as they were popularly known. From this period come two of the classic combat handguns of all time: the German army Luger, the Pistole 08, and the US Army's M1911 Colt Browning. These guns typify radically differing approaches to combat-pistol shooting on the opposite sides of the Atlantic. The German gun, small and somewhat delicate, fired a comparatively small-diameter 9mm bullet (actually ·357in) with surprising accuracy; the American gun, sturdy and comparatively simple, fired the man-stopping ·45 ACP with acceptable accuracy.

The European shooting scene spawned a myriad shooting clubs like the famous Baerenzwinger Club in Berlin, numbering among its members Georg Luger and the renowned authority on pistol-shooting, Gerhard Bock. The clubs' patrons were often drawn from the aristocracy, their social success was considerable and their stilted disciplined shooting styles greatly influenced military practice. Though the value of accuracy was propounded constantly, no attempt was made assess the known effects of combat stress or to combine accurate shooting with more stressful rapid fire. Even in the 1930s, many army manuals − British, Belgian, German and French alike − show the same rigid stances and the same emphasis on scores.

During this period, few restrictions were placed on the

The Borchardt (see page 11) led to the Borchardt-Luger pistol, better known as the 'Parabellum' or the 'Luger'. The gun shown here is an example of the Old Model, adopted by the Swiss army in 1900. (Courtesy of John Walter.)

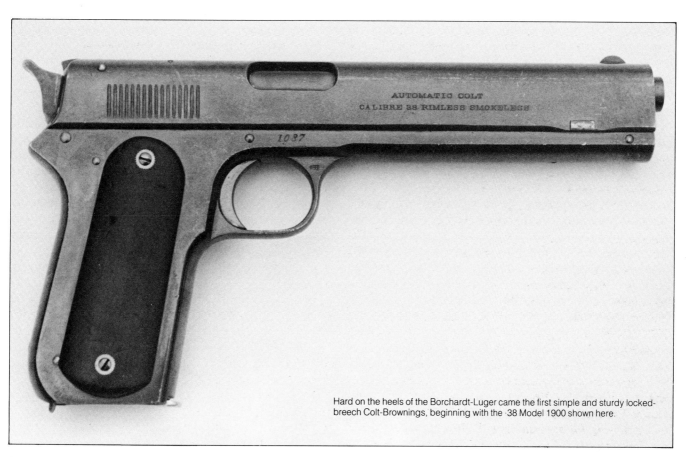

Hard on the heels of the Borchardt-Luger came the first simple and sturdy locked-breech Colt-Brownings, beginning with the ·38 Model 1900 shown here.

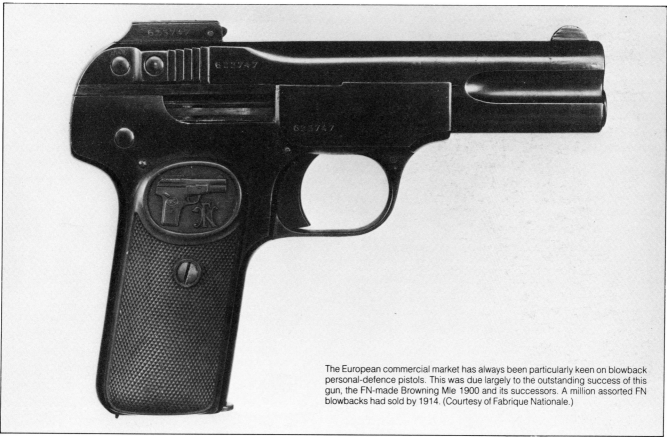

The European commercial market has always been particularly keen on blowback personal-defence pistols. This was due largely to the outstanding success of this gun, the FN-made Browning Mle 1900 and its successors. A million assorted FN blowbacks had sold by 1914. (Courtesy of Fabrique Nationale.)

purchase, wear and use of firearms. The police, whether uniformed or plain-clothed, were universally armed (except in Britain). However, as most of the Continental European population could also be armed when necessary, the law-enforcement agencies had no monopoly on firearms; additionally, 'street shooting' was not considered a primary police role, as each citizen was allowed to defend not only himself but other people when the need arose. As time passed, this concept was being challenged by nationalists, anarchists and revolutionaries, whose successes included the assassination of the Archduke Franz Ferdinand at Sarajevo in 1914, precipitating the First World War , and the murder of the King of Yugoslavia in Paris in 1934. The exploits of these forerunners of modern urban guerrillas even caused the formation of what would now be called counter-terroriest units in France and other European countries. Yet the handgun still remained a very close combat weapon with no specialist training other than wholly inappropriate long-range military style practice: most of the contemporary reports indicate that the ratio of hits to shots fired was very poor indeed, due not to the inaccuracy of the guns but simply to the lack of 'combat training'.

Gradually, increasing political instability caused the steady restriction of guns to 'acceptable' agencies; for example, the British Firearms Act of 1920 began a cycle of legislation that not only finally curtailed the private ownership of handguns but also destroyed the British handgun-making industry. Even in the Germany of the Third Reich, a national law passed in 1938 successfully removed firearms from the hands of many private individuals. The German occupation of large tracts of Europe deprived the indigenous population of guns, the cumulative effect of such acts being, in the final analysis, to ensure that handguns are less common in the modern Europe than they were seventy years ago.

Colt's ·34 Government Model (·45 Automatic Pistol, Model of 1911) was a simplification of the earlier 'parallel motion' guns of 1900-7, using a single link to unlock the tipping barrel from the breech.

Shortly after the adoption of the Colt automatic, these US Army men proudly display their new issue sidearm. (US National Archives, photograph 165-CB-3216.)

V. The USA scene, 1918-41

Among the early US automatics were the Savages, a ·32 version of which was developed after a ·45 gun had been submitted (unsuccessfully, as it turned out) to the US Army pistol trials of 1906-7. Smith & Wesson's ·35 gun appeared in 1913, but the company soon discovered that the odd chambering adversely affected sales and a ·32 version was substituted in 1924. A few years earlier, the best US-made pocket pistol of the early twentieth century — the Pedersen designed Model 51 — had been marketed by Remington in ·32 and ·380 ACP. Unfortunately, the Model 51 was comparatively expensive, and its promising career was cut short by the Depression; by 1934, sales had been discontinued.

Despite the development of the automatic pistol, revolvers remained the principal American combat handgun during the inter-war period. One of the first classic designs, the S&W Hand Ejector Military & Police, appeared in 1899 and is still in production as the Model 10 (see directory section). Another important early Smith & Wesson was the ·44 Hand Ejector of 1908. This was the precursor of all the later large-frame S&W magnums, including the Models 25, 26, 27, 28, 29 and 57. During the 1930s, Smith & Wesson continued to develop their revolver line with the ·38/44 Heavy Duty (1930), which was followed in 1935 by the legendary ·357 Magnum.

In 1927, Colt had begun to tap a large market among police and civilians for ·38 Special revolvers expressly designed for concealment. The resulting Detective Special was the classic 'snub' of the next three decades of cinema films. Though the short-barrelled Smith & Wesson Military & Police revolver had been available for some years, the first true S&W 'snub' was the Chief's Special of 1950.

By the time of the US entry into the Second World War, at the end of 1941, only the commercial variants of the ·45 Colt Government Model and the Colt-Browning pocket pistols had made much of a dent in the supremacy of the excellent Colt and S&W revolvers.

The 1910-model FN-Browning blowback was another of the popular European personal-defence guns. (Courtesy of Fabrique Nationale.)

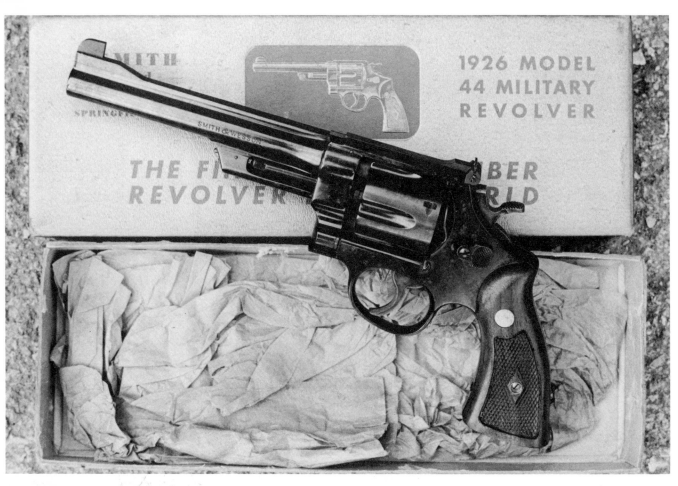

The Smith & Wesson N-Frame ·44 Special revolver was a predecessor of the ·44 Magnum, and an effective combat handgun in its own right.

Smith & Wesson's ·38/44 'Outdoorsman', introduced in 1931, was the immediate precursor of the ·357 Magnum.

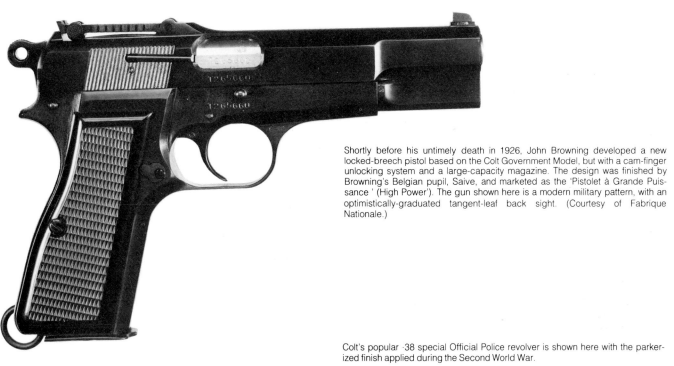

Shortly before his untimely death in 1926, John Browning developed a new locked-breech pistol based on the Colt Government Model, but with a cam-finger unlocking system and a large-capacity magazine. The design was finished by Browning's Belgian pupil, Saive, and marketed as the 'Pistolet à Grande Puissance ' (High Power'). The gun shown here is a modern military pattern, with an optimistically-graduated tangent-leaf back sight. (Courtesy of Fabrique Nationale.)

Colt's popular ·38 special Official Police revolver is shown here with the parkerized finish applied during the Second World War.

The Walther P.38, adopted by the German army in 1940, is one of the better natural pointers among automatic pistols, balancing quite well for instinctive fire.

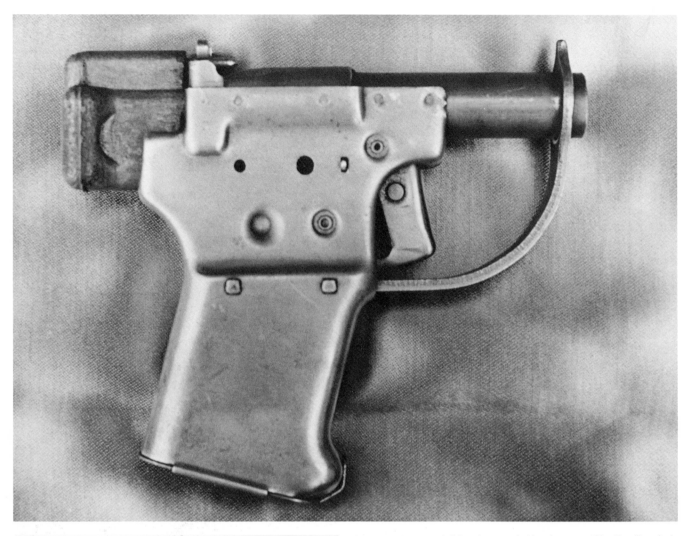

VI. The modern era

One of the cheapest of all American combat handguns was this ·45-calibre single shot 'Liberator', produced for the OSS at a cost of $1.71.

The aftermath of the Second World War prevented many European handgun manufacturers recommencing production, particularly as those in Germany were banned from making warlike goods. However, as the Allies were contemplating wholesale rearmament, Fabrique Nationale was able to establish a near monopoly by supplying the excellent FN-Browning Pistolet à Grande Puissance ('High-Power') worldwide. To date, the gun has sold to the military or police forces in nearly seventy countries. Beretta began production of locked-breech pistols in the early 1950s, simply by adapting the efficient Walther P.38 breech-lock — though without the pioneering double-action trigger system of the German prototype. By the late 1950s, however, Walther had recommenced production of the P.38 and the stage was set for the renaissance of the Germano-Swiss handgun industry: the products of Walther and Heckler & Koch in Germany, together with SIG in Switzerland, are now widely seen. And, despite the attempts by Manurhin and others to establish a recognizably European revolver, the automatic pistol remains the favoured combat handgun

outside the USA. In addition to the powerful military-style guns, which are not always acceptable for personal defence, a large number of smaller guns are available. Among the best of these are the compact 9mm Parabellum types, such as the Heckler & Koch PSP (P7) and 7.65mm and 9mm Auto (·32 and ·380 ACP) blowbacks such as the FN Model 140 DA and the essentially similar Berettas.

The 1950s proved an especially fruitful decade for US combat handguns. The government was searching for a replacement for the venerable Colt Government Model, whereupon both the Colt Commander and the Smith & Wesson Model 39 were developed for consideration. Both have since received wide combat acceptance, with the Model 39, particularly, helping to drive a small wedge into the traditionally revolver-dominated US police market. 1955 brought the introduction of two classic fighting revolvers; Smith & Wesson announced the ·357 K-Frame Combat Magnum in response to pleas from Bill Jordan and other police officers for a more portable ·357, and Colt countered with its classic Python to make it a truly vintage year for such powerful designs. A year later, Smith & Wesson produced the ultra-powerful ·44 Magnum for those wanting ultimate knock-down capabilities.

It took Clint Eastwood, however, to popularize the Model 29 as a fighting revolver. Another important S&W innovation was the use of stainless steel for the Model 60 (1965). Many who carry a handgun constantly in an open holster, or close to the body in a humid climate, have learned to appreciate the importance of stainless steel in a duty gun.

During the period 1965-75, the growth of American interest in the automatic pistol as a combat weapon was stimulated by the late George Nonté's advocacy of the Smith & Wesson Model 39 and Jeff Cooper championing Colt's Government Model and Commander. The concurrent development of effective handgun ammunition such as Super-Vel, which will expand at the comparatively low handgun velocities, enhanced the combat efficiency of automatic and revolver alike. Policemen and civilian enthusiasts started buying automatic pistols in greater numbers, while International Practical Shooting Confederation (IPSC) competitions efficiently polished shooting techniques. The latest US JSSAP military trials to select a 9mm Parabellum gun to replace the ageing Colt Government Model have added impetus to the distribution of autoloaders.

As a direct result of increased law enforcement interest, in 1971, Smith & Wesson introduced the large-capacity variant of the original Model 39 known as the Model 59 —

though a secret silenced predecessor of this gun had been developed some years earlier for the US Navy SEAL teams.

Another recent trend in combat autoloaders has been towards building concealable weapons chambering authoritative cartridges. The Detonics line of small ·45 ACP guns, and the recent introduction of the comparably powerful Colt Officer's Model, have given those needing power in a small package a more effective choice. Compact double action 9mm automatics have also gained popularity; to meet this demand, Smith & Wesson has added the Model 469 to its product range, while Detonics has introduced the Pocket-9. Though chambering the ineffectual ·25 ACP round, another important design is the Seecamp LWS-25 — an extremely safe and reliable design, and possibly the best small automatic ever produced in the USA.

Two long-awaited large-bore pistols are now also entering production. The Bren Ten, touted by Jeff Cooper as the 'ultimate combat autoloader', and the Smith & Wesson Model 645 were both released in 1985. For those favouring the Colt Government Model, the current Colt Series IV will shortly be offered in stainless steel to increase its utility as a heavy-duty belt gun.

Their progress will be watched with interest.

USAF pilots during the Korean War period (1950-3) wore combat handguns for protection should they be downed behind enemy lines. Note the revolver worn by the man second from the right.

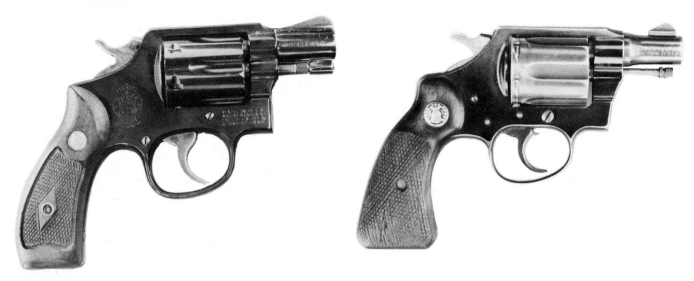

The special combat revolvers developed for the USAF included these alloy-framed Smith & Wesson (left) and Colt (right) 'Aircrewman' guns.

Two US Army military policemen and a local sheriff display the traditional US military and police handguns: the ·45 Government Model Colt-Browning and a ·38 Special Smith & Wesson revolver.

The Hi-Standard ·22-calibre over-and-under derringer achieved popularity as a police 'back-up' gun during the 1960s and 1970s.

A Colt 'snub' revolver, with the trigger guard cut away and the hammer bobbed for combat use. (Courtesy of Bob Arganbright.)

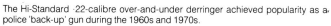

The small size of the obsolescent Smith & Wesson Model 61 pistol is evident when compared with the 1½in-diameter medallion.

Although the powerful ·44 Auto Mag was never intended as a combat handgun, it sprang to public attention in the recent 'Dirty Harry' film *Sudden Impact*.

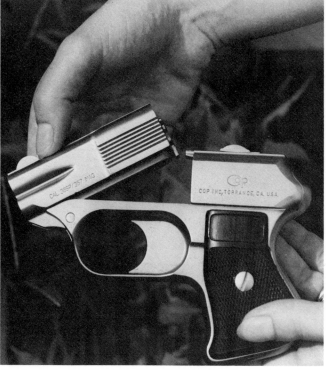

A recent, short-lived American 'back-up' gun was this COP ·357 Magnum.

24

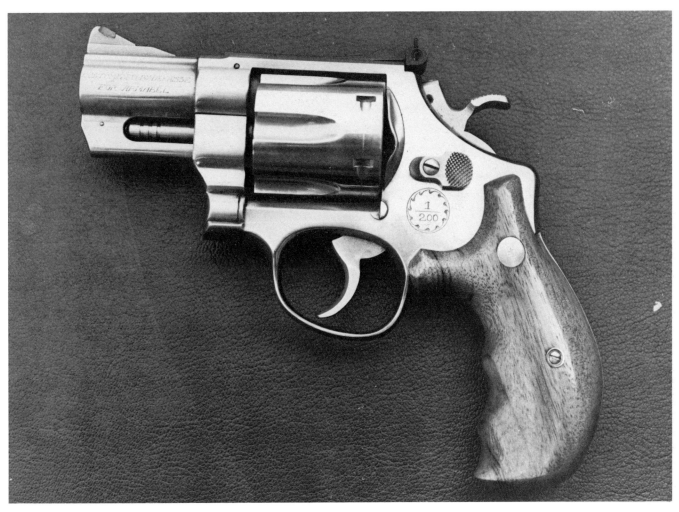

A very good example of European customizing: a Smith & Wesson Model 629 'De Kaisse-Armabel Killer Stopper' with a shortened 2in barrel and new grips.

A gun has no value in combat if it cannot be controlled; here, Leroy Thompson stops the Detonics Mark VII at the peak of its recoil arc, ready for a quick recovery and a second shot.

Combat handgun shooting

I. Military progress

Until comparatively recently, with the notable exception of the specialized counter-terrorists units, few military authorities considered the handgun particularly combat-worthy. To most, it has become a symbol of authority for officers and senior NCOs or a confidence-boosting 'last resort'.

The handgun is not really indispensable for military purposes, as few situations arise where the handgun could effectively substitute for an assault rifle, a combat shotgun or submachine-guns such as the Uzi, the Mini-Uzi, the Sterling, the Ingram, the Heckler & Koch MP5 or the Beretta M12S. However, even armies such as Finland, where the handgun was rejected totally in the 1970s, have recently purchased 9mm automatic pistols. Until recently, few attempts were made to study, develop and teach military handgun shooting owing to uncertainty about the handgun's combat efficacy. The exceptions have concerned small specially-trained groups detached for particular purposes, formed from specialists who are neither bound by traditional engagement rules nor restricted to conventional training. For the remainder, the training is archaic; though it may lead to marksmanship badges and sharpshooters' qualifications, these are almost always obtained from generously-timed and unrealistically static shooting.

Until recently, the choice of a military pistol was governed by convention. The abandonment of the revolver in European armies (generally in the period 1900-35, though the laggardly British retained the Webley until 1957) was accompanied by widespread, largely unfounded fears about the safety of the automatics. Consequently, excepting the Walther P.38, the classic military pistols have all been single action, regulations forbidding them to be carried cocked-and-locked ('Condition One' carry). Chambers should be empty and the hammer down, requiring the slide to be retracted, using both hands, before the gun can fire. The ultimate expression of this is seen in the Russian Tokarev, adopted by most Eastern European countries prior to the introduction of the Makarov, which has no manual safety at all; the choice is simply to carry the gun with an empty chamber, or to lower the hammer to its 'safe' half-cock position and risk carrying the gun loaded.

The attitude of military authorities has often been that the handgun is as dangerous to the firer as the intended target, and that every precaution should be taken to prevent accidental discharge. Clues to this are provided by the proliferation of superfluous magazine safeties, excessively heavy trigger pulls and (in most cases) poor sights. For example, the trigger pulls of the single action FN-Browning High-Power pistols delivered to the Belgian army must be at least 3.5kg, ever since an official board of inquiry ruled that a training accident was partly due to too light a trigger. One can only wonder at the wisdom of handicapping the High-Power, until recently the best all-round military/police/defence handgun, with an unnecessarily heavy trigger and additional 'magazine security'.

The High-Power magazine safety was considered a sales-worthy innovation by its designers, preventing the release of the hammer when the magazine was removed, but clearly demonstrates lack of faith in the firers. Obviously, it was deemed far too dangerous for the average soldier or civilian to remove the magazine and thus gain the impression that his gun was unloaded even though a round could still be chambered. However much the trained combat shooter may curse the magazine-safety concept, which can immobilize the gun unless reloading is undertaken before the last round is fired, many military personnel (and even some policemen) receive guns simply because of their official status — yet would pass few practical pistol courses without extensive training, and cannot be relied upon to 'unload and show clear' by removing the magazine and manipulating the slide.

Specialized military units such as the British SAS, West German GSG-9 (actually part of the Bundesgrenzschutz, the border guards), French GIGN and Belgian ESI act as the equivalent of the US SWAT police teams — unknown in Europe, apart from a few German cities - and are among the best-trained in the use of differing weapons, including handguns. None the less, owing to their military status, they are still widely restricted to 'issue' equipment: for example, members of GIGN are issued with the MR 73 revolver. Though the Manurhin is excellent, its limited cylinder capacity is a great disadvantage against some of the current automatics, which can fire, in the case of the Steyr GB-80, three times as many shots without reloading. This can easily put the revolver-firer at risk in prolonged combat, as even the best revolver speedloaders are less efficient than replacing a box magazine.

The American JSSAP has undoubtedly played a major role in shaping the current generation of automatic pistols, particularly in Europe where most of them are made. It is less well known that the Europeans began the cycle with two such programmes; in 1975, for example, following the disaster at the 1972 Munich Olympic Games, an effort was made to reform the German state police forces and standardize 9mm Parabellum ammunition. Oddly, each of the three competing designs — the Walther P5, SIG P225 (P6) and the Heckler & Koch PSP (P7) — was adopted, as all three had proved sufficiently effectual. Apart from large-capacity magazines, the West German specifications all but predicted those of the JSSAP. Guns such as the Beretta 92SB, FN-Browning BDA, Star 30M, Llama Omni, Steyr GB-80 and Glock 17 all draw heavily on the lessons of the German police and JSSAP trials.

This picture, taken from a 1930s-vintage training manual, emphasizes the static military shooting style that has persisted to the present day.

Raymond Sasia, a Controller-General of the French national police and instigator of the FBI-inspired 'Sasia Method' of revolver shooting.

II. The police

The police use of handguns is controversial, and often ineffectual. Incidents in Europe have shown this clearly as when, for example, two out of four plain-clothes men were killed and a third injured by the handful of gunmen they intercepted when on patrol; when four experienced policemen fired fifteen rounds from a distance of two metres at an aggressor passing a doorway, without a hit; when a uniformed policeman attempting to stop a robbery was killed largely because his High-Power pistol contained only three rounds and had no spare loaded magazines; or when élite police 'marksmen' stopped a car in a crowded street and fired a dozen shots at close range without killing the presumed target (fortuitously, as it was the wrong man).

There are countless successes to balance against these few tragedies, but it is clear that the average policeman is far from expert in a combat situation. His guns, ammunition, holsters and ancillary equipment are often completely inadequate. Even in 1986, many policemen, security guards and others whose lives may depend on their guns still carry ineffectual 7.65 and 9mm Auto-calibre pistols, or ·38 Spe-

cial revolvers loaded with cheap, under-powered cartridges. In 1983, according to a professional policeman, the French national force officially used 28 different handguns in eight calibres. For a long time, too, many US police forces were satisfied with the notoriously weak ·32 revolver cartridges, none of which had much stopping power. To economise, weak ·38 Special often serves as 'training' for the powerful ·357 Magnum . . . with potentially unfortunate results when accuracy matters most and the additional recoil of the service round proves too hot to handle..

Prior to 1960, when crime and street-violence were still relatively minor, European police forces had no consistent shooting doctrine. In the USA, training was undertaken more professionally, under the guidance of experienced combat-shooting names such as Askins, Applegate, Keith, Weaver and Jordan, together with the influence of legendary performers such as Ed McGivern (whose close range simultaneous two-hand rapid-fire records stood until comparatively recently). European training was restricted to static scenarios, with conventional (but unrealistic) paper targets, miserly issue of ammunition and commensurately minimal mandatory shooting qualification requirements.

Modèle R.S.

The 'Sasia Target', based on an FBI prototype. Only a single target is used in the fifty-round 'Police Course', which is always fired in the same order, from the same positions and at the same distances.

René Smeets (standing) participates in a realistic police contest based on the Sasia Method in 1982. In this competition, revolvers and automatic pistols alike are loaded with five rounds, all spare ammunition being carried in the pocket. Neither speedloaders nor spare magazines are allowed.

Though outstanding marksmen did emerge from this system, they were few and far between.

Traditionally, street patrol was undertaken by cool, experienced uniformed policemen, usually respected by the population, while more complex problems were entrusted to plain-clothes men relying more on brains than brawn. During the 1960s, however, the old order changed perceptibly. Problems were evident in many European countries, none more so than in the France of Charles de Gaulle. De Gaulle, acting against the counsel of many advisers and the wishes of many French émigrés, granted independence to Algeria in 1960 after a bloody struggle against nationalist guerrillas. The grant of independence precipitated riots, even mutiny among some élite French army units, and a secret terrorist group calling itself the OAS was created in France. The ultimate target was de Gaulle himself, as depicted so graphically in Frederick Forsyth's book *The Day of the Jackal*.

Against this backcloth, Raymond Sasia, a noted French judo and self-defence instructor, was given the task of protecting the President as head of the special security group responsible for the head of state. Sasia determined to re-organise the shooting training of the entire French police, visiting the FBI Academy in Quantico in 1961 to assimilate the then-current revolver orientated methods that culminated in the famous 'Hogan's Alley' training course.

Back in France, Sasia opted for the revolver, eventually asking Smith & Wesson to make the special 'S&W 19/3 RS' ('Raymond Sasia') with a 3in barrel, fixed sights and narrow grips. He then created a complete method, which he called 'Le Tir Rapide', based around a fast draw from the back of the hip and instinctive one-handed rapid fire at close range. Two-hand stance was permitted for medium and long-range shooting, but the gun was carried with the chamber empty and the hammer down. The 'bowling draw' was to be accompanied by simultaneously retracting the slide, were the revolver to be substituted by an automatic pistol.

Sasia also adapted the typical FBI-style silhouette target,

28

a stiff and unnatural pose scoring 1-5, the bottle-shaped '5' (or 'bowling pin') being the 'stopping zone' and a central 'playing card' being the 'kill-zone'. Sasia also adapted the FBI practical pistol course for his own purposes, requiring the trainee to fire 50 rounds in about five minutes, beginning with an empty gun and having to load and reload systematically at each stage. The course was always performed in the same order, with the same positions and the same distances − better than nothing, but by no means ideal. Finally, Sasia created the police shooting school (the Centre National de Tir) to train instructors in the 'Sasia Method'. Almost every country sent selected personnel to CNT sessions. The essentials of the Sasia Method were incorporated in the German PDV 211 system, development of which began soon after 1972.

American influence was evident even in these early European efforts. Among the US masters, Jeff Cooper, the promoter of the Bren Ten, was to play a major role. Beginning in the 1950s, he had established his own combat-training method, based on the effectiveness of a simple fast draw with the upper part of the body remaining very straight, adapting the well-known body position and two-hand grip of the 'Weaver Stance'. Despite publishing the *Complete Book of Modern Handgunning* in the early 1960s, Cooper is not a man to rest on his laurels and has constantly striven to refine his techniques.

Many people interested in combat handgunning − on personal or professional bases − have contributed to the perfection of techniques, assisted (particularly in Europe) by the growth of specialist magazines devoted to handgun shooting rather than more traditional historical studies. During the past few years, a very few books have appeared on the subject; however, not all of their recommendations are realistic, and a few are downright dangerous.

In the period 1965-75, the Europeans began to appreciate the advanced US handgunning techniques, and began to experiment with revolvers, ·22 rimfire pistols, tied-down Western-style holsters, the Sasia Method and improvised targets − only to discover that no European manufacturer made the slide- or speed-holsters they sought, all of which had to be imported from the USA. During the 1970s, Jeff Cooper came to Europe, organized some seminars, met police authorities and civilian enthusiasts, and explained his 'new pistol' project to potential manufacturers. Though he gained the firm impression that no-one understood the purpose of the design that was to become the Bren Ten, and though few of the police authorities were forward-looking enough to grasp the merits of his method, Jeff Cooper had convinced many of the civilian enthusiasts of his goals.

The German Siegfried Hubner forged his own policy, organizing courses and seminars, writing books, and training some of the German police units with other instructors such as Max Wiegand.

The Belgian Roger Swaelens followed Cooper's path, being the only European (and one of few non-Americans) to

Jeff Cooper, pictured during a seminar in Belgium; August 1982.

be recognized as an instructor by the master himself. After acquiring a reputation as a fantastic teacher, Swaelens and some friends formed one of the few private European academies specifically devoted to training law enforcement personnel. Dramas like the Munich Olympic Games massacre, the kidnapping and murder of important people like Aldo Moro or Martin Schleyer, the Patty Hearst affair, assassination attempts on President Reagan and the Pope, machine-gunning synagogues, attacks on airline offices and widespread hijacking have accelerated the development of police equipment and training methods more quickly than 25 years of conventional street-crime.

During the 1980s, however, the outlook has changed. For example, many new types of target have been developed, and several companies have created moving-target systems. These range from inexpensive computer-based units capable of progamming control of movement, delay and obscuration of up to ten targets, to the most super-sophisticated system imaginable. Currently, the Riyadh range is probably the most complete police and counter-terrorism range in the world, where targets may move in any direction or under the influence of sensors activated by the firer. There are also complete vehicle courses, multiple video systems and 'fun houses'.

Obviously, most authorities cannot afford such luxuries, particularly where ranges must be shared with target shooters from varying disciplines. However, judicious use of cheap material enables even these facilities to be transformed for realistic police shooting, using Olympic rapid-fire targets as moving ones, or metal 'Pepper Poppers' to demonstrate the need to place shots accurately to get the best from stopping power.

More and more contests are testing the growing skill of the practical handgunner, some events rapidly attaining an international reputation. Last, but not least, the incredible diversity of new guns — and the replacement of many old 7.65mm Auto guns with others in 9mm Parabellum of ·357 Magnum — has greatly increased interest among law-enforcement agencies.

This small computer 'brain' controls the movement of five 4-position targets, plus five additional 'pop-up' patterns. The increasing popularity of these comparatively inexpensive systems has revolutionized combat shooting training, enabling techniques to be refined appreciably.

Roger Swaelens (left) instructing members of a municipal SWAT team in the use of riot-guns and pistols.

Police are now making their training increasingly realistic. Here, a policeman practices shooting from a type of Volkswagen popular throughout Europe.

In a search for realistic targets, leading cartoonists were asked to collaborate.

a.

b.

c.

d.

e.

Realistic training demands an appropriate setting — such as this bullet-riddled Peugeot, accompanied by Sasia Targets ·.. and a distinctive white 'hostage' shot only at the firer's peril!

The ·41 Magnum has great advantages in stopping vehicles. Even practised shooters do not always realize that a powerful gun is needed to penetrate a windscreen from any angle.

The results of training. Two people, author Smeets with a pistol and a revolver-firing police officer, achieve similar results in the 'Step Back' despite no prior acquaintanceship (though sharing instructors). When the moving targets appear, the firers must move to the rear, draw and place two shots in the K-zone within one second.

Civilian ranges can easily be adapted for police shooting. In this instance, the target-returning system is used to provide a 'moving aggressor'. The instructor controls the progress of the target, the trainee commanding the 'aggressor' to stop; if the target does not do so, the trainee must fire only at close range.

The metallic 'Pepper Popper' is a legacy of IPSC shooting. A realistic target is fixed to the Pepper Popper, which will fall only if vital zones are hit. The non-vital zones overlap the backing and bullets will simply pass through uneventfully. An 'innocent bystander' is sometimes placed close to the 'aggressor', falling if hit to dramatize the firer's error.

One of the numerous advantages of combat handgun training is the opportunity to talk with people; here, having passed a 'corner', René Smeets is ordering an innocent target to show his hands and evacuate the danger zone. The instructor follows progress intently.

René Smeets passing a corner in a 'fun house', during a police course 'house clearance'. In this technique, the gun is pulled down immediately after the shot (or shots) to see whether the target has fallen.

Part of the vast choice of modern 9mm Parabellum ammunition.

III. Personal defence

There is little scope for the personal-defence pistol in Europe - quite unlike the United States of America — and the enthusiast almost has to teach himself. Specialized magazines are rare, and the space devoted to personal-defence guns is restricted by comparison with the combat handguns. Few suitable shooting schools can be found, though multi-European champion Bob Dunkley organizes praiseworthy courses in Britain. Siegfried Hubner offers 'Civil Combat Courses' and FN-Browning once ran a training school based on the Sasia Method. Though the FN school was advertised as 'open to the public', most of its students were members of security companies. Its ultimate failure was ascribed to the restriction of private handgun ownership in Belgium, leaving the IPSC to provide the only readily accessible personal-defence training facilities in Europe.

The effect of French SFM Alia super-perforating ·357 Magnum bullets, fired at 16mm steel plate — from a 6in-barrelled revolver - at a range of 3 metres. This is outstanding penetration for handgun ammunition.

The SFM-made THV rounds, shown here in ·357 Magnum, are probably the best 'man-stoppers' in the world, excepting the soft- or hollow-points. They will penetrate 5-6mm steel plate at close range (bottom). The flat-shooting ultra-light weight bullet, owing to its high velocity, tends to shoot low unless sights are adjusted. The hollowed bullet permits additional propellant to be squeezed into the cartridge.

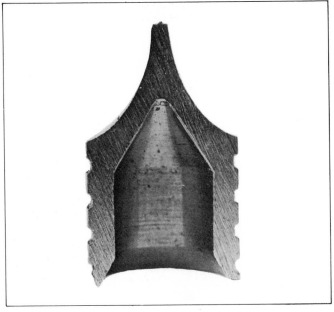

The complete series of Senix 'High-Perf' ammunition, relying on a sabot with an extra-hard sub-calibre point. From left to right: ·223 and ·222 Remington, ·30 M1 Carbine, ·357 Magnum, ·38 Special, ·22 Winchester Magnum Rimfire, ·45 ACP, 9mm Parabellum and ·22in Long Rifle Rimfire. The ·22 LR was the first to be introduced. Senix ammunition combines a devastating effect on light armour with excellent stopping power.

The 9mm Parabellum Geco 'Actiongeschoss' or 'Quick Defense' (left), and the MEN 'Deformation-geschoss' (right) are specifically intended to provide a combination of good stopping power and excellent tyre-deflating capabilities. The axial tunnels through the bullets are covered by a super-light plastic point prior to firing.

The ·38 Special Norma Magnum is one of the very best man-stopping cartridges. In Europe, however, many countries prohibit official issue of hollow or soft-point ammunition — largely by misinterpreting international conventions, but often disadvantaging their law-enforcement personnel compared with civilians bound by no such restrictions.

Choosing a combat handgun

The selection of a gun is based on several criteria. A police officer will often choose a different weapon to a civilian, while a plain-clothes or undercover police officer will require a different gun compared with his uniformed colleagues. The availability of suitable holsters and ammunition is also important, as it is important that a gun must fit the firer's pocket as literally as figuratively: there is no point owning a combat handgun, however ideal it may be, if the ammunition is too difficult or too expensive to obtain.

Choosing the gun requires more than a superficial knowledge of the subject. The advantages and disadvantages of each gun are vitally important, together with an idea of the differing models and the reliability of the manufacturers, wholesalers and retailers. Do not buy a particular gun if you suspect that the manufacturer may go bankrupt tomorrow, if spares are in short supply, or if the local gunsmiths cannot handle repairs. Advertising material and the reviews published in the specialist magazines should be read carefully, remembering that claims of 'fantastic technical advance' and gimmickry are *not* the most important considerations. A gun is not a toy, and it is stupid to own or carry a gun on which you cannot rely in a crisis. However formidable, bright and expensive it looks, the name of the game is to stay alive with the help of the gun rather than its hindrance.

In Europe, even professionals (such as police) may be restricted to one gun; thus, the choice is almost always the most versatile gun, role-adjustments then being made by selecting differing ammunition or holsters. Even in the USA, where guns can usually be acquired for specific purposes, the 'one gun' concept has great advantages — not least being familiarity which, instead of 'breeding contempt', will enable the firer to deliver his shots with the confidence born of constant practice, rather than interchanging guns whose handling/firing characteristics may be totally dissimilar.

The European 'one gun' choice is generally between a **9mm Parabellum** automatic pistol and a revolver chambering ·38in Special or (in some cases, *and*) ·357 Magnum. Some police units still favour pistols chambering the ineffectual 7.65mm or 9mm Auto (·32 and ·380 ACP) or the powerful man-stopping ·45 ACP. The 7.65mm and 9mm Auto rounds are often fired from pistols small enough to be concealed as 'back-up' weapons, though this concept is far more popular in the USA than in Europe; the latter's police and paramilitary are rarely permitted to carry more than a single pistol. Cartridges as small as ·22 LR rimfire and 6.35mm Auto (·25 ACP) have also been used in these personal protection pistols, but, provided recoil is not too fierce, the largest-possible calibre is preferable.

The US combat handgun scene is dominated by revolvers. The most important calibres are ·38 Special and ·357 Magnum, which are interchangeable in the best guns, though ·44 Magnum is favoured for long distance work and military-style ·45 ACP also has its champions. In addition, ·44 Special confers the advantage of 'back-up' potential for a large ·44 Magnum service revolver, and the venerable ·45 Colt offers excellent knock-down power without the vicious recoil of the ·44 Magnum.

Though this book is principally concerned with the guns, some idea of the diversity of available ammunition is useful. Modern loads include efficient super-penetrating bullets, such as the French Arcane, SFM Alia, SIB 'hautes Performances' and 'Perforantes', available in most calibres from 7.65mm Auto to ·45 ACP. The best results are often obtained with ·357 Magnum, one SIB Perforante bullet breaking the steel-plate liner of one of the best available '.44 Magnum bullet and 12-gauge slug'-proof jackets at 2 metres.

Among the best of the dual-purpose penetrating/man-stopping cartridges is the French SFM 'Très Haute Vitesse' (THV, 'very high speed'), available in 9mm Parabellum, ·357 Magnum and ·38 Special, with 7.65mm and 9mm Auto and ·45 ACP obtainable on special request. The ·357 THV load offers a rifle-like velocity of about 800 m/sec (2,625 ft/sec) with its 43gn lightweight special-profile bullet. This provides enormous stopping power, with two additional advantages: first, it loses velocity rapidly after 100m to minimise danger to innocent bystanders, and secondly, it has excellent short-range penetration. The SENIX 'High Perf' is available not only in the classic combat-handgun calibres, but also in ·22 LR and WMR together with such rifle cartridges as ·222 and ·223 Remington and ·30 M1 Carbine. The hardened sub-calibre point gives very good penetration and stopping power, plus an excellent temporary shock cavity.

In addition to widely distributed jacketed soft- and hollow-point ammunition, there are special 'super stoppers' such as the German 9mm Parabellum MEN Deformationsgeschoss or Geco Actionsgeschoss (or 'Quick Defense'), the latter being sold in the USA in ·357 Magnum. Both of these proprietary bullets have a very light 'point' covering an axial cavity; the point is lost when the gun is fired, the tunnel allowing excellent expansion in the target. These loads are particularly good for deflating tyres, the air passing through the central channel with unusual efficiency.

Europe has traditionally depended on American-made holsters, such as the products of Bianchi, Safariland, Strong and de Santis. Recently, however, indigenous companies such as Sickinger (Austria), Gil Holsters (France) and Horseshoe Leather (Britain) have made inroads in the US-dominated market, while many small-scale custom and semi-custom leatherware makers are now active in Belgium, Britain, France and Germany. The rapid rise of IPSC-style and combat shooting has played a major role in shaping the growth of this European industry.

Before moving on to the directory, however, it must be reiterated that training is vital to the combat handgunner. It is not enough to be able to place shots adequately on a paper target, with an Olympic-quality matching pistol, on a quiet indoor range. Without proper practice and the right equipment, even these marksmen can be a liability in a 'combat' situation.

THE DIRECTORY

Beretta 92SB

Type: double-action semi-automatic pistol.
Maker: Pietro Beretta SpA, Gardone val Trompia (Brescia), Italy.
Calibre: 9mm Parabellum (7.65mm Parabellum optional).
Overall length: 220mm, 8.66in.
Barrel length: 125mm, 4.92in.
Weight, empty: 960gm, 33.9oz.
Magazine capacity: 15+1.
Construction: alloy frame, fixed sights.

Other models include the **92SB Compact** (198mm/8.80in overall, 875gm/30.90z, magazine 13+1) and the **92SM Compact** M (similar to the Compact, but with an eight-round magazine and weighing only 860gm/27.5oz).

Established in Gardone since 1680, Beretta was better known for its fine shotguns and submachine-guns prior to the recent adoption of the 92F pistol by the US Army. However, the company has made excellent, reliable semi-automatic pistols – popular among European military and police forces – since the First World War.

The earliest pistols chambered weak ammunition, such as the ·32ACP and ·380ACP, which allowed them to be small and handy. Simple blowback operation was also permissible, owing to the ineffectual cartridges. In the early 1950s, Beretta adapted the recoil-operated breech-lock of the Walther P38 for the Mo.51, though a double-action trigger system had to await the introduction of the Mo.92 in 1976. The Mo.92 initially displayed such poor features as the curious lateral magazine lock, situated low on the left grip, and the transverse safety. However, Beretta was attracted by the US JSSAP trials, intended to find a replacement for the venerable M1911A1 Colt, and gradually transformed the Mo.92 into the 92SB and 92F – by way of the 92S and 92S-1.

Delivered with only a single magazine, the Beretta 92SB is by no means small, but the good-quality alloy frame minimizes weight. The slide features the quintessentially Beretta cutaway top, but is so well designed that no reflection occurs to disturb the sight picture. The firer is completely unaware of the exposed barrel.

The dismantling lever, the slide stop, the de-cocking lever and the magazine catch all appear on the left side of the pistol, a complication that is by no means its best point. Unlike many guns, the slide-stop notch is cut on the inner edge of the slide and is not apparent from the outside.

The locking system of the Beretta 92SB is simply borrowed from the Walther P38: short straight recoil, with the barrel initially locked into the slide by two lateral 'wings', until an actuator, pushing against the standing frame, forces the wings down into recesses in the frame. The barrel then stops, and the slide reciprocates alone to complete the loading/cocking cycle – extracting, ejecting, cocking the hammer, chambering a fresh round and forcing the barrel forward until the two lock-wings re-enter the slide recesses.

This system is exceptionally robust, minimizes breakages, promotes accuracy and avoids a removable barrel bush of Colt-Browning type. Furthermore, the cartridges are presented by the magazine almost directly behind the chamber, avoiding a conventional feed ramp and permitting hollow-point and other specially-bulleted ammunition to be used without difficulty.

One of the most important components of the trigger system is the trigger bar. In single-action, one element of this bar disconnects the firing-pin safety and another breaks the contact between the hammer and the sear to allow the hammer to fall onto the firing pin. In double-action mode, a protrusion on the trigger bar cocks the hammer, a second element prevents the hammer being caught by the sear, and the third disconnects the firing-pin safety. The trigger bar also acts as a slide safety, disconnecting the whole mechanism unless the slide, having returned to its proper locked position, allows the tail of the trigger bar to rise.

Another characteristic of the Beretta 92SB family is the multiplication of the safeties, some being, in many people's view, completely superfluous. The slide safety has already been mentioned. The gun is also equipped with a loaded-chamber indicator, combined with the extractor. There is also a firing-pin safety, which blocks the separate rear part of the firing-pin system; only a deliberate trigger pull can move this block upwards to release the firing-pin spindle and allow the hammer to strike the firing pin.

The principal safety is the conventional de-cocking system, actuated by the ambidexterous lever on the slide. The spindle of the de-cocking lever disconnects the sear from the cocked hammer, allowing the latter to fall towards the firing-pin head. However, the separate rear part of the firing pin assembly is raised to prevent the hammer transferring a blow to the front portion of the pin, which is still locked by its trigger-actuated safety mechanism. The de-cocking lever does not automatically re-set itself, and can be used as a 'manual safety'; however, it is insanity to keep a double action pistol with the hammer down and blocked in this way.

If the gun exhibits pleasant handling characteristics, the trigger pull on the test gun was decidedly 'military' – 6.5kg (14.3lb) in double-action mode, with a long-but-regular travel, and more than 3kg (6.6lb) in the otherwise crisp, short single-action. The Beretta is extremely accurate, with little sensation of recoil, and allows easy rapid fire. The slide of the trial gun failed to remain open after the last shot, even with powerful FN factory cartridges; only really 'hot' hand-loads managed to block the slide with the magazine follower. This could be very dangerous in situations where the firer does not realize he holds an empty gun.

It is interesting that Forjas Taurus, in Brazil, produces a version of the Mo.92 under licence. The Taurus PT-92 has a squared trigger guard, and the safety lever will be found on the frame rather than the slide in the manner of the original Beretta Mo.92.

In January 1985, the US Army announced that a minor modification of the 92SB, the 92F, had been chosen as the standard US martial handgun under the designation '9mm Pistol, M9'. The principal differences concern the squaring of the trigger guard to promote two-hand grip, matt finish, differently shaped grips and restoration of the magazine floor-plate design featured on the early Compacts.

The Beretta was selected after protracted trials involving many of the world's leading designs, such as the SIG-Sauers, Heckler & Kochs and Smith & Wessons. Beretta had previously staged a brilliant commercial coup, replacing the S&W revolvers of one American State's Police with 92SB pistols free of charge, but this costly operation may now be seen as a clever investment. The political and economic relationship between the USA and Italy has also played its role, but the Beretta is indisputably an excellent design.

The forerunner of the 92SB and the 92F was the Modelo 92, shown here. Note the absence of a slide-mounted safety catch/de-cocking lever. (Courtesy of Pietro Beretta SpA.)

A left-side view of the 92SB; note the number of protruding levers and buttons! (Courtesy of Pietro Beretta Spa.)

The Beretta is by no means small, but handles well.

A right-side view of the 92SB showing the dismantling lever head (1) and the trigger bar (2) let into the frame.

The barrel of the Beretta, showing the pivoting locking piece. Note the actuator projecting rearward; this strikes the standing frame to force the 'wings' of the locking piece down into the frame and release the slide.

The frame of the 92SB. Key: *1*, the head of the trigger bar, acting as the disconnector; *2*, the firing-pin safety lever; *3*, the de-cocking bar, *4*, the locking-piece recesses in the frame; *5*, the internal portion of the slide-stop, which remains on the frame after the gun is field-stripped; and *6*, the feed ramp.

Beretta 84BB

Type: double-action semi-automatic pistol.
Maker: Pietro Beretta SpA, Gardone val Trompia (Brescia), Italy.
Calibre: 9mm Short (·380 ACP).
Overall length: 172mm, 6.77in.
Barrel length: 98mm, 3.86in.
Weight, empty: 660gm, 23.3oz.
Magazine capacity: 13+1.
Construction: blued steel/anodised alloy, fixed sights.

The 84BB is one of the newest examples of the Beretta 'Series 81' personal defence pistols, which has included the original Models 81 and 84 (in 7.65mm Auto and 9mm Short respectively) and the similar, but newer 81BB and 84BB with large-capacity magazines and firing-pin locks. The models 82BB and 85BB are identical with the 81BB and 84BB respectively, but have single-row magazines (9+1 and 8+1) and non-reversible safety catches. The Model 87BB is a ·22 Long Rifle training/sport pistol.

The Beretta 84BB is a typical double-action European-style personal defence pistol, drawing much of its inspiration from the original Walther Polizei-Pistole. It is a very elegant design, with a rounded trigger guard — facilitating holstering — and a cut-away blued steel slide so typical of its manufacturer. The frame is an anodised aluminium alloy. Among the best features is the ambidexterous safety catch, perhaps a little inconveniently placed at the rear of the grip but easy to apply and reset. The magazine catch is a reversible crossbolt behind the trigger guard, while the slide-stop is inset at the top of the left grip. A left-handed firer can release the slide-stop with the trigger finger but, as the catch is not truly ambidexterous, must change his handgrip.

In the absence of a de-cocking system, lowering the hammer onto a loaded chamber should be exercised with care — particularly on the obsolescent Model 84, which has no firing-pin lock. Once the hammer has been lowered, the slide can be locked by pushing the twin manual safety levers (on the rear of the frame above the grip) upward to cover the red dot on the slide. A firing-pin safety lever on the 84BB, sharing the hammer spindle, prevents the firing pin reaching the primer of the chambered round except during the final stages of the trigger pull. The Beretta pin-lock is not as substantial as some rival designs, but appears durable and efficient enough for its task.

Field-stripping is comparatively simple. Once the gun has been unloaded, and the chamber checked, the dismantling button on the left side of the frame must be depressed while simultaneously rotating the dismantling lever (on the right) downward. The slide, barrel and spring assembly can be pulled forward and off the frame. Once the recoil spring and its guide rod has been removed, the barrel can be detached for inspection. Reassembly is the reverse of dismantling, care being necessary to ensure that the barrel is replaced properly in the slide, the extractor (which doubles as a loaded-chamber indicator) is correctly positioned, and the head of the recoil-spring guide rod is properly centred below the breech.

The 84BB has a reasonable trigger system, both pulls being a little stiff on the test gun (the double action being 7kg, 15.4lb) though travel and break-points are quite acceptable. Owing to the low power of the 9mm Short cartridge, recoil is comparatively light and the Beretta is eminently controllable. This is particularly important owing to the poor man-stopping qualities of the cartridges which, unless loaded with jacketed hollow-point bullets, may require a rapid follow-up shot. The Beretta pistols are supplied with attractive smooth-finished wood grips with inset medallions, but the optional chequered plastic variety gives a better grip in conjunction with the grooved backstrap. This prevents the gun slipping in the firer's hand.

The fixed sights are adequate, and sufficiently well rounded to prevent undue snagging during a fast draw. The back sight can be driven across its dovetail to correct imperfections in lateral shot placement. The sample gun proved accurate enough at combat ranges, achieving group diameters of 12-15cm at 25 metres.

Owing to the thirteen-round magazine capacity, and the excellent manufacturing quality, the Beretta is among the best of its type. It is appreciably simpler than the CZ 83 (q.v.) and has found many champions as a 'back up' gun owing to its attractive combination of good firepower and comparatively small size.

In addition to the Berettas, an adaptation of the basic design is made in Belgium by Fabrique Nationale (a company with a substantial shareholding in Beretta). The FN variant, the 140 DA, has a closed-top slide but is otherwise much the same as its Italian prototype apart from the slide-mounted safety lever. Advocates of FN's ribbed top closed-slide construction claim that it minimizes reflection compared with the Italian pattern, which is not proven, and — possibly more realistically — that it restricts the entry of dirt and dust into the mechanism. The 140 DA, known in the USA as the BDA 380, has replaced the venerable Mle 125 on the FN production line.

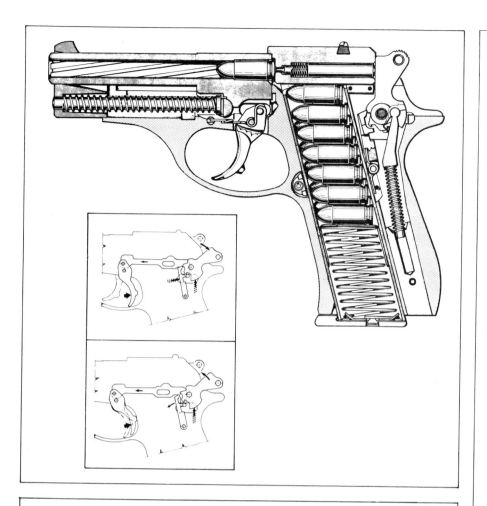

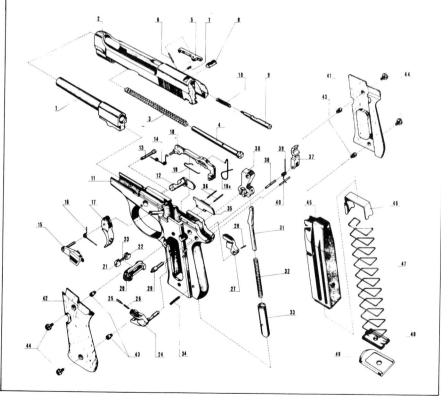

	Key
1	Barrel
2	Slide
3	Recoil Spring
4	Recoil Spring Guide
5	Extractor
6	Extractor Pin
7	Extractor Spring
8	Rear Sight
9	Firing Pin
10	Firing Pin Spring
11	Frame
12	Takedown Latch
13	Takedown Latch Release Button
14	Trigger Spring
15	Slide Catch
16	Slide Catch Spring
17	Trigger
18	Trigger Bar
19	Trigger Bar Spring
19A	Magazine Safety Spring
20	Magazine Release Button
21	Magazine Release Button Spring Bushing, Left
22	Magazine Release Button Spring Bushing, Right
23	Magazine Release Button Spring
24	Left Safety
25	Safety Spring Pin
26	Safety Spring
27	Right Safety
28	Safety Pin
29	Hammer Pin
30	Hammer
31	Hammer Spring Strut
32	Hammer Spring
33	Hammer Strut Guide
34	Hammer Strut Guide Pin
35	Ejector
36	Ejector Pin (2 Pieces)
37	Sear
38	Sear Pin
39	Sear Spring
40	Sear Spring Pin
41	Right Grip
42	Left Grip
43	Grip Bushing (4 Pieces)
44	Grip Screw (4 Pieces)
45	Magazine Box
46	Magazine Follower
47	Magazine Spring
48	Magazine Plate
49	Magazine Bottom

The standard Modelo 82B, chambering the ineffectual-but-popular 7.65mm Auto pistol cartridge (·32 ACP). (Courtesy of Pietro Beretta SpA.)

The FN DA 140, sometimes also known as the BDA 380, can be obtained chambering 7.65mm or 9mm Auto pistol cartridges (·32 and ·380 ACP), the latter being preferable for combat — though, at best, a marginal load. (Courtesy of Fabrique Nationale.)

Browning GP Mle 35 ('High-Power')

Type: single-action semi-automatic pistol.
Maker: Fabrique Nationale SA, Herstal, Belgium.
Calibre: 9mm Parabellum (a few exist in 7.65mm Parabellum).
Overall length: 197mm, 7.76in.
Barrel length: 117mm, 4.61in.
Weight empty: 910gm, 32.1oz.
Magazine capacity: 13 + 1
Construction: all steel, fixed sights.

Numerous other models exist, including several made for the US market with special finishes. The current military model – the **Vigilante** – has a half-moon blade front sight: the original military variant, no longer made, had a tangent-leaf back sight graduated to 500m and a noticeably higher front sight blade. The **Sport** model now has a fully adjustable back sight and a high rectangular front sight. In 1983, FN introduced the Mark 2, with ambidexterous safety, better sights, matt finish and neoprene grips to enhance handling. This model, with additional dots on the sights, has been adopted by special units of the Belgian state police. An alloy-frame version was introduced some years ago for the Belgian constabulary, but was withdrawn and revised after the powerful FN-loaded 9mm cartridges used by the police fractured too many frames.

The legendary High-Power – or 'Pistolet à Grande Puissance' – was the last design of the greatest genius of them all, John M. Browning. Patents for what would become the most widely distributed military pistol of all time were sought as early as 1922, but perfection was only achieved some years later. However, even the first guns showed some of the features that were to become world-famous, including the large-capacity staggered double-row magazine. Only the external hammer was missing from the guns designed in 1922-3. Unfortunately, Browning died in 1926, leaving completion of the High Power to his pupil, Dieudonné Saive, who was later to design the FAL (light automatic rifle). By 1927, the High-Power was being illustrated in FN catalogues in a form very close to the final design.

Made for the Germans during the Second World War – as well as in Canada, for the Canadians, British and Chinese – the High-Power has since equipped almost every country in the Free World. It is still, for example, the official sidearm of the British Army and the SAS.

It is no surprise that Browning used short recoil principles on his last handgun, as this had been included in the first patents ever sought for his pistols (1897) and developed, through several intermediate stages, into the US Army's M1911 Colt-Browning. The original intention was to reduce the shocks absorbed by the fabric of the gun with powerful cartridges, which could not be used safely with the fixed-barrel blowback system. Browning's solution was to let the barrel and the slide, locked together, travel backwards before being separated by a downward move of the barrel, letting the slide reciprocate alone to complete the operating cycle. This slowed the separation sufficiently for the chamber pressure to drop to a safe level.

The principal objective of the High-Power seems to have been the adoption of 9mm Parabellum, smaller than the US .45 ACP, together with a large-capacity magazine. The High Power was the only mass-produced service pistol to successfully incorporate a detachable butt-mounted box magazine containing more than ten rounds until the S&W Model 59 appeared in 1971.

Browning apparently decided that the stirrup-like trigger system used in the M1911 Colt-Browning – and many of the earlier FN-Browning blowback designs – could not be used with so wide a magazine, though the subsequent example of the S&W Model 59 and the FÉG DA, among others, have proved that he was mistaken.

Comparing the High-Power with the Colt Government Model, Browning's two classic handguns, the major differences are the suppression of the removable muzzle bushing, changes in the recoil spring system, the introduction of an unlocking ramp in place of the original articulated lug, a change in the mainspring, the elimination of the grip safety, and the addition of a magazine safety. Most importantly, the simple stirrup trigger was replaced by a much more sophisticated trigger bar/sear system. Unfortunately, the stirrup allows a plain trigger with a straight pull (and, incidentally, great adaptability), while the High-Power pattern has a lateral bar system with a pivoting trigger that gives a longer, less consistent pull. The FN-Browning mechanism is infinitely more complicated and, though usually regarded as exceptionally reliable, undeniably more fragile than the original Colt-Browning. In addition, the 9mm Parabellum cartridge is harder on the gun than the powerful-but-slow ·45 ACP.

I have already fired more than twenty thousand rounds in High-Powers, trusting my life to my own customized gun (see Appendix 1). The HP is one of the most promising of all guns 'from the box' but requires minor modifications; for example, the superfluous magazine safety (to be removed immediately!) contributes to an undesirable double-action pull exceeding 6kg/13.2lb. Removing the safety reduces the pull to about 4kg (8.8lb), better than the original but by no means outstanding. The sights supplied with the Vigilante are poor, though greatly improved on the Mark 2. The best combat pistol choice is the Sport model, which can then be customized as required. As supplied from the factory, the HP's slide, slide catch and magazine catch are all easy to operate; however, the ridiculously small manual safety lever is generally very stiff. The extended ambidexterous safety of the Mark 2 is a vast improvement.

Despite these numerous minor problems, easily eliminated by customizing, the High-Power is an extremely accurate, reliable tool. It is not entirely coincidental that many of its more recent rivals have borrowed so many of its features . . . or even, in some cases, its entire external appearance.

The 'Captain', a name applied to the military version of the High-Power in the early 1980s. Note the tangent-leaf back sight, which has no place on a combat handgun, and the lanyard ring. (Courtesy of Fabrique Nationale.)

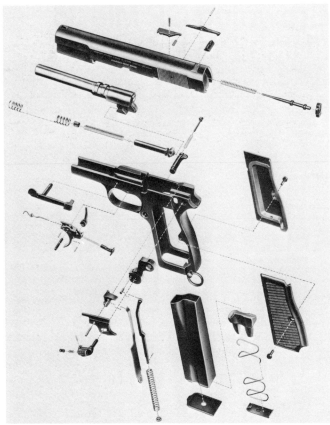

An exploded view of the High-Power. (Courtesy of Fabrique Nationale.)

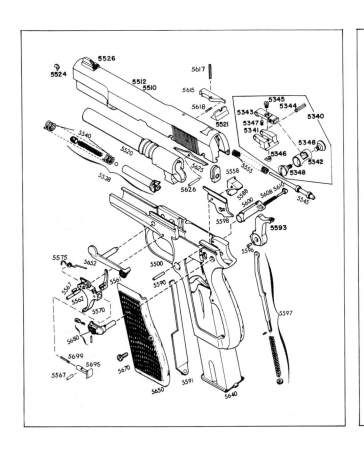

Key

5500	Frame	5625	Sear Lever
5520	Barrel	5626	Sear Lever Pin
5598	Ejector	5590	Sear Pin
5615	Extractor	5591	Sear Spring with Button
5617	Extractor Pin	5340	Rear Sight Complete, Adjustable Sight Model
5618	Extractor Spring		
5545	Firing Pin	5341	Rear Sight Base (A.S.M.)
5555	Firing Pin Spring	5342	Sight Aperture—Rear (A.S.M.)
5558	Firing Pin Retaining Plate		
5567	Trigger Spring Retaining Pin	5343	Sight Aperture Housing— Rear (A.S.M.)
5650	Grip Plate—Left— French Walnut	5344	Sight Aperture Housing Pin— Rear (A.S.M.)
5670	Grip Plate Screw	5345	Sight Elevation Screw—Rear (A.S.M.)
5593	Hammer (New Type)		
5597	Hammer Strut Assembly with Mainspring, Mainspring Support Pin, & Nut	5346	Sight Elevation Screw Spring—Rear (A.S.M)
		5347	Sight Elevation Spring—Rear (A.S.M.)
5596	Hammer Strut Pin		
5640	Magazine Complete	5348	Sight Windage Screw—Rear (A.S.M.)
5600	Magazine Latch		
5608	Magazine Latch Spring	5521	Sight—Rear
5610	Magazine Latch Spring Guide	5524	Sight—Front
5695	Magazine Safety	5526	Sight—Front (A.S.M.)
5699	Magazine Safety Spring	5510	Slide
5567	Magazine Safety Pin & Trigger Spring Pin	5512	Slide (A.S.M.)
		5652	Slide Stop
5540	Recoil Spring	5570	Trigger
5538	Recoil Spring Guide Assy. with Slide Stop Retaining Ball, Spring & Cap	5561	Trigger Lever
		5562	Trigger Pin
5680	Safety Assembly Complete	5575	Trigger Spring
5588	Sear		

The 'Vigilante' model of the military High-Power. The factory sights are not particularly good for combat handgunning, though the hole in the trigger reveals that the unnecessary magazine safety has already been removed.

The new High-Power Mark 2, with revised sights, neoprene grips, and an ambidexterous manual safety — far better than its predecessor. (Courtesy of Fabrique Nationale.)

A three-quarter view of the Mark 2 High-Power, showing the shape of the new front sight and the squared notch of the back sight. (Courtesy of Fabrique Nationale.)

Browning BDA-9

Type: double-action semi-automatic pistol.
Maker: Fabrique Nationale SA, Herstal, Belgium.
Calibre: 9mm Parabellum.
Overall length: 200mm, 7.87in.
Barrel length: 117mm, 4.61in.
Weight, empty: 900gm, 28.8oz.
Magazine capacity: 14 + 1.
Construction: all steel, fixed sights.

Fabrique Nationale offers several variants of the BDA-9, including the super-compact **BDA-9C**, with a 96mm/3.78in barrel, a shortened slide, and a greatly abbreviated grip for a special 7-round magazine (the standard magazine can be used, but protrudes below the butt). With the normal 7-round magazine, the BDA-9C measures 173mm (6.81in) overall and weighs 745gm or 23.8oz. The **BDA-9M** ('Medium') combines the short slide/barrel of the BDA-9C with the full-size butt of the standard pistol, with a result that is 178mm/7.01in overall and weighs 855gm (27.4oz).

The BDA — 'Browning Double Action' — answers the problem facing Fabrique Nationale, Colt and other makers of traditional, classic pistols: maintain the fabulous image, yet meet competition by modernising the basic design. Until the arrival of the Smith & Wesson Model 59 in the early 1970s, the High-Power was the only large-magazine full-bore pistol made in significant quantities by a major manufacturer, enabling FN to capitalize on the success for almost forty years. 'Baby' 6.35mm and 7.65mm Mle 10/22 pistols were made in some numbers, but none could compare with the success of the High-Power.

In 1980, FN proposed the very interesting, technically advanced (but now cancelled) 'Fast Action' derivative of the High-Power. This combined the traditional external appearance with a much more sophisticated trigger mechanism that allowed the gun to be cocked and the hammer de-cocked simply by pushing the hammer forward. When the trigger was pulled, effectively in single-action mode, the result was a very fast double movement of the hammer ('fast action') to give the first and all subsequent shots with the same firing characteristics. Carrying the gun cocked, with a manual safety applied, was thus eliminated. The system, confidentially presented to the US JSSAP trials and demonstrated to some interested parties elsewhere, was too complicated and fragile to withstand rigorous testing — to the great disappointment of the FN research and development team.

The Fast Action was replaced by a more conventional double-action system, developed in parallel as a safeguard against the failure of its more ambitious rival and sharing as many parts as possible. Exploded views and documentation of all three FA and DA variants were available by the summer of 1981, and, in September 1983, I was the first journalist to test the brand-new standard BDA-9.

Externally, the pistol is very similar to the High-Power, though closer examination reveals many minor differences of line and finish. The sights are greatly improved, an ambidexterous de-cocking lever replaces the traditional safety, a one-piece wraparound neoprene grip improves handling, and the trigger guard has a squared extention to facilitate a two-hand grasp.

The BDA bears little mechanical resemblance to the High-Power. Not only has the design of the recoil-spring guide rod been changed, but the entire trigger-bar/sear system has been replaced by a more conventional bar directly from the trigger to the sear and disconnector. The safeties are completely different from the old design; the superfluous magazine safety, for example, has been discarded. The firing-pin safety is an original conception in which a firing-pin 'door' blocks the rear portion of the firing pin until pushed upward by a pull on the trigger. This raises the disconnector, which in turn pushes up on the 'door', freeing the firing pin to be struck by the hammer. Accidental firing is impossible, and only a pull on the trigger can fire the gun. The firing-pin safety pivots on the edge of the slide, above the disconnector. The latter is pushed down if the slide is not properly forward, immobilising the firing pin until slide/barrel lock has been successfully completed.

The single action is quite conventional, the trigger pull (2.5kg, 5.5lb, on the test gun) tripping the sear and hammer, through an intermediate bar, and releasing the firing-pin safety 'door'. The rearward movement of the slide disconnects the trigger and re-cocks the hammer. The double action relies on the ovoid disconnector, which releases the hammer before the sear can catch.

Once dismantled, with the grip removed, the BDA-9 exhibits not only the sophisticated trigger mechanism but **also the new frame and squared butt. None of the parts will interchange with the High-Power: even the magazine is unique, holding fourteen rather than thirteen rounds. The BDA magazine has two lateral locking notches, permitting the release catch to be inverted in a few seconds to suit left-handed marksmen.**

The double de-cocking levers are similarly ambidexterous. A lug on the spindle forces the sear to release the hammer when the catch-lever is pushed upwards, but an eccentric on the axle cushions the hammer fall. When the de-cocking lever spring returns the lever to its down position, the hammer gently comes to rest.

The BDA-9 was tested at varying distances, with differing ammunition, with praiseworthy accuracy and reliability. **I had the opportunity to test it during a practical training course, along with my own customized High-Power, achieving similar scores slightly more slowly, largely because I could not let the BDA magazine fall to the ground as it lacked a bumper pad. The wide BDA trigger allows an acceptable first double-action and subsequent single-action shots with an unchanged trigger-finger position, though the angle of pull is rather different. Neither travel was exceptional, though both were acceptable.**

The short lived FN-Browning 'Fast Action'.

The trigger mechanism of the 'Fast Action': cleverly designed and very sophisticated, but insufficiently robust to withstand rigorous service.

A right-side view of the BDA. Note the new extractor, the extended trigger guard, the ambidexterous decocking lever and the reversible magazine-catch spindle.

A left-side view of the BDA, cocked. The new magazine-release button and one-piece neoprene grip are noteworthy.

(Below) the BDA-9M ('Medium') and (opposite page top) BDA-9C ('Short') variants of the BDA. Note the latter's extraordinarily abbreviated grip. (Courtesy of Fabrique Nationale.)

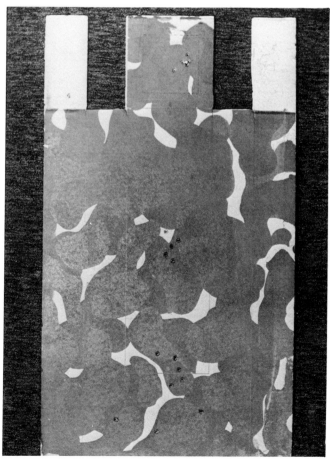

The accuracy of the BDA is excellent: the 'head' group was fired at 7 metres, the 'chest' at 15 metres. The 'stomach' contains four double taps from 10 metres.

The BDA field-stripped. The end of the recoil-spring guide rod is now completely symmetrical.

Field-stripped, the frames of the High-Power (top) and the BDA (bottom) display obvious differences.

Charter Arms Bulldog

Type: double-action revolver.
Maker: Charter Arms Corporation, Stratford, Connecticut, USA.
Calibre: ·44 Special
Overall length: 197mm, 7.75in.
Barrel length: 76mm, 3.0in.
Weight, empty: 625gm, 22oz.
Cylinder capacity: 5.
Construction: stainless steel, fixed sights.

The introduction of the Bulldog in 1974 was an important milestone in modern US combat handgun development. Although the idea of a compact revolver chambered for a fullbore cartridge with good man-stopping qualities was old – both US and British 'Bulldog' revolvers in ·44 and ·45 dated back to the late nineteenth century – the Charter Arms Bulldog marked the first modern attempt to produce such a gun, on a small or medium frame that would enhance concealability.

The result is clearly a winner. Even in its anaemic standard loading, the ·44 Special round is a better man-stopper than the ·38 Special. Federal's 200gn semi-wadcutter hollow point increases lethality, and a good handload with a semi-wadcutter bullet improves this aspect still more. Unlike the ·357 Magnum 'snubs', which provide its main competition, the Charter Arms ·44 Bulldog does not generate excessive muzzle blast. As the ·44 Special gets its stopping power more from its heavy well-shaped bullet rather than high velocity (at least in the case of the semi-wadcutters), the short barrel of the Charter Arms revolver is not at as great a disadvantage as cut-down ·357 Magnum rivals. These generate power through high velocity, a substantial portion of which is lost in a short barrel.

The Charter Arms Bulldog is also extremely comfortable to carry, being, at 22oz, comparable with most small-frame ·38 'snubs'; the Smith & Wesson Model 60, for example, weighs in at 19oz, while the ·357 Magnum S&W Model 66 (with a 2.5in barrel), one of the Charter ·44's main competitors, weighs a substantial 31oz. The 'pocket hammer' is another advantage of the ·44 Bulldog, as it offers less to catch during the draw. Unfortunately, the hooked serrated-ramp Patridge front sight is a disadvantage and can catch on a lining. On the new 2.5in-barrelled Bulldogs, a full-length ramp front sight enhances 'drawability'.

An interesting feature of Charter Arms revolvers is that the cylinder can be released by either pushing the cylinder-release catch forward or pulling the ejector rod toward the muzzle. Some shooters, who find that the bulky cylinder-release catch cuts their hand during firing, remove it and simply rely on the ejector rod to release the cylinder. Others who have never been 'bitten' simply leave the catch in place.

The travel of the ejector rod is not sufficient to fully eject the remaining rounds, so it is advisable to invert the gun and give the rod a sharp tap to ensure rapid extraction. The ·44 Bulldog cylinders only hold five rounds, but five rounds of ·44 Special is nonetheless a potent pocketful. The restricted capacity is necessary to restrict cylinder bulk. The cylinder itself shows thoughtful design, the bolt cuts being offset to avoid weakening the thinnest part of the cylinder walls. However, only factory-loaded ·44 Special rounds (or factory-equivalent handloads) should be used. The Federal 200gn semi-wadcutter bullet is ideal.

I chose a ·44 Bulldog made of stainless steel, owing to its greater durability, though the Charter Arms 'stainless' alloy is rust-resistant rather than truly rust-proof. Though this is true of many 'stainless steel' guns, the Charter Arms finish, in my experience, has not proved as durable as those used by Colt, Ruger and Smith & Wesson. However, only a light coat of surface rust will occur, even in harsh salty and humid conditions. I have used my ·44 Bulldog in some very moist places and the rust traces – little more than slight spotting along the front sight ramp – can usually be removed by vigorously rubbing with an oily cloth.

On the range, the ·44 Bulldog performed admirably. Though recoil is noticeable, owing to its light weight and the impulse of a comparatively heavy bullet leaving the barrel at an appreciable velocity, it is not hard to handle. The neoprene grips certainly help, and are highly recommended; in fact, they are virtually a necessity unless ultimate concealability is desired (when I would substitute the grips from a Charter Undercover revolver, accepting the greater recoil sensation they bring).

Personal experience with the Federal 200gn semi-wadcutter, developed with the ·44 Bulldog in mind, taught me that this was an accurate load with which to undertake testing. At 10 yards, the diameter of rapid-fire double-action groups rarely exceeded 3in. Interestingly, much the same results were obtained at 15 yards. The test gun shot slightly to the right, but not enough to matter at the short distances for which the gun is intended (point blank to 15 yards). The 3in barrel gives a reasonable sight radius, which enhances accuracy. Despite the noticeable recoil and muzzle flip, inherent in a light gun, the comfortable neoprene grips shorten recovery time in rapid double-action shooting. The double-action trigger pull is excellent, being smooth, crisp and relatively light; the single action will be rarely used, since most situations in which the ·44 Bulldog will be fired demand a fast first shot, invariably fired simply by pulling through on the trigger.

The Charter Arms ·44 Bulldog receives a high rating as a combat handgun. It is light, reasonably compact, accurate at short range and chambered for a good man-stopping cartridge. It is at its best in situations where a police officer, for example, needs a light concealable weapon powerful enough to stop an assailant high on drugs. The ·44 Bulldog is a particularly useful back-up for the policeman whose service handgun is a ·44 Magnum: ·44 Special rounds carried on the belt may be fired in either gun. The ·44 Bulldog also has attractions for personal protection, allying, as it does, effective stopping power with comparatively poor penetration.

The Charter Arms ·44 Bulldog is one of the few currently-available revolvers that packs truly fullbore punch in a compact weapon – the perennial goal of handgun designers.

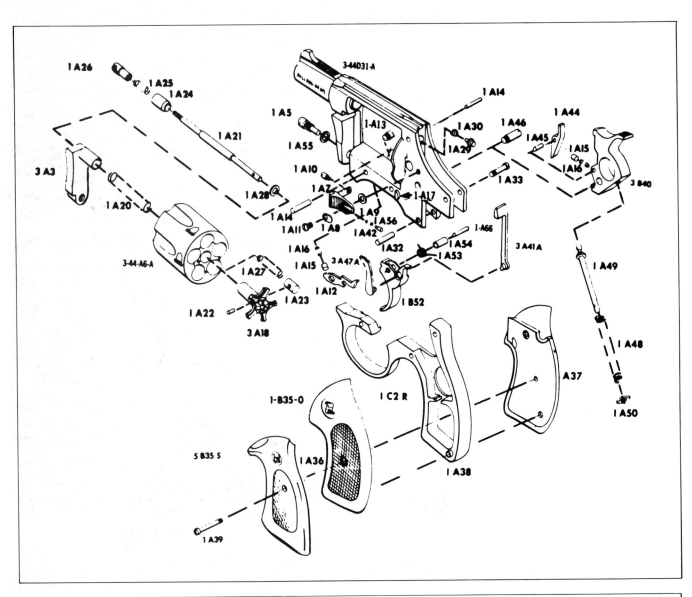

Key

1C2R	Grip Frame with Grip Locating Pin	1A13	Cylinder Stop Bushing	1A25	Ejector Rod Collar Spring	3B40	Hammer	1A56	Cylinder Latch Spring
3A3A	Crane	1A14	Cylinder Stop & Firing Pin Retaining Pin	1A26	Ejector Rod Head	3A41A	Hammer Block Assembly	1A66	Trigger Pin
1A5	Crane Screw	1A15	Cylinder Stop & Hammer Pawl Plunger	1A27	Ejector Rod Lock Spring	1A42	Cylinder Latch Plunger		
3-44A6A	Cylinder			1A28	Ejector Rod Washer	1A44	Hammer Pawl		
1A7	Cylinder Latch	1A16	Cylinder Stop, Hammer Pawl Spring	1A29	Firing Pin	1A45	Hammer Pawl Pin		
1A8	Cylinder Latch Cover Plate			1A30	Firing Pin Spring	1A46	Hammer Screw		
1A49	Cylinder Latch Washer	1A17	Ejection Stud	3-44D31A	Frame & Barrel	3A47A	Hand Assembly		
		3A18	Ejector	1A32	Frame Assembly Screw	3A48	Mainspring		
1A10	Cylinder Latch Release Screw	1A20	Ejector Return Spring	1B350	Grips, Bulldog	1A49	Mainspring Guide Rod		
		1A21	Ejector Rod	5B35S	Grips, Square Butt	1A50	Mainspring Seat		
1A11	Cylinder Latch Retaining Screw	1A22	Ejector Rod Assembly Pin	1A36	Grip Escutcheon	1B52	Trigger		
		1A23	Ejector Rod Bushing	1A37	Grip Escutcheon Nut	1A53	Trigger Spring		
1A12	Cylinder Stop	1A24	Ejector Rod Collar	1A38	Grip Locating Pin	1A54	Trigger Spring Bushing		
				1A39	Grip Screw	1A55	Crane Screw Washer		

The ·44 Bulldog. Note that the cylinder can be released either by pushing the frame latch or by pulling the ejector rod.

Neoprene combat grips are a real asset on the ·44 Bulldog.

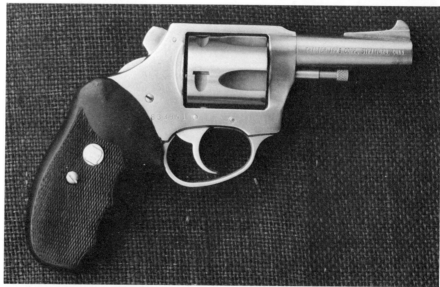

By limiting cylinder capacity to five rounds, Charter Arms has given the ·44 Bulldog good wall thickness. Note that the bolt-cuts are offset to conserve strength; the gun would have been seriously weakened had they lain over the thinnest part of the cylinder wall. The impressive-looking chambered rounds are 200gn Federal hollow-point semi-wad-cutters.

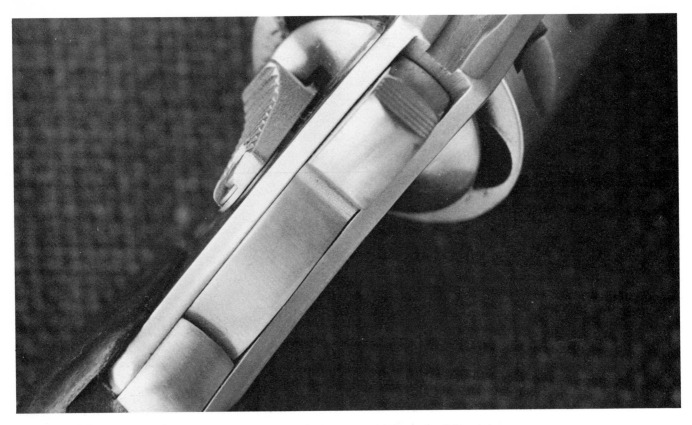

The ·44 Bulldog's spurless pocket hammer prevents it snagging clothing during a draw.

The Bulldog does have a substantial recoil, even with standard ·44 Special ammunition.

15 yard double-action groups obtained from the ·44 Bulldog.

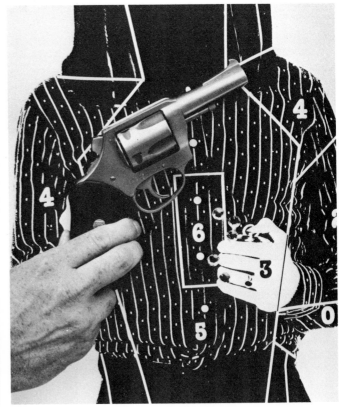

Charter Arms Bulldog Tracker

Type: double-action revolver.
Maker: Charter Arms Corporation, Stratford, Connecticut, USA.
Calibre: ·357 Magnum.
Overall length: 191mm, 7.5in.
Barrel length: 63mm, 2.5in.
Weight, empty: 595gm, 21oz.
Cylinder capacity: 5.
Construction: blued steel, adjustable sights.

The forté of Charter Arms is offering reliable revolvers at reasonable prices, and the Bulldog Tracker is firmly in this tradition. The grip on all Charter revolvers is basically the same, though the portion of the frame containing the cylinder is somewhat strengthened on the 'Bulldog' line. The Bulldog frames are, in fact, solid steel.

A snub-nose ·357 revolver, such as the Bulldog Tracker tested, is generally a compromise between compactness and power. The ·357 Magnum gets much of its power from high velocity, which necessitates a relatively heavy gun to handle the resulting pressure safely. The Bulldog Tracker, however, is the lightest of the ·357 'snubs' by a substantial margin, despite being a good size. For carrying purposes — when concealment is important — the Charter Arms Undercover grips, preferably the older smooth type, may be substituted for the larger, squared chequered-walnut Bulldog pattern. The smaller grips make the gun harder to control, but appreciably easier to conceal.

The Bulldog Tracker's five-round cylinder offers additional strength by giving greater cylinder-wall thickness. The heavy 'bull' barrel adds strength and stability, weight at the muzzle helping to counter muzzle flip — along with muzzle blast, a primary problem with ·357 'snubs'. Like all Charter Arms revolvers, the cylinder of the Bulldog Tracker may be released by pushing the cylinder latch forward or by pulling the unsupported ejector rod toward the muzzle. The open cylinder displays the counter-bored recesses for the case heads, a traditional feature of the S&W ·357 Magnum revolvers dating from the days when the cartridge was 'the most powerful in the world' and doubts were expressed whether revolvers could handle it safely.

One of my few objections to Charter Arms revolvers is that the cylinder, when open, does not always rotate as smoothly as those of Colt, Ruger or Smith & Wesson guns. Neither does the ejector rod always operate as smoothly. However, roughness in the cylinder and ejector system does not compromise reliability or safety.

Even though its weight is good, and the click-adjustable back sight is compact, the 'hooked' Patridge-type front sight ramp prevents the Bulldog Tracker being an optimum pocket revolver. Instead, it is a compact holster gun. I normally prefer smaller guns for concealment, but will admit that the standard Bulldog grips are well designed and help with both recoil and 'pointability'. The black neoprene grips available with the Charter Arms Bulldog can also be considered, as they are more compact and should cushion the recoil of the ·357 Magnum better than the standard wood ones.

For safety, the Bulldog Tracker uses a hammer block, which prevents the hammer reaching the firing pin unless the trigger is pulled. I believe that a combat revolver should always be used exclusively in double-action mode, not only increasing reaction speed but also eliminating many of the accidents caused while manoeuvering with a cocked revolver. However, the Charter's safety remains useful, as it will also prevent discharge should an uncocked gun be dropped. The firing pin is made of an alloy of beryllium and copper, being sufficiently durable to allow practice dry-firing.

Both single- and double-action trigger pulls were reasonably smooth and crisp on the test gun, though all shooting was performed simply by pulling through on the trigger. The double-action pull would have been better had it been a couple of pounds lighter, but it was acceptably smooth and had no perceptible increase in pressure before let-off.

Testing — exclusively with full-power ·357 Magnum loads — was undertaken at 10, 15 and 25 yards, using 110gn CCI-Lawman, 110gn and 125gn Federal jacketed hollow point loads. The Bulldog Tracker obtained the best results with the 125gn Federal bullet, though all three types performed reliably. At 15 yards, the diameter of rapid-fire double action 5-shot groups averaged about 3in. The best group at this distance was just over 2in. Groups opened out at 25 yards, but were still normally under 6in and often measured 4-5in. As one would expect from a short-barrelled lightweight ·357, recoil, muzzle blast and flip were all noticeable. However, accuracy was good and the Bulldog Tracker came through the shooting tests quite well.

The greatest advantage of the Bulldog Tracker is its combination of a lot of power in a reasonably small package at a very attractive price. However, ·357 Magnum 'snubs' are not widely favoured, as a 4in-barrelled gun carries almost as a 2in-barrel variety. The Bulldog Tracker also faces formidable competition in the form of the short-barrel Colt Python and Lawman, the Ruger Security Six, or the Smith & Wesson Models 19 and 66, and has not achieved widespread police acceptance. It still has merits for personal defence, though, as its reliability and accuracy are unquestioned.

Although the short barrel and small frame help to make the Bulldog Tracker an excellent concealment gun, the grips and the hooked front sight are unsuitable for this role.

One real asset is the compact adjustable back sight of the Bulldog Tracker. Though bulky, the grips aid rapid shooting.

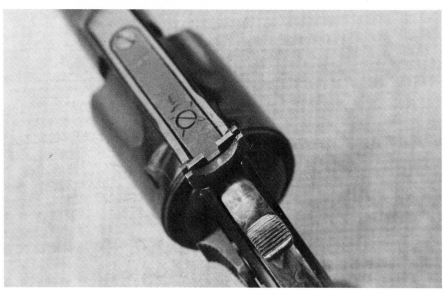

The back sight of the Charter Arms Bulldog Tracker, an especially compact and desirable pattern.

To allow greater cylinder-wall strength in a small-frame revolver, Charter Arms reduced the cylinder capacity of the Bulldog Tracker to five rounds.

In rapid fire, the Bulldog Tracker shows a tendency towards muzzle climb but is soon mastered with practice.

15 yard double-action group obtained from the Bulldog Tracker.

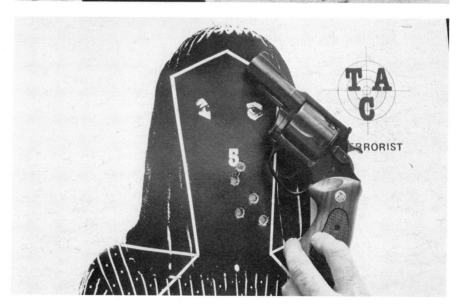

Charter Arms Off-Duty

Type: double-action revolver.
Maker: Charter Arms Corporation, Stratford, Connecticut, USA.
Calibre: ·38 Special.
Overall length: 159mm, 6.25in.
Barrel length: 51mm, 2.0in.
Weight, empty: 455gm, 16oz.
Cylinder capacity: 5.
Construction: matt-black steel, fixed sights.

Although Smith & Wesson's airweight Chief's Special is slightly lighter, the Off-Duty revolver shares its title of the most compact ·38 Special revolver on the market with the essentially similar Charter Arms Undercover. The company has established its reputation by making attractively priced, reliable and serviceable weapons, a tradition in which the Off-Duty is firmly rooted.

Like S&W's J-Frame ·38 revolvers, the Off-Duty has a five-round cylinder to restrict its width to merely 1.25in. Reducing cylinder bulk is an important step in producing a true concealment revolver, as cylinder bulge is the hardest part of a revolver to hide. The Off-Duty is very easy to conceal, though. While small, the Off-Duty's cylinder and frame are both all-steel (though the grip is alloy) and durable enough provided standard ·38 Special loads are used.

In typical Charter Arms fashion, the cylinder can be released either by pushing the cylinder latch forward or by pulling the ejector rod forward. The ejector rod is not long enough for full extraction so the gun needs to be tilted 'barrel-up' to ensure reliable extraction. The ejector does not work as smoothly as one expects on a Smith & Wesson, Colt or Ruger, but still does its job reliably.

Despite the small size of the Off-Duty frame, the trigger guard is roomy enough to allow the trigger to be reached quickly and easily. The trigger itself is grooved longitudinally to prevent slipping, and allows a comfortable reach for a normal-size hand. The optional spurless 'pocket hammer' is useful, as it will not catch during a rapid draw from (for example) inside a jacket. The trigger pull on the test gun was about average, the double-action mode being smooth if a little heavy.

The Off-Duty's rudimentary fixed square-notch back sight is typical of small 'snub' revolvers, but is quite sufficient at the close ranges for which the gun is intended. The red-dot insert in the front sight greatly assists rapid sight alignment.

Although many shooters dislike the tiny smooth walnut panel-style grips, I find them a bonus: they not only facilitate concealment, but also lack the chequering that can abrade the hand while shooting. With this small gun, sharp chequering would have been noticeable even with standard velocity ·38 Special loads. However, medium-size hands and a strong grip are both advantageous when using the Off-Duty.

The Off-Duty has an excellent flat black matt non-reflective finish, ideal for combat use and enhancing concealability. The gun performed well on the range, considering the limitations of its diminutive size. All testing was undertaken at 10 and 15 yards, where it was possible to keep all five rounds, fired double action, in the chest cavity of a figure target. Group diameter at 15 yards averaged 4-5in, particularly when 158gn Federal semi-wadcutter loads were used; 158gn CCI-Speer semi-wadcutter and 158gn Federal round-nose bullets also performed adequately. Many shooters fire '+P' loads in light Charter Arms revolvers, but the lower pressure standard-velocity loads are preferable.

The handling characteristics of the Off-Duty were also good. Muzzle flip was as noticeable as with any comparably light compact ·38 Special revolver, but the Off-Duty could be hauled back on target relatively quickly for repeat shots and sighting was enhanced by the red front-sight insert. Like all such 'snubs' — especially the ultra-compact ones — mastering the Off-Duty requires a certain amount of patience and tolerance. Its convenient size makes the effort worthwhile.

The Off-Duty is at its best as an undercover or 'hideout' weapon, where its small size, pocket hammer and matt finish all assist concealment. It is highly concealable, yet it hits with authority - the two principal attributes of a good hideout gun for police officer and civilian alike. However, practice on the range is required to get the best out of the Off-Duty: purchasing the gun, loading and hiding in a drawer, without learning to handle it first, courts disaster.

One of the guns the US firearms industry makes best is the ·38 'snub', and the Charter Arms Off-Duty is in the tradition of its champions.

The Off-Duty. Note the small plain grip-panels, greatly favoured for concealment.

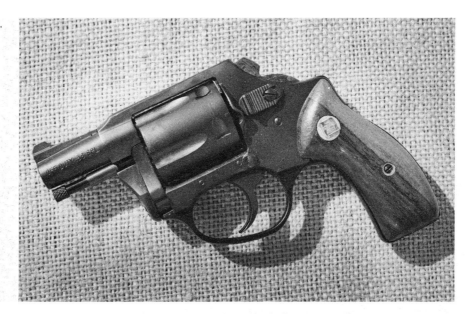

Even though the Off-Duty is the most compact ·38 Special revolver on the market, it is still an easy gun to shoot. The full-size trigger guard allows rapid access to the trigger.

The front-sight insert on the Off-Duty assists rapid sight alignment.

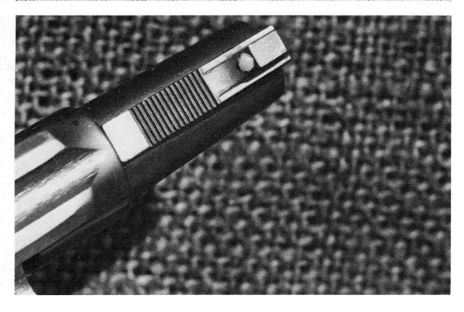

The pocket hammer allows the Off-Duty to be concealed and drawn easily.

Despite the Off-Duty's small grip and light weight, handling full-power ·38 Special loads presented few problems.

A typical 15 yard double-action group obtained with the Charter Arms Off-Duty.

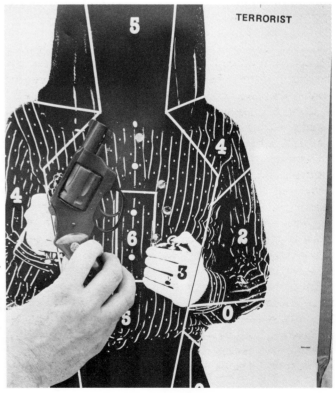

Colt Agent

Type: double-action revolver.
Maker: Colt's, Inc., Hartford, Connecticut, USA.
Calibre: ·38 Special.
Overall length: 168mm, 6.63in.
Barrel length: 51mm, 2.0in.
Weight, empty: 480gm, 17oz.
Cylinder capacity: 6.
Construction: parkerized, fixed sights.

Colt pioneered the snub-nose ·38 Special revolver with the Detective Special in 1927. A variant of this snub, with an alloy frame and a shortened grip, was introduced as the 'Agent'. There was also an alloy-frame twin of the Detective Special, known as the Cobra, until Colt dramatically rationalized its handgun line a few years ago. Only the Detective Special survived, with a new heavy barrel and a distinctive ejector shroud. In 1982, however, Colt re-introduced a new version of the Agent to compete with inexpensive ·38 snubs such as the Charter Arms Undercover.

The new Agent is akin to the old Cobra, as it is really no more than an alloy-framed Detective Special without the Cobra's cosmetic improvements. To keep costs down, the Agent is parkerized rather than blued and the smooth walnut squared-butt grips are unfinished. Parkerization is advantageous on a combat gun, as it is non-reflective and wears better than blued steel. The smooth grips are a mixed blessing since they have more of a tendency to shift in the hand than chequered grips, but handle recoil more comfortably with the full-power ·38 Special loads.

Despite the Agent's lack of frills, it is still well made. Though it is a subjective test, I always evaluate a revolver by the sound of the cylinder closing, and the Agent has the 'bank vault click' one expects from a Colt or Smith & Wesson. The Agent cylinder holds six rather than five rounds, making it a competitor of the Smith & Wesson Model 10 rather than the S&W Model 36 or Charter Arms Undercover revolvers. The cylinder release has to be pulled backward, in typical Colt fashion. The ejector rod — like many other 'snubs' — does not travel far enough to fully extract fired cases unless the Agent is held 'barrel up' during extraction, a technique recommended for all such guns. The cylinder latch on Colts is relatively bulky, but does not normally interfere with speedloaders and reloading time is at least average.

The heavy barrel and shrouded ejector rod give the Agent a very sturdy appearance. The weight of the muzzle also helps to counter muzzle flip. The ramp-type front sight is not grooved, but this is not obviously disadvantageous on a close-quarters weapon. The Agent's fixed sights offer average efficacy. Firing at 15 yards, the sights on the test gun were found to be a couple of inches high and a shade to the left. All three loads tested — 158gn Federal and Remington lead semi-wadcutters, and 158gn Federal lead round-nose bullets — shot high. Group diameters at this distance generally measured 3-4in, the best being achieved with the 158gn Federal semi-wadcutter.

Only double-action fire was used during tests. In 2- or 3-round strings, recovery time was about what would be expected for a gun weighing just 16oz. The Agent was easier to bring back on target than its J-Frame Smith & Wesson rivals, but not as fast as the larger S&W K-Frame guns. The double-action pull was quite heavy, and had a tendency for pressure to increase just before let-off. The test gun would undoubtedly have benefitted from shooting-in, or the work of a competent gunsmith on the trigger system to hone the pull. The thin trigger is not grooved.

The overall handling characteristics of the Agent are very good. It balances well, and points instinctively enough to facilitate shooting. The grip is full enough for all three fingers to fit around it, enhancing control and 'drawability'; when pulling the Agent from a holster, one can rapidly achieve a good grip. The reach to the trigger is comfortable enough, though long-fingered firers - even if their hands are only medium-size — may find it easier to use the middle segment of the finger on the trigger.

Accepting that the best and most concealable 'snub-nose' revolvers are those with small frames, the Agent offers very good value at a reasonable price. It is especially well suited to home-defence, particularly where its owner is not particularly interested in firearms. Though a longer barrel is normally preferable in a 'home gun', the Agent has certain advantages: it is harder, for example, for an intruder to grab a short barrel, which also denies him satisfactory leverage. The Agent will also fit into a drawer or a pocket better than a long-barrel revolver.

As most non-firearms enthusiasts rarely wish to spend more money than necessary on a personal defence gun, yet need reliability on which their lives can be staked, the good-quality inexpensive Agent is an attractive proposition. In addition, the parkerized finish will wear well.

The Colt Agent offers good value for money. Though the Smith & Wesson J-Frame revolvers may be preferable for the off-duty police officer (as the J-Frame is easier to conceal), the Agent is ideal for home defence. However, in common with any 2in-barrel revolver with fixed sights, practice is required to master the Agent effectively. And choice of ammunition is important, owing to the combination of a short barrel and an alloy frame. My tests indicate that the 158gn Federal semi-wadcutter is the best factory load, acquiring its stopping power, as it does, from a blunt heavy bullet fired at medium velocity. This facilitates better gun control than would be possible with a higher velocity high-pressure load.

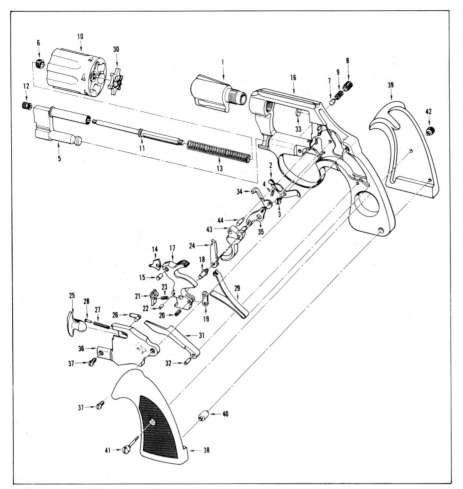

The clean lines of the Agent, together with its heavy barrel and ejector-rod housing, are obvious in this side view.

Note the flat parkerized finish of the Agent, and the distinctive Colt cylinder-release latch.

The Agent's smooth walnut grips are inexpensive, but minimize recoil sensations since there is no chequering to abrade the hand. However, smooth grips can be disadvantageous if they permit the gun to shift in the hand during firing.

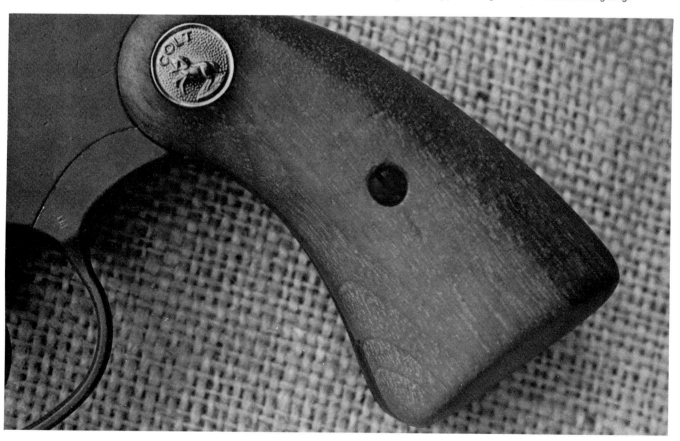

Heavy barrel, shrouded ejector rod and a long ramp-mounted front sight are among the Agent's most prominent features.

Despite light weight, the recovery time on the Agent is surprisingly good; this photograph was taken after two shots had been fired, yet the muzzle-flip is minimal.

A typical rapid-fire double-action group obtained from the Agent at 15 yards.

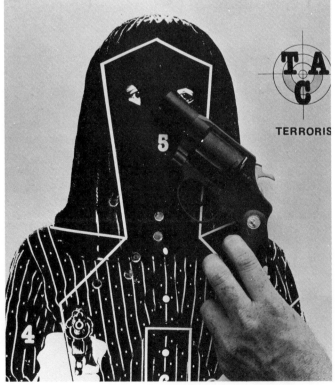

Colt Diamondback

Type: double-action revolver.
Maker: Colt's, Inc., Hartford, Connecticut, USA.
Calibre: ·38 Special.
Overall length: 229mm, 9.0in.
Barrel length: 102mm, 4.0in.
Weight, empty: 808gm, 28.5oz.
Cylinder capacity: 6.
Construction: blued steel, adjustable sights.

The Colt Diamondback was introduced in 1966 as a luxury version of Colt's classic lightweight Police Positive Special revolver, one of the company's most popular revolvers for over fifty years despite its inadequate sights and muzzle-lightness. Taking the Police Positive frame (the D-Frame) as the basis, Colt engineers designed the Diamondback as a scaled-down Python lookalike.

Despite its superficial resemblance to the Python, the Diamondback remains a small-frame revolver — though, owing to its heavy barrel, it weighs 6oz more than the earlier Police Positive Special. However, the Diamondback is sufficiently sturdy to be considered safe with high velocity '+P' ·38 Special loads. The heavy Python-style barrel with ventilated rib and under-lug not only adds to the Diamondback's appearance, but also helps dampen muzzle flip with heavier loads or during rapid fire. The rib and top strap have a glare-restricting matt finish, though the remainder of the gun is brightly blued.

The back sight is click-adjustable laterally and vertically (for 'windage' and elevation respectively). Adding a white front sight insert and a white-outline back sight blade facilitates rapid aiming.

The cylinder remains that of a light gun, the wall thickness not being very great. However, the offset bolt-cuts ensure that the cylinder is quite sturdy. In typical Colt fashion, the cylinder release latch operates rearward; in addition, the cylinder rotates clockwise, locking up tightly when the trigger is pulled and the hammer drops. The trigger is standard, but the hammer is of target type.

The fit of the large chequered walnut target-type grips on the trial gun was poor, allowing the frame to shift within them and showing an unwarranted lack of acceptable quality control that the purchaser has a right to expect on a comparatively expensive gun such as the Diamondback.

The factory grips proved uncomfortable for combat shooting and were replaced with neoprene Pachmayr grips. Many women find that shooting the Diamondback is helped by fitting the smaller grips from the Police Positive, additionally enhancing concealability. Another real advantage of the Diamondback is the existence of a ·22 version, ideal for training purposes. The ·22 Diamondback is a twin of the ·38 pattern, except for being slightly heavier owing to the greater amount of metal left in the barrel and cylinder. Inexpensive familiarization and practice can be undertaken with the rimfire gun before moving on to its full-bore twin. Though a great deal of experience with ·38 Special service ammunition is necessary to perfect combat shooting, practice gained with the essentially similar ·22 version usually proves valuable.

The double- and single-action trigger pulls on the test Diamondback were both heavy, though the single-action pull was relatively crisp. Since the gun was used almost entirely in its double-action mode, however, the undesirable tendency of the double-action pull to increase just before let-off made smooth rapid-fire shooting difficult. Though the Diamondback resembles the Python externally, it is obvious that the action does not receive the Python's hand-fitting.

Even with the heavy double-action pull, the Diamondback grouped well. Using 158gn CCI-Speer or Federal semi-wadcutters, 125gn CCI-Speer and 110gn Federal jacketed hollow-point ammunition, double-action group diameters averaged 2-3in at 15 yards. These groups opened up a bit at 25 yards, though staying around 3in with 125gn CCI-Speer jacketed hollow-points and 158gn Federal semi-wadcutters. The heavy barrel helped recovery time in rapid shooting. Even with '+P' loads, the Diamondback was comfortable to shoot, though the sharp chequering on the factory target-type grips cut into my hands.

The Diamondback is one of the best ·38 Special revolvers on the market. It offers a good compromise between convenient concealability and a sturdiness that allows the more deadly ·38 Special loads to be used. With Police Positive or Detective Special grips, which adjust the trigger-reach for smaller hands, the Diamondback not only conceals well but also makes a comfortable woman's gun. Along with the Smith & Wesson Models 10 and 15, the Diamondback ranks as one of the best duty-type ·38 Special revolvers on the market. It is useful not only for police duty, but also for home defence and personal protection.

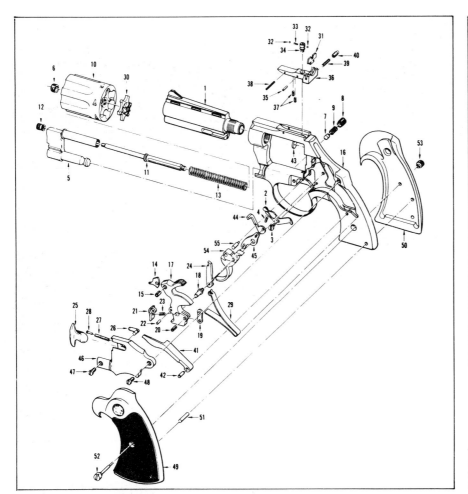

The external similarity of the Diamondback to the Python is clearly evident by comparing this view with the picture on page 81. The barrel rib and the underlug help reduce muzzle flip.

The Python-type Diamondback grips are not to my liking, as they are uncomfortable and too sharply chequered.

Though the Diamondback greatly resembles the Python, its cylinder is not as large as the latter's.

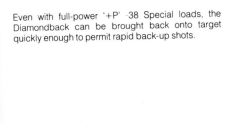

Even with full-power '+P' ·38 Special loads, the Diamondback can be brought back onto target quickly enough to permit rapid back-up shots.

A double-action group achieved with the Diamondback at 15 yards.

Colt Government Model Mark IV

Type: single-action semi-automatic pistol.
Maker: Colt's, Inc., Hartford, Connecticut, USA.
Calibre: ·45 ACP.
Overall length: 216mm, 8.5in.
Barrel length: 127mm, 5.0in.
Weight, empty: 1,105gm, 39.0oz.
Magazine capacity: 7+1.
Construction: blued steel, fixed sights.

There are many who consider the Colt Government Model the combat handgun, and though I do not include myself in the group, I certainly give it high marks. Originally conceived as a military sidearm, the Government Model has also established a good reputation for police and civilian use. The very fact that it remained the official US service handgun for nearly 75 years says much for the durability and reliability of the big Colt. The fact that John Browning designed the Government Model is also a telling point in its favour, since the Ogden Maestro rarely made mistakes.

The Government Model utilizes a breech system based on a link below a barrel, which cams the latter out of engagement with the recesses in the slide after the slide/barrel group, locked together, has travelled a short distance backward. This system works particularly well with the ·45 ACP round. Dismantling the Government Model for normal maintenance is reasonably easy, though more complicated than some newer designs. With practice, however, the ·45 Colt automatic can be field-stripped quite rapidly. When the Mark IV Government Model is field-stripped, it becomes clear that the barrel bushing fits more tightly around the barrel than on the older military or commercial guns. This improves accuracy considerably.

Despite its large calibre and hefty size, the Government Model is eminently concealable. Apart from the protrusion of the slide stop and the safety, the side of the slide is quite flat. On the standard Government Model (but not the Gold Cup variant), the sights are rudimentary − though adequate out to 25 yards and compact enough to minimize snagging clothing during a rapid draw.

The Government Model safety is placed so that it can be flicked off without changing the hand-grasp. Operating the slide stop and the magazine-release button, however will usually require a shift in grip. The magazine release lies in a typical Colt-Browning position, on the frame behind the trigger guard. The Government Model grip is reasonably comfortable for a medium or large hand. Some shooters find that the hammer has a tendency to 'bite' them as it is cocked by the slide, while others find that the grip safety hinders a proper grasp. However, it is not advisable to disconnect the grip safety, especially on guns carried cocked-and-locked ('Condition One') − a practice I do recommend.

The Government Model's magazines play an important part in reliable functioning, and their lips must be checked frequently to ensure they are not bent. Followers and follower springs must also be checked frequently. Magazines are, of course, important to the working of all semi-automatics, but this is particularly true of the Government Model. The magazine will normally fall free easily when the release button is pressed, aiding rapid reloading.

The trigger pull on the test gun was rather heavy, but the design of the parts is such that any good pistolsmith can smooth the action. On the range, the gun performed reasonably well. As might be expected, the best performance was obtained with 230gn Remington full metal-case (FMC) bullets, which went into 3.5-4in diameter groups at 25 yards. Federal's 230gn FMC and 185gn jacketed hollow-point loads performed almost as well.

Though the slam of the recoiling Government Model slide disconcerts many inexperienced shooters, practice usually makes perfect. Much of the fear of using this ·45 gun stems from the reminiscences of poorly-trained military personnel issued with well-worn guns. However, small hands are not really compatible with the Government Model even though many outstanding women shooters have proved that the big Colt can be a satisfactory unisex weapon.

The Colt Government Model is worthy of consideration for military, police or civilian combat/defence purposes. The ·45 ACP is a good man-stopper with metal-jacketed 'hardball' ammunition, though Silvertips or Glaser Safety Slugs enhance its performance. Though it is considered a 'large auto', the Government Model carries reasonably well, though at something of a disadvantage to the Colt Lightweight Commander or ·45 Officer's Model where concealment is concerned. The Government Model makes a good holster gun, preferably carried cocked-and-locked ('Condition One' provided suitable care is taken with the chambered round. The gun is valuable for home- or personal-defence use in the hands of an experienced firer, but is not recommended for the occasional shooter for whom the Government Model is too powerful a handful. Survivalists also like the ·45 ACP Colt, owing to the wide availability of spares and ammunition − in addition to its durability and proven knockdown capability.

One of the most impressive features of the Government Model is its businesslike appearance. There is little doubt that it is intended for combat.

The well-placed magazine release, safety and slide stop are all obvious from this view. However, sights are minimal.

The Government Model's grip safety, though useful, prevents some shooters gripping the Government Model properly.

(Above) The new-pattern muzzle bushing helps improve the accuracy of the Government Model.

(Right) The Government Model really does not have an uncontrollable recoil: note that the ejected spent case is still in the air, yet the gun is being returned to the target. However, the slam of the slide has a recoil-magnifying effect that may disconcert in-experienced firers.

A 25 yard group obtained with the Government Model.

Colt Officer's Model

Type: single-action automatic.
Maker: Colt's, Inc., Hartford, Connecticut, USA.
Calibre: 45 ACP.
Overall length: 184mm, 7.25in.
Height: 127mm, 5in.
Width: 35mm, 1.37in.
Barrel length: 89mm, 3.5in.
Weight, empty: 964gm, 34oz. (unloaded).
Sights: front – blued post with white dot, rear – square notch with two white dots.
Stocks: blackened, chequered walnut.
Finish: stainless steel, fixed sights.
Capacity: 6+1.

The Colt Officer's Model marks a new responsiveness on the part of Colt to the desires of shooters. For many years anyone wanting a compact ·45 auto had to either have a custom gunsmith alter a full-sized Government Model or be content with a Detonics. With the introduction of the Officer's Model, however, a highly concealable Colt ·45 auto is now available from the factory. There are four versions available: blued steel; blued Lightweight, with an alloy frame; stainless steel; and matt nickel. My personal favourite for carrying would normally be a Lightweight version; however, since one was not available for testing as this book went to press, I have evaluated my second choice, the stainless steel Officer's Model.

One of the big points in the Officer's Model's favour is that it is chambered for the potent ·45 ACP cartridge yet is still quite compact. This combination is hard to beat for someone who carries a gun professionally. Of course, the Officer's Model's concealability is still relative since I would rate it a holster gun rather than a pocket pistol. The Officer's Model is, in fact, slightly bulkier than the Detonics, partially due to a slightly longer grip, which most find more comfortable. Personally, I don't really see that it makes much difference in shooting the two guns. One thing I really do like, though, is that, unlike the Detonics, the Officer's Model incorporates a grip safety. Even though I've carried autos cocked and locked for twenty years, such carry still makes me a trifle nervous, and the grip safety lessens that nervousness somewhat. The Officer's Model also incorporates the old-style flat mainspring housing, which certainly makes sense on the shorter grip. The Officer's Model shares the ringed hammer with the Colt Commander, and this is a good choice for concealment arm since it is less likely to snag while drawing the arm.

One feature the Officer's Model shares with the Detonics is the use of the coned barrel for lockup at the muzzle. I've always preferred this system to the use of a barrel bushing, but the Officer's Model uses both the cone system and a bushing. Like the Detonics, the Officer's Model also uses a double recoil spring to dampen recoil and cushion the slam-

ming of the slide. This combination makes for good accuracy and reliability with the Officer's Model, but I dislike the fact that the Officer's Model is more difficult to field strip for cleaning than either the full-sized Government Model or the Detonics MC-1.

In addition to the grip safety the Model incorporates a normal Colt-type safety on the left side of the frame, which is well located for quickly flicking off in a combat situation. There is also a 'half-cock' safety which will prevent the hammer from hitting the firing pin if the gun is dropped or the hammer released in some other manner than pulling the trigger. The firing pin itself is an inertia firing pin, which needs a hammer blow before it can hit the primer on a cartridge. This firing pin also incorporates a lock to prevent its movement until the trigger is pulled. In combination, these safeties offer many failsafes to prevent an accidental discharge though, as always, with firearms great care must still be exercised!

To allow accurate sighting the top of the slide has a matt finish to reduce glare. The front and rear sights on the stainless steel model tested were blued and incorporated white dots for quick acquisition. Though these are fixed combat sights rather than adjustable target sights, they function very well for the ranges likely to be involved in using the Officer's Model. The square notch on the rear sight is open enough to allow easy acquisition, and with a little practice, one can align the three dots on the sights very quickly.

The grips are of black chequered walnut and offer a good gripping surface. In fact, I find the Officer's Model the most comfortable Colt ·45 auto I've ever fired; its grip actually fits me better than a full-sized Government Model. The magazine release is located on the frame in standard Colt/Browning position for easy engagement, though from the factory the magazine does not drop free when the release is pressed. Those desiring faster reload capability will want to have a custom gunsmith work on this. Also, as with other Colts the Officer's Model comes with only one magazine. I've always felt that an auto pistol should be supplied with at least two and preferably three magazines. The inclusion of a spare magazine and of a test target to show the gun has been tested are both aspects of European autoloaders I much prefer over American autoloaders.

Tests were carried out with 100 rounds of Federal 230 gn FMC ammo, 50 rounds of Federal 185gn JHP ammo, and 50 rounds of CCI 200gn JHP ammo. All 200 rounds were fired in one session, and the Officer's Model performed excellently, feeding all flawlessly and providing good accuracy with all three loadings. Most testing was done at 15 yards, with some fast shooting at 10 yards and a couple of magazines full at 25 yards. At 15 yards 6-shot groups usually ran in the 3-4in range. These groups were normally fired off-hand fairly quickly. As might be expected, muzzle flip and recoil were slightly more noticeable than with a full-sized Government Model, but they were certainly not more than an experienced shooter can handle with ease. I found that the Officer's Model handled very quickly when used to engage multiple targets, a real plus for a real-world combat weapon.

Overall, I give the Officer's Model very high marks. It is compact yet authoritative. It is very reliable and very accurate. I like the stainless steel version I tested a great deal, but would recommend the Lightweight version for anyone needing a gun to be carried constantly. Those ten ounces less make a big difference when the weight is tugging at one's belt. For a house defence gun, an outdoorsman's gun, or a boat-owner's gun, however, the stainless steel version should get the nod.

Just how compact the Officer's Model is can be seen from this comparision with a Smith & Wesson J-frame revolver which has a barrel 1½ inches shorter and holds 2 less cartridges.

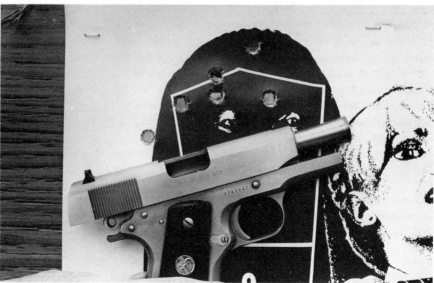

This 15-yard group illustrates that the Officer's Model is quite capable of good combat accuracy.

Colt Python

Type: double-action revolver.
Maker: Colt's, Inc., Hartford, Connecticut, USA.
Calibre: ·357 Magnum.
Overall length: 286mm, 11.25in.
Barrel length: 152mm, 6.0in.
Weight, empty: 1,235gm, 43.5oz.
Cylinder capacity: 6.
Construction: stainless steel, adjustable sights.

It is often said that the Python is the Rolls-Royce of revolvers and, even though the description is hackneyed, the phrase remains apt. Like the Rolls-Royce, the Python is a cut above its competitors, both in quality and price. Introduced in 1955 as a target revolver, the Python has since achieved great popularity as a combat and sporting gun. From the beginning, Colt has lavished more hand fitting and polishing on the Python than on any other revolver, and the result has been a superior product.

Accuracy standards, for example, are quite high for Pythons; and each one is bore-sighted with a laser. The components of the trigger system are hand-honed, resulting in a smooth and crisp action, generally conceded to be the best 'out of the box' pull obtainable. The standards of external finish on Pythons are normally substantially better than average.

The Python's outstanding performance is matched by its classic looks. The heavy ribbed barrel, with its under lug, is one of the most admired and most copied features of modern revolver design. Not only is this heavy barrel aesthetically pleasing, but it is also a real boon in countering muzzle flip. It is both handsome and functional. Although the 4in barrel is more practical for combat use, the popularity of the 6in Python with police officers influenced selection of the test gun.

The Python uses the Colt I-Frame which, though sturdier than the Smith & Wesson K-Frame, is not really large. However, it is certainly heavy and strong enough for the ·357 Magnum round. The Python's cylinder is also strong enough, though not as hefty as those of the Smith & Wesson Models 27 or 28. The absence of counter-bored chambers is one of the few poor features of the Python. As one expects with a superior weapon, the Python cylinder locks with that 'bank vault click' denoting solidity. The ejector rod also glides as smooth as silk. In normal Colt fashion, the cylinder revolves clockwise and locks up tightly as the hammer falls.

I have a slight preference for Smith & Wesson's rather than Colt's adjustable sights, principally because the former's micro-adjustable back sights are supported at the rear of the frame. The back sight on the Python (and some other Colts) is not supported in the same manner, though strong and easily caught by the eye. The Colt sights are blackened to prevent glare, while the top strap and the top of the rib have a glare-restricting matt finish.

Fittingly, the Python, Colt's first stainless gun, displays one of the most carefully finished stainless finishes ever examined even by a particular fan of such work. The single- and double-action trigger pulls are both smooth and crisp. I dislike the standard wood Python grips, owing to their shape and sharp chequering, and fitted the test gun with the optional Colt 'Gold Medallion' Pachmayr pattern. The Pachmayr grips comfortably and effectively cushion recoil with full-power ·357 Magnum loads, though the weight of the Python also helps to minimize apparent recoil.

On the range, the Python lived up to its reputation and proved the most accurate US-made revolver tested for this book, achieving 2in-diameter double-action groups at 15 yards. At 25 yards, sub-3in groups were also common. The most accurate load was the 125gn Federal jacketed hollowpoint, but the similar 125gn Remington, 140gn CCI-Speer and 158gn Federal bullets also performed well. The combination of the long, heavy barrel and smooth double-action trigger pull allowed swift recovery during rapid fire.

Overall, the Python performed outstandingly. It's that exception in today's commercial world: an item which lives up to its billing and its price tag. Though the gun is expensive, the purchaser can console himself with one of the finest handguns in the world.

The Python is certainly not everyone's choice for combat, but I recommend it highly to those wanting a ·357 Magnum holster gun...assuming they can afford the outlay. As a police duty weapon, the Python is excellent. Many policemen are willing to pay the price to ensure that the principal tool of their trade is the best. The Python is also a good choice for the civilian who appreciates the best, and is willing to pay well for a personal defence gun he can treasure as well as trust. Many shooters use a Python for hunting, silhouette shooting and even plinking. For such versatility, the 6in-barrelled Python — as tested here — is a good choice, even though I would prefer the 4in barrel in combat.

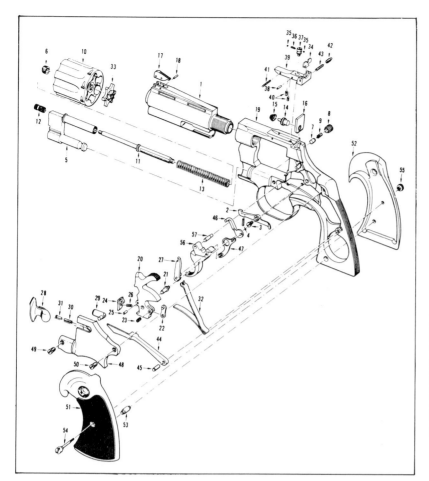

Key

1	Barrel	31	Latch Spring Guide
2	Bolt	32	Main Spring
3	Bolt Screw	33	Ratchet
4	Bolt Spring	34	Rear Sight Blade
5	Crane	35	Rear Sight Detent Balls (2)
6	Crane Bushing	36	Rear Sight Detent Spring
7	Crane Lock Detent	37	Rear Sight Elevating Screw
8	Crane Lock Screw	38	Rear Sight Elevating Screw Pin
9	Crane Lock Spring	39	Rear Sight Leaf
10	Cylinder	40	Rear Sight Leaf Elevating
11	Ejector Rod		Springs (2)
12	Ejector Rod Head	41	Rear Sight Leaf Pin
13	Ejector Spring	42	Rear Sight Windage Screw
14	Firing Pin	43	Rear Sight Windage Spring
15	Firing Pin Spring	44	Rebound Lever
16	Firing Pin Stop	45	Rebound Lever Pin
17	Front Sight Blade	46	Safety
18	Front Sight Pins (2)	47	Safety Lever
19	Frame	48	Side Plate
20	Hammer	49	Side Plate Screw (Front)
21	Hammer Pin	50	Side Plate Screw (Tgt.
22	Hammer Stirrup		Stocks)
23	Stirrup Pin (Roll Pin)	51	Stock—Left Hand
24	Hammer Strut	52	Stock—Right Hand
25	Hammer Strut Pin	53	Stock Pin
26	Hammer Strut Spring	54	Stock Screw
27	Hand	55	Stock Screw Nut
28	Latch	56	Trigger
29	Latch Pin	57	Trigger Pin
30	Latch Spring		

The sleek lines of the Colt Python are emphasized by the comfortable Pachmayr grips.

The 6in barrel gives the Python attractive proportions.

Among the most distinctive features of the Python is its barrel, with a rib and heavy underlug.

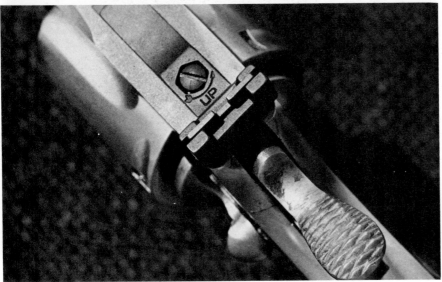

The Python has an adjustable back sight and a semi-target hammer, visible in this close-up view.

Despite the heavy barrel, there is still some muzzle flip in rapid double-action firing with full-power loads. The Python is, however, eminently controllable.

The Python proved to be the most accurate of the US-made revolvers tested for this book, as this 15 yard double-action group testifies.

CZ 75

Type: double-action semi-automatic pistol.
Maker: Přesné Strojírenství, Uherský Brod, Czechoslovakia.
Calibre: 9mm Parabellum.
Overall length: 205mm, 8.07in.
Barrel length: 115mm, 4.53in.
Weight, empty: 1,000gm, 35.3oz.
Magazine capacity: 15+1.
Construction: all steel, fixed sights.

One of many pistols made in Eastern Europe specifically for export, the sturdy CZ 75 was the first large-capacity magazine double-action pistol to be made entirely in steel, the Model 59 Smith & Wesson (except for one small batch) being made exclusively with an alloy frame. The CZ 75 is an intelligent combination of the general dimensions of the FN-Browning High-Power with some of the attributes of the SIG P 210. However, these characteristics have been refined into a functional and thoroughly modern design. The grip of the CZ 75, for example, is appreciably better than the High-Power — so good, in fact, that it was crudely copied by the designers of the Bren Ten.

The P 210 provides the 'button-hole' unlocking device, a closed-path lug replacing the links or cam-blocks of the Colt-Browning and the High-Power systems. Like its Swiss prototype, the Czech gun has a slide running inside the grooves cut in the frame. The first impressions of the pistol are very favourable though, oddly, documentation was curiously absent from the box. Had it not been for the fact that dismantling parallels the High-Power, this surprising omission may have caused insuperable problems. There is no dismantling notch on the slide, the slide stop being removed when two small marks on the frame and slide are aligned. This can be difficult, as the weak hand is needed to retain the slide while the slide stop is removed.

A puzzling feature of the CZ 75 is the 'magazine brake', which prevents the magazine being ejected when the release catch is pushed. However, this simple — and somewhat unnecessary — piece of folded sheet-steel can be removed at will.

One original feature of the CZ 75 is the manual hammer-locking safety, rarely found in a double-action trigger, which permits the gun to be carried cocked-and-locked ('Condition One'). Unfortunately, the manual safety is fitted at the expense of a de-cocking system; thus, the trigger must be pulled and the hammer very gently lowered by shooters who do not like to carry the gun cocked on a chambered round. Lowering the hammer in this way is potentially dangerous, requiring not only great prudence but also the need to point the gun in a safe direction.

The well raked grip gives exceptional handling characteristics - among the CZ 75's best features — and the slide-stop, safety and magazine catch are easily operated. The back sight notch is to shallow for some tastes and, in conjunction with the low front sight, gives a bad sight picture except under ideal light conditions. However, this is a minor criticism and can easily be rectified by judicious customizing.

The trigger pull is excellent in both single and double action, (2.1 and 4.6kg respectively on the trial gun (4.6 and 10.1lb), the travel being superior in single action or very good in double-action mode. The CZ is better in this respect than most 'out of the box' factory guns. Its design is comparatively simple, with only 51 parts (including five in the magazine), but there are nine springs and complete dismantling in neither easy nor advisable. The mechanism is classic in its simplicity, except for a disconnector actuated by both sides of the slide rather than just one.

The CZ 75 functioned flawlessly during testing and Practical Pistol courses on the range: 'Pepper Poppers' — collapsing targets — went down easily up to 30 metres, and good scores were obtained on police 'realistic targets' during rapid fire. The CZ 75 is among the best European combat pistols, with a large capacity magazine, an excellent trigger system, good accuracy and sturdy all-steel construction. The design is rated so highly, indeed, that it has been copied by two Western European manufacturers with purely minor modifications to the safety system. The Italian Tanfoglio TA-90 and the Swiss ITM AT 84 are a tribute to the inspiration of the CZ 75.

The CZ 75 is supplied in an unattractive cardboard box.

The right side of an early CZ 75, with the short slide/frame grooves. Newer guns resemble the CZ 85 (q.v.).

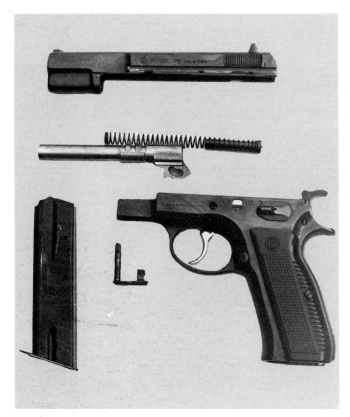

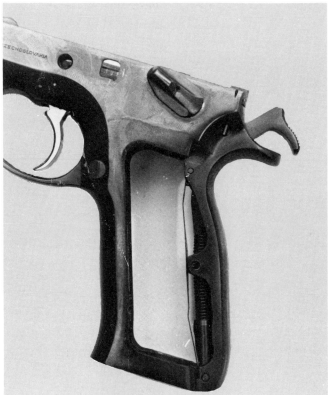

The CZ 75 field-stripped, showing some of the High-Power influences but also the closed SIG-style cam-path in the barrel depressor block.

The combat handgunner should immediately discard the useless CZ 'magazine brake', the spring-strip visible in the magazine-well ahead of the mainspring.

The CZ 75 is pleasant to fire and easily controlled.

The CZ 75: to the head from 10 metres.

An excellent 'body group', achieved with the CZ 75 from 15 metres.

CZ 83

Type: double-action semi-automatic pistol.
Maker: Presné Strojírenství, Uhersky Brod, Czechoslovakia.
Calibre: 7.65mm Auto and 9mm Short (·32 and ·38 ACP)
Overall length: 174mm, 6.85in.
Barrel length: 95mm, 3.74in.
Weight, empty: 735gm, 25.9oz.
Magazine capacity: 15+1.
Construction: all steel, fixed sights.

Production of the new CZ 'small automatic' began at the end of 1983, following the success of the earlier CZ 50 and CZ 70, its design incorporating features protected by no less than six national patents. The CZ 83 is a blowback, with its barrel fixed securely to the frame and the recoil opposed only by the mainspring (surrounding the barrel) and the inertia of the moving parts. As the slide reciprocates, the chambered case is extracted and ejected, the hammer is cocked and a fresh round is stripped into the chamber as the breech closes. This system is more than adequate for the low-power 7.65 and 9mm cartridges, but is rarely suited to powerful catridges such as 9mm Parabellum.

The inspiration for the CZ 83 is clearly the Soviet Makarov (q.v.), and thus, ultimately, the Walther Polizei-Pistole of 1929. Dismantling is controlled by the Walther trigger-guard latch which, when pulled down, allows the slide to be moved back and upward from the frame. The grip of the CZ 83 is unusually thick, which is hardly surprising considering a cartridge capacity three greater than rivals such as the FN DA 140 and the Beretta Mo.81. However, this is advantageous to men with average-size hands and contributes greatly to the pistol's pleasant handling characteristics. The large trigger guard will also accept a gloved finger.

Like the larger CZ 75, the CZ 83 incorporates double-action lockwork and a manual hammer-locking safety lever. The absence of a de-cocking system is less important in the CZ 83 than in the CZ 75 owing to the inclusion of a firing-pin safety; after the initial movement of the hammer when the trigger has released it, under thumb control, a horizontal bar prevents the hammer reaching the firing pin and the gun will not fire even if the hammer slips from the firer's thumb. When the trigger is pulled, the trigger bar raises the safety until, corresponding with a cutout in the hammer-body, it allows the latter to strike the firing pin.

The CZ 83 also features a truly ambidexterous magazine catch, which can be actuated from either side of the gun with equal facility. The magazine-lock is placed centrally in the magazine well and pivoted on the trigger-guard. The magazine cannot be inserted while the trigger guard is depressed during dismantling. Though the ambidexterous magazine release may seem an obvious advantage, such a crossbolt system must protrude on both sides of the frame and the trigger finger can sometimes inadvertently prevent magazine ejection! Moreover, when the catch is pressed, the average hand - protruding below the short grip — can simply block the magazine. The system will function only with a bit of training. Fast reloading is not only problematical, but pointless if another magazine is not available: only one magazine is supplied with the gun, which also arrives without additional documentation. This is an unfortunate omission, because the CZ 83 is particularly complicated and has an incredible number of parts. Owing to the absence of information and the sophisticated design, no attempt was made to dismantle the test gun: according to Czech sources, it contains no less than 133 parts.

The gun is completely ambidexterous, apart from the slide stop, with the magazine catch and manual safety on both sides and excellent shaping of both grips. The slide stop can be operated by the trigger finger of a left-handed firer, a trick that is easily mastered.

Chambering such an innocuous cartridge as the 7.65mm Auto (·32 ACP) results in unimpressive stopping power. However, mastering the CZ 83 is easy; the sights are good; the trigger pull is exceptional in single action (2kg) or very good in double-action mode (4.75kg); and the gun gives a good account of itself with a two-hand grip and Weaver Stance. Few problems will be encountered in accurately placing very tight groups in rapid fire.

Used with jacketed bullets, the CZ 83 is among the best available 'back up' guns, combining enormous firepower with good concealability and a laden weight of only 850gm. Used with Silvertip ammunition, the CZ 83 can even serve as a main gun for those who seek respectable stopping power with discretion.

A left-side view of the CZ 83, hinting at the curious vertical movement of the ambidexterous safety catch.

A right-side view of the CZ 83, showing the ambidexterous magazine catch positioned for a left hander.

The CZ 83 field-stripped. Though Walther and Makarov influences are detectable, the CZ is appreciably more complicated than either.

Firing the CZ 83 on an indoor police range.

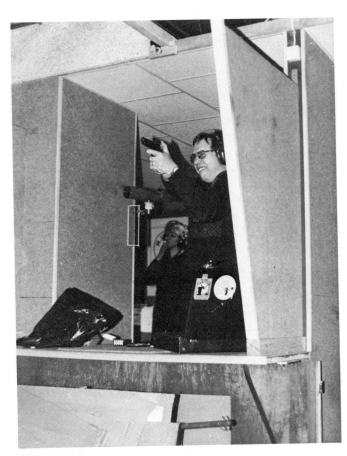

(Below left) The CZ 83 is surprisingly accurate, as attested by this group achieved from 12 metres.

(Below) As the CZ 83 is accurate, the shot in the hostage's hip was entirely my fault . . . !

CZ 85

Type: double-action semi-automatic pistol.
Maker: Přesné Strojírenství, Uherský Brod, Czechoslovakia.
Calibre: 9mm Parabellum.
Overall length: 205mm, 8.07in.
Barrel length: 115mm, 4.53in.
Weight, empty: 1,000gm, 35.3oz.
Magazine capacity: 15 + 1.
Construction: all steel, fixed sights.

The CZ 85 may be obtained in several models. The **Model 06** is finished in matt black and has fixed sights; the **Model 07** is blued with fixed sights; the **Model 08** is a blued 'Sport' model with a fully adjustable back sight; and the **Model 09** is a 'Combat' model with an adjustable back sight, a squared trigger guard and walnut grips.

Though the CZ 75 remains an excellent combat pistol, the Czech designers obviously concluded that revisions were necessary to remain in the forefront of technology. They had already succeeded in refining what had already become a classic handgun by lengthening the slide/frame support, a feature added to the CZ 75 after the initial production runs and perpetuated on the CZ 85 — interestingly, more than ever like the SIG P 210.

The CZ 85 is the same size as the CZ 75, being delivered in a similar cardboard carton with the same lack of information. The modifications are largely external, initially seeming purely cosmetic until further examination reveals that all but one improve the basic design. The new squared-off slide stop and safety levers reduce the possibility of thumb-slip, albeit at the expense of some of the previous elegance. The grips have also been modified, giving the impression, during firing trials, that handling had been improved by very good chequering and astute re-shaping of the upper portions to accommodate the thumb. Owing to the ambidexterity of the gun, the grips remain symmetrical.

The top portion of the slide has also received attention, with an additional broad glare-suppressing band — a minor modification, as the design of the CZ 75 caused no real problems and its excellent fixed back sight prevented slide reflections distracting the firer. The slide-retracting grooves have reverted to a conventional flat design at the expense of the original recessed pattern. I feel that this is a retrograde step, as the older design, one of the most interesting features of the CZ 75, permitted easy retraction of the slide and all but prevented the cocking-hand slipping.

The drastic modifications are restricted to the ambidexterous safety (not new in handgun design) and the ambidexterous slide stop, never previously encountered on a production combat pistol. This lever is completely symmetrical and allows perfect manipulation for right- and left-handed firers alike. As this system works so perfectly, one wonders why the clever CZ designers did not add an ambidexterous (or at least reversible) magazine catch to the CZ 85, making it the first completely ambidexterous modern combat handgun since the Heckler & Koch P7M13 — but with more conventional handling characteristics and two extra shots.

The field-stripping sequence, which parallels the CZ 75, is not initially obvious. The pin of the left-hand lever is simply surrounded by the hollow spindle of the right-hand lever. The spindle is retained in the frame by a wire spring, the squared tip of the opposing pin entering a recess in the base of the spindle to ensure that the two slide stops act in concert.

There were two minor irritations with the test gun, a Model 06; the lacquered finish was not very durable, and the superfluous sheet-steel magazine brake was immediately removed. The trigger pull on the sample gun was not as good as the CZ 75: though excellent in single-action mode, the double-action pull was heavy and erratic. Extremely accurate, very easy to operate, with a large-capacity magazine and improved ambidexterity compared with the CZ 75, the CZ 85 could be what Jeff Cooper had in mind when he was developing the Bren Ten. And chambering the CZ 85 for such a widely distributed cartridge as the 9mm Parabellum neatly avoids the problems of obtaining rarely encountered 'one off' types.

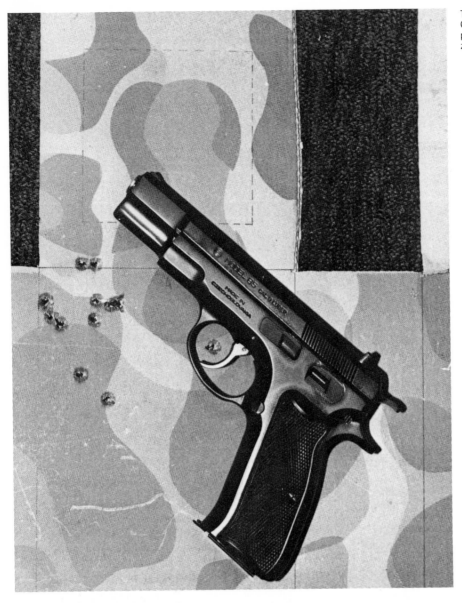

The CZ 85 is a straightforward modernization of the CZ 75. This ten-shot group was fired from 12m in poor light, the aim-point being the light-coloured zone to left of the trigger-guard.

One of the improvements the CZ 85 offers, compared with its predecessor, is the ambidexterous safety catch and slide stop. This gun exhibits the full-length slide/frame support, shared with the later production models of the CZ 75.

The slide-stop lever, viewed from the right side of the frame when the gun is field-stripped, displays the rectangular aperture for the spindle of the corresponding stop on the left side.

On test, the CZ 85 proved one of the most impressive of all combat pistols.

A full magazine at 15m, fired in light conditions paralleling those of the 12m group. The gun is impressively accurate.

Detonics MC-1

Type: single-action semi-automatic pistol.
Maker: Detonics Associates Inc., Seattle, Washington, USA
Calibre: ·45 ACP.
Overall length: 172mm, 6.75in.
Barrel length: 89mm, 3.5in.
Weight, empty: 820gm, 29oz.
Magazine capacity: 6+1.
Construction: stainless steel, fixed sights.

The Detonics MC-1 was specifically designed to be a powerful, yet compact autoloader. Detonics Associates specializes in small automatics chambered for the 9mm Parabellum and ·45 ACP rounds, the guns being highly regarded by professionals requiring a powerful concealed handgun.

Externally, the MC-1 resembles a scaled-down Colt Government Model, though there are some obvious differences such as the lack of a grip safety. The slope at the rear of the slide is also noteworthy, theoretically allowing faster hammer cocking with a round chambered and the hammer down on a loaded chamber ('Condition Two' carry). Owing to the slope, the easy-to-use square notch back sight lies much further forward on the slide than many shooters like. Though this system shortens sight radius by about an inch, it is none the less possible to shoot well with an MC-1.

Many of the MC-1's most outstanding features are internal, intended to enhance reliability and accuracy. The internal parts are all carefully finished and polished. The cone-type barrel centring system aids accuracy and reliability by eliminating the original barrel bushing. The recoil spring-within-a-spring is also noteworthy, as it helps to dampen recoil despite the small size of the gun.

Among the 'customized' reliability features are a throated barrel, a polished feed ramp and a relieved ejection port. To facilitate rapid magazine changes, the magazine well is also bevelled. The additional polishing of the internal components gives the MC-1 a very smooth trigger pull. These extra features improve the combat capabilities of the MC-1. Though they raise the price, the alterations are cheaper than having a custom gunsmith convert a standard Government Model.

The only safety is the tried and well-tested thumb lever on the frame; though no safety should be considered foolproof, I rely on this device and carry the MC-1 'cocked and locked' (Condition One). Handling the Detonics MC-1 immediately indicates how much smaller it is than the Government Model. Many people find the position of the little finger below the grip disconcerting, though gripping room must obviously be traded for concealability. The factory-chequered grips are comfortable, though optional Pachmayr neoprene grips are also available from Detonics.

The MC-1 is made of stainless steel, a point I consider in its favour as the finish is matt, unpolished steel and far less reflective than usual. Detonics' stainless steel guns are durable, in addition to their proven reliability, since great care is taken in selecting a combination of steels that will not fret.

Range tests with the MC-1 produced outstanding results, especially for a gun of its size, and reaffirmed that Detonics products are accurate and reliable. I found neither the short grip nor the abbreviated sight radius bothersome. At a range of 15 yards, 3in-diameter groups were obtained consistently; at 25 yards, 4-5in groups were common. I also tried some rapid-fire at 50 yards, striking a 9in-diameter gong at least five times out of seven and sometimes even with all seven. Successful trial loads included 230gn Remington full metal-case, and 185gn Federal and 200gn CCI-Speer jacketed hollow-points. The 185gn Federal bullet gave the best accuracy; all types fed flawlessly. The recoil of the MC-1 actually seems to be less than with a full-size Government Model, a noteworthy fact I attribute primarily to the 'spring within a spring' recoil system helping to absorb some of the force.

All cartridges fed flawlessly, muzzle flip was minimal, and it was easy to haul the MC-1 back onto the target for quick follow-up shots. The overall performance of the MC-1 was outstanding; it proved reliable, accurate and comfortable to shoot. Adding its compactness to the ·45 ACP chambering provides an excellent combat automatic.

The MC-1 is one of my personal 'top choices' for combat and is by far my favourite ·45 semi-automatic. It is at least as concealable as a ·38 'snub' revolver, yet packs two more rounds than the smaller revolvers and chambers a more potent cartridge. It is also a more accurate weapon, owing to its comparatively lengthy barrel. Unlike the small ·38s, the MC-1 does not have a bulging cylinder and is very easily concealed.

I rate the Detonics MC-1 as the best combat handgun on the market for someone needing good knockdown power and concealability in the same package. No other gun offers this combination as efficiently as the MC-1 and, despite the expense, one gets an 'off the shelf' quality usually associated only with specialist customization.

Undoubtedly at its best as a high-powered 'carry gun', the MC-1 can also serve as a compact home-defence or personal protection gun, a survival tool or a military back-up — particularly where it is the second gun to a ·45 ACP Government Model. Unlike many handguns used for combat, the MC-1 was specifically designed as a 'street fighter' and succeeds in that capacity unusually well.

This view of the MC-1 shows the safety catch, and the back sight mounted well forward above the slide-retraction grip.

The ejection port of the MC-1 is relieved to enhance reliability.

The Detonics double-spring system helps to cushion recoil, as well as enhancing reliability with heavy loads.

A tapering-cone barrel lock-up on the MC-1 aids accuracy and reliability.

Though the double-spring system helps cushion recoil, this photograph shows that the MC-1 still has substantial muzzle flip.

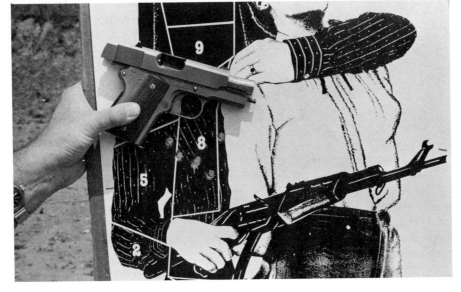

This 15 yard rapid-fire group shows that the Detonics MC-1 is capable of excellent accuracy despite its small size.

Detonics Pocket 9

> **Type:** single-action semi-automatic pistol.
> **Maker:** Detonics Associates Inc., Seattle, Washington, USA.
> **Calibre:** 9mm Parabellum.
> **Overall length:** 146mm, 5.75in.
> **Barrel length:** 76mm, 3.0in.
> **Weight, empty:** 175gm, 28oz.
> **Magazine capacity:** 6+1.
> **Construction:** stainless steel, fixed sights.

Detonics has established its reputation as a firearms manufacturer by producing compact automatics chambered for full-power cartridges. The Pocket 9 is the latest in a line of innovative semi-automatics and is the smallest 9mm autoloader on the market. It is so compact, in fact, that it is actually smaller in length, height and width than even the small Smith & Wesson J-Frame ·38 snub-nosed revolvers, yet it has a longer barrel, a greater magazine capacity and a more potent cartridge.

Unlike most 9mm semi-automatics, the Pocket 9 is not a locked-breech design. Instead, it is a delayed blowback which utilizes a heavy spring, a barrel bushing and a heavy slide to handle the pressure generated by the 9mm cartridge. This system, combined with the small size of the Pocket 9, results in a heavier than normal recoil. However, this increase is more than repaid by the savings in bulk. The Pocket 9 is well designed for concealment, with few protrusions. The design of the post-and-notch sights is especially effective, since they are inset into the top of the slide. Here they are well protected and greatly reduce the chance of snagging during the draw. At combat ranges, these sights are effective enough to facilitate alignment.

Additional streamlining is evident in the ambidexterous safety, which protrudes only about 0.13in on each side of the slide, and the compact hammer. The trigger guard is hooked and grooved, theoretically facilitating a two-hand hold with one finger of the weak hand curled around the guard. Since few shooters actually use this shooting technique, I would prefer a less obtrusive rounded guard.

The magazine release button lies, in standard US fashion, on the frame behind the trigger guard. Only one magazine is furnished with the gun, a point I consider a disadvantageous since spare Detonics magazines are in short supply. At least one spare (preferable two) should be furnished with each gun. The Lexan grips are very good, being a matt black colour and very slip-resistant.

The Pocket 9 offers double action for the first shot, and single action for subsequent rounds. Unlike most double-action autoloaders, the gun does not use a de-cocking system. Instead, when applied, the safety rotates the firing pin into the frame so that the hammer can be safely dropped on a loaded chamber by squeezing the trigger and lowering the hammer with the thumb (cf., CZ 83). Thus, the safest way to load the weapon is to apply the safety before chambering the first round. The hammer can then be safely lowered. For those seeking additional security, the safety can be left engaged and only released prior to firing an initial double-action shot. However, since the primary advantage of a double-action system is its instant availability for action with a single pull on the trigger, I disengage the safety and rely on the inertia-type firing pin – though, it should be noted, a firing pin of this type may occasionally fire the gun if the latter is dropped.

My primary criticism of the Pocket 9 is its field-stripping procedure. Theoretically, one can dismantle the Pocket 9 by pulling down on the dismantling block and pulling the slide back and upward to disengage it from the frame-rails. The slide can then be slid off the front of the frame, and the barrel and spring can be removed for maintenance. Unfortunately, it is often virtually impossible to proceed even this far, because the tiny dismantling block is hard to hold without additional assistance. The problem undoubtedly arises from the necessity to keep the Pocket 9 as compact as possible, but the dismantling difficulties are a real disadvantage.

Detonics has had extensive experience with stainless steel and, as a result, has learned how to perfect weapons using this material. To avoid fretting, two different alloys are used for the slide and frame. I would like to see an unpolished slide, to reduce unwanted reflection, but the construction and finish are otherwise satisfactory.

For the range tests, fifty rounds of each of four different loadings were used: 100gn CCI-Speer jacketed hollow-points, 115gn Federal and Remington jacketed hollow-points and 125gn CCI-Speer jacketed soft-points. The Pocket 9 handled all two hundred without malfunctioning. Accuracy was not outstanding, rapid-fire group diameters usually running to 4-5in at 15 yards, but was acceptable enough for combat ranges. Since most groups were fired with the first-round double action, the heavy trigger pull often added a couple of inches to the groups. While I rarely have trouble adapting to the differing trigger pulls inherent in double-action autoloaders, the pull on the Pocket 9 was so heavy that I had trouble compensating. The single-action pull was a little heavy, but crisp. Owing to severe recoil, however, the recovery time was not as good with the Pocket 9 as with its larger rivals.

The gun has some definite disadvantages, particularly its strong recoil, a heavy trigger pull (particularly in double action), and the quirky dismantling procedure; but it is still a highly effective combat handgun. Its combination of small size and reliability, together with the excellent 9mm Parabellum cartridge, make it a potent concealment weapon. Its advantages definitely outweigh its disadvantages, but it is not a weapon for an amateur or someone merely keeping a handgun around the house. It is a professional's gun, and demands an experienced firer who will expend sufficient range time to master it.

This view shows the Pocket-9's bright-finish slide, hooked safety guard and ambidexterous safety catch.

Note the ambidexterous safety (cf., above) of the Pocket-9, in addition to the bobbed hammer spur. The 'high tech' appearance of the gun and its grips is noteworthy.

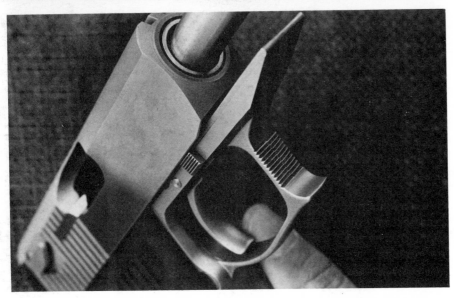

Although I do not like the grooved and hooked trigger guard, it is undeniably one of the gun's most prominent features.

When the Pocket-9 safety is applied, the firing pin is retracted within the slide. The hammer must still be lowered manually.

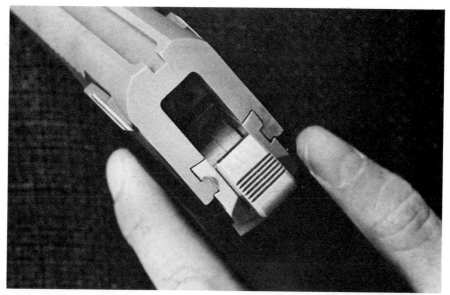

In spite of noticeable recoil, recovery time is quite good; this photograph shows the sights rapidly returning to the target.

Although 15-yard accuracy is not outstanding, the Pocket-9 is still acceptable for combat.

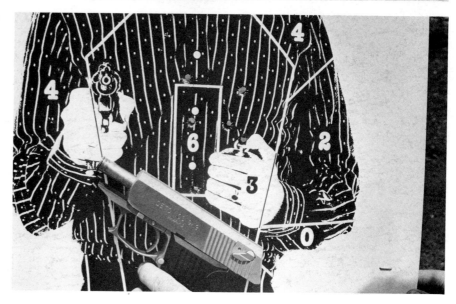

FÉG P9R 'Double Action System'

Type: double-action semi-automatic pistol.
Maker: Femaru és Szerszamgépgyär NV, Budapest, Hungary.
Calibre: 9mm Parabellum.
Overall length: 199mm, 7.83in.
Barrel length: 117mm, 4.61in.
Weight, empty: 985gm, 34.8oz.
Magazine capacity: 15+1.
Construction: blued steel, fixed sights.

The **P9RA** is similar to the P9R, with an alloy frame; the single action High Power-lookalike **FP9** has a ventilated barrel and bobbed hammer.

Apart from the Czech firearms industry, which continues to promote indigenous designs, the other constituents of the Eastern Bloc either cling to Soviet designs or shamelessly copy Western guns. It came as no surprise, therefore, when I originally encountered the FÉG 9mm Parabellum SA (now known as the 'FP9') — a blatant copy of the FN-Browning High-Power, except for the ventilated rib atop the slide. The test gun performed very well, as accurately as its prototype, but none of the parts were interchangeable owing to minor differences in tolerances.

Towards the end of 1984, I first learned of the FÉG P9R; and, being the first journalist to test the then-new FN-Browning BDA, I found it intriguing that the Hungarians should have copied the Belgian design so quickly. However, when I obtained the FÉG, I realised that it was not a copy of the BDA, but simply an adaptation of the Smith & Wesson Model 39 — with the fifteen-round magazine of the Model 59 — in High-Power cladding. When S&W upgraded the Model 39 to provide a fifteen-shot magazine, renaming it the Model 59, several modifications were made to the safety system. The FÉG clearly uses the earlier action, together with the Smith & Wesson-type barrel-locking ramps, the trigger mechanism (including the trigger stirrup), the back sight, the safety/de-cocking system, the assembling pin/slide stop and the disconnector. The High-Power pro-vides the external appearance, together with the elimination of the barrel bushing, the basic design of the magazine, the twin-lug system of locking the barrel into the undersurface of the slide, the grips, the magazine catch, the front sight and the fixed ejector.

The few original features include the enlargement of the High-Power magazine to hold fifteen rounds, the chequered back of the butt, the ingenious cut-out front of the butt (facilitating withdrawal of the magazine) and the method of retaining the spring-guide rod beneath the barrel: nothing of importance, but, together with the elimination of the magazine safety, at least a minor improvement on both its prototypes.

The action of the trigger and locking systems are described in the sections devoted to the High-Power and the S&W Model 39.

On the range, the P9R demonstrated excellent accuracy and flawless reliability, nothing surprising considering its antecedents. Operation of the magazine catch, the slide stop and the safety/de-cocking lever was stiff 'out of the box', and much manipulation (and dry firing) was necessary before the action achieved smoothness. Even initial dismantling was difficult; unlike the High-Power, there is no dismantling notch in the slide (owing to the S&W-type safety) and the slide must be held to the rear with one hand while removing the dismantling pin with the other.

When satisfactorily 'run in', the gun performs very well. The back sight notch is too small, however, and combines badly with the thick front-sight blade. The only other problem concerned the wood grips for, after dismantling, I tightened the grip screws so far that the magazine could not be released for reloading. The trigger-pull weight is excessive in both modes (more than 3kg/6.6lb single action, 8kg/17.6lb double), and though the single-action pull is short and crisp, double action is long and inconsistent. With a little work on the trigger, however, the P9R is a good choice for those who do not like to carry a gun cocked-and-locked (Condition One carry). As 9mm Parabellum is not used officially in the Eastern Bloc, it is clear that the FÉG is designed exclusively for export.

Excepting the distinctive ventilated rib, the single-action FÉG is a very close copy of the FN-Browning High-Power. None of its parts will interchange with the originals, owing to differing manufacturing tolerances.

The left side of the double-action FÉG pistol, an obvious combination of the external appearance of the High-Power with that of the Smith & Wesson Model 39.

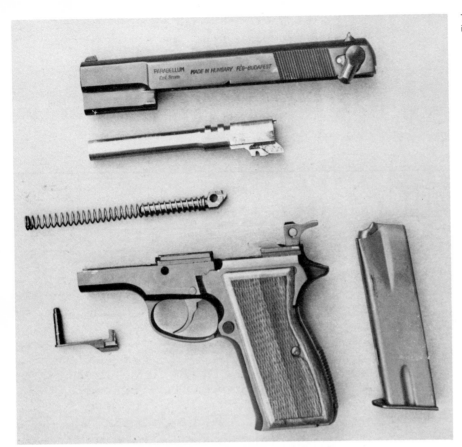

The FÉG P9R. Once field-stripped, the pistol shows its affinity with the S&W Model 39 more clearly.

A typically good group obtained from the FÉG, scarcely surprising considering that not only is the gun very well made, but also that it is based on two successful predecessors.

Glock 17

Type: 'safe action' semi-automatic pistol.
Maker: Glock GmbH, Deutsch-Wagram, Austria.
Calibre: 9mm Parabellum.
Overall length: 203mm, 8.0in.
Barrel length: 114mm, 4.5in.
Weight, empty: 650gm, 22.9oz.
Magazine capacity: 17 + 1.
Construction: steel/plastic, fixed sights.

First seen in 1982 by privileged people at IWA, Nuremburg, this pistol is the first important breakthrough since the perfection of the Walther P38, the first fullbore double-action military pistol.

Apart from the Browning inspired short-recoil operation, the Glock introduces several features and — uniquely — a one-piece plastic frame. As the magazine is also plastic, the gun only weighs 860gm with its eighteen rounds (seventeen in the magazine and one in the chamber). In a brave attempt to explore these revolutionary constructional techniques, Glock has developed a plastic holster and even delivers the gun in a waterproof plastic box with a central hole designed to receive retaining bars.

Even some parts of the mechanism, including the trigger and the safety system, are made of plastic or light alloy. The exceptions are the slide, the barrel, the firing pin and the spring. Narrow metal strips are set into the frame to receive the slide, and similar reinforcing pieces strengthen the lips of the magazine.

The smooth-shaped Glock lies surprisingly low in the hand, despite the recoil spring in its classic position under the barrel. The recoil sensation is minimal considering the low gun-weight.

The only protruding parts are the slide stop and the double dismantling latches (well protected in recesses in the frame), and the unusually stiff magazine catch. The design of the gun is such that there are only 29 parts, four of which constitute the magazine. The Glock slide is locked to the barrel during the initial recoil movement, before the barrel is pushed down and the slide reciprocates alone. Apart from the extensive use of plastics in its construction, the P17 has two idiosyncrasies. One takes the form of an inverted V-spring, which replaces the conventional hammer/firing pin assembly. In most guns, the firing-pin spring keeps the pin from the chambered cartridge, until the hammer-strike forces it sufficiently far forward; in the Glock, however, the spring is permanently compressed around the firing pin. When the slide runs backward, the 'sear' portion of the trigger system catches a protrusion on the firing-pin and retains it as the slide closes. When the gun is manually cocked for the first shot, or after each succeeding shot, the firing pin is held back until it is released by a pull on the trigger depressing the bar acting as a sear. Thus, the Glock qualifies as striker-fired.

In addition to its unusual ignition system, the Glock is notable for the absence of a manual safety. The effective 'Safe Action' system is simply built into the trigger mechanism, the firing pin safety allowing the gun to be carried cocked-and-locked ('Condition One') perfectly safely. The gun can be operated simply by pulling the trigger, which disconnects the mechanical safety: with a Glock, just draw and fire.

The system is amazingly simple. A second 'trigger', placed inside the main lever and sharing its pivot, protrudes some distance forward of the main trigger. At the back, its extension is blocked by the frame. The firer first has to pull the subsidiary trigger (pull weight 125gm, travel 11mm), which then allows a pull of 2.25kg on the sample gun to release the striker and fire the gun. The trigger pivots on the trigger bar, each reciprocation of the slide forcing the bar downward and resetting both triggers.

Retracting the slide manually with the weak hand (never change your grasp!) is not especially easy, and the magazine catch on the test gun was exceptionally stiff. However, the handling characteristics are otherwise excellent provided the firer remembers to compensate for the appreciable change in balance as the cartridges are fired - with only one cartridge remaining, the weight has dropped by about 170gm or about 20 per cent of the full-load figure. The muzzle has a tendency to drop, as the equilibrium between the steel slide/barrel mass and the loaded magazine is disturbed.

The Glock has excellent sights and is, perhaps, the most accurate of the European combat guns tested for this book. The unusual firing pin leaves a distinctive signature on fired primers, and the rifling profile is claimed by the manufacturer to be a compromise between traditionally grooved rifling and the Heckler & Koch polygonal system. Whatever the claims, the certainly of ignition is excellent and the accuracy outstanding enough to show that Glock's engineers got their calculations right.

The 'plastic gun' is not to everyone's tastes. However, the Austrian army, before adopting it as the P80, submitted the Glock to rigorous testing; including the adverse-conditions trials, the P17 performed a minimum of 15,000 shots without breakages. This is hardly surprising considering that few of the parts are submitted to strain, but only service experience will show whether adoption in preference to more conventional alternatives was justified. The external finish of the trial gun, for example, showed wear after only a few hundred shots.

In sum, the interesting Glock undoubtedly ranks among the best of the modern combat pistols.

The Glock pistol and its synthetic holster. Note the double-trigger system: the gun cannot be fired until the firer has pulled the 'insert trigger', which otherwise locks the main trigger into the frame. (Courtesy of John Walter.)

The plastic 17-shot Glock magazine is very reliable.

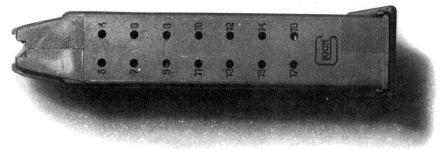

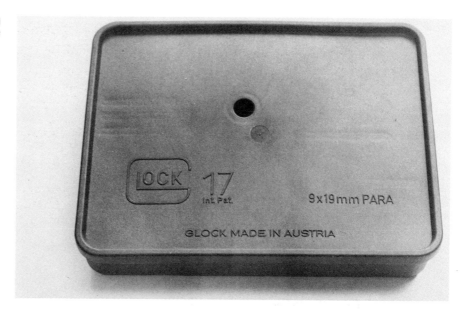

The plastic box of the Glock 17 is cleverly designed to be locked by passing a securing bar through the central hole.

The field-stripped Glock, with the firing pin and extractor removed.

The Glock has some of the best handling characteristics among combat pistols.

There are eighteen shots in this rapid-fire group, obtained with the Glock from 10m. The pistol proved to be one of the most accurate tested for this book.

Heckler & Koch P7M13

Type: double action semi-automatic pistol.
Maker: Heckler & Koch GmbH, Oberndorf/Neckar, West Germany.
Calibre: 9mm Parabellum.
Overall length: 166mm, 6.54in.
Barrel length: 105mm, 4.13in.
Weight, empty: 880gm, 31.0oz.
Magazine capacity: 13+1.
Construction: blued steel, fixed sights.

Heckler & Koch also makes the P7M8, with an eight-round magazine, and a new 'convertible' (0.22in LR, 7.65mm Auto and 9mm Short) P7K3 to replace the old HK4. A ·45 ACP version of the P7 has also been developed, and is being readied for series production.

The original Polizei-Selbstlade-Pistole (PSP), together with the Walther P5 and the SIG-Sauer P225, competed in the programme of 1975 intended to regularize the weapons of the German state police forces. The goals included the standardization of 9×19mm (9mm Parabellum) and selection of a pistol that could be carried safely, but fired without requiring a manual safety to be re-set. Eventually, all three of the main participants were passed for service, as the P5 (Walther), P6 (SIG-Sauer) and P7 (PSP).

The only possible way to comply with the carrying restrictions appeared to be a double-action trigger system, selected by SIG and Walther, but − typically − Heckler & Koch sought a new solution. The P7 is one of the most intriguing pistol designs ever to be perfected for service. It shares the polygonal rifling of the P9 and P9S, and a delayed blowback system. However, the delay is provided by allowing a portion of the propellant gas to vent through a gas port near the breech into a chamber beneath the barrel, where a piston pushes the slide forward until the gas pressure drops to a level safe enough to allow the breech to open. The slide then reciprocates, extracting and ejecting the fired case, recocking the firing pin (the gun being hammerless) and returning to strip a fresh round out of the magazine and into the chamber.

Although seemingly complicated, the P7 mechanism is simple and efficient. The firing-pin spring is reversed compared with most traditional designs, in which the spring keeps the pin away from the cartridge until struck by the hammer. In the P7 and the Glock, the firing-pin spring is compressed by the cocking of the gun, being held by a searbar until the trigger is pulled. The safety system of the P7 is also astutely conceived. When the grip is pressed, it forces the cocking bar to the rear and cocks the striker; however, when the grip is released, the firing-pin returns to its normal position, uncocking the gun. An additional mechanical safety is provided by the slide, which depresses the trigger bar to prevent release of the firing pin until the slide is completely closed.

The main disadvantage of the original P7 was its limited magazine capacity (8+1) and the position of the magazine catch on the heel of the butt. Reloading required two hands, restricting speed. Though Heckler & Koch had complied with all the terms of the 1975 German police programme, the advent of the US JSSAP led to improvements necessary to satisfy the US Army. The result was the P7M13 (1984), with a large capacity magazine, an ambidexterous magazine catch in the frame and a greatly revised grip.

I had little enthusiasm for the original P7, manipulating the action of which was totally alien to my combat-shooting training. For example, depressing the grip bar twice after inserting a new magazine (to close the slide and chamber a new cartridge) seemed less desirable than simply pressing the slide stop with the right thumb to release the slide and load the gun. The stiff pull necessary to cock the system (about 8kg/17.6lb in a new gun), the poor magazine capacity and awkward magazine-catch position made me feel that a promising concept had been let down by poor execution - even though the fixed-barrel polygonally rifled P7 was reliable, accurate and eminently controllable owing to its low profile in the hand.

The test of the P7M13, therefore, was eagerly awaited. I was impressed by the large-capacity magazine and the greatly improved ambidexterous safety catch on the frame. I was a bit anxious about the handling characteristics, because even the preceding P7 grip had been bulky and here was a gun containing five more rounds. Previous experience had taught me not to fear the idiosyncratic cocking grip: when the P7 was drawn, I discovered the grip was pressed naturally and quite unconsciously even before the weak hand reinforced the strong hand in a two-hand grip, and lost no time compared with more conventional designs.

However, during the test, I made a mistake that would not have been so funny had it occurred in combat. When I attempted a 'fast reload', I tried to release the slide by pressing the 'slide stop' through force of habit; unfortunately, this button is actually the magazine catch on the P7M13, and I ended up with an open slide and the magazine on the ground. The P7 family requires intensive familiarization, particularly for shooters who have been used to more conventional designs.

Once unfamiliarity has been overcome, the P7 is a great combat design and probably one of the safest pistols ever proposed. It has the immense advantage of a consistent trigger pull, compared to the differing weights and trigger travel associated with dual-purpose single/double action systems.

Particularly 'hot' cartridges, like the FN factory loads, gave excessive recoil and bad groups owing to handling problems. With normal ammunition, however, the P7M13 is very accurate and pleasant to fire, its 1.6kg (3.5lb) trigger pull contributing to easy manipulation. I am not particularly enthusiastic about the various dots and lines on the sights, though those on the P7M13 are better than others I have tried.

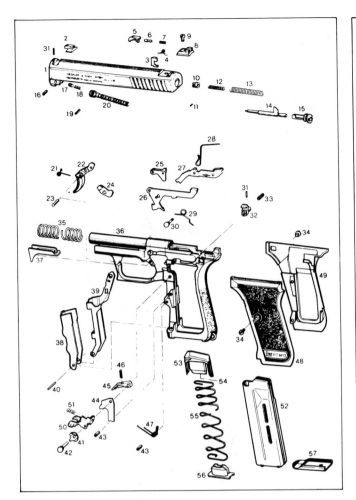

Key

1. Slide
2. Front sight
3. Drop safety catch
4. Drop safety catch spring
5. Extractor
6. Extractor spring guide
7. Extractor spring
8. Rear sight
9. Rear sight screw
10. Firing pin collar
11. Firing pin collar pin
12. Inertia spring
13. Firing pin spring
14. Firing pin
15. Firing pin bushing
16. Piston pin
17. Piston detent
18. Piston detent spring
19. Piston retaining pin
20. Piston
21. Trigger spring
22. Trigger
23. Trigger pin
24. Transmission lever
25. Disconnector
26. Slide catch lever
27. Sear bar
28. Sear spring
29. Rocker spring
30. Rocker spring axle
31. 2 × Front sight/ slide retainer pin
32. Slide retainer
33. Slide retainer spring
34. 2 × Grip screw
35. Recoil spring
36. Receiver with barrel
37. Cover for trigger guard
38. Squeeze cocker
39. Drag lever
40. Squeeze cocker axle
41. Rocker
42. Magazine catch axle
43. 2 × Stop pin
44. Stop
45. Cocking latch
46. Cocking latch spring
47. Squeeze cocker spring
48. Grip-shell left
49. Grip-shell right
50. Magazine catch
51. Magazine catch spring
52. Magazine housing
53. Follower
54. Follower insert
55. Follower spring
56. Locking plate
57. Magazine floor plate

The compact P7M13 has remarkably neat lines owing to the absence of conventional safety catches.

Comparing the P7M13 with the High-Power shows the added concealability of the Heckler & Koch design, though magazine capacity is identical.

The P7M13 field-stripped, showing the fixed barrel and its annular mainspring. This construction allows a very low profile in the hand.

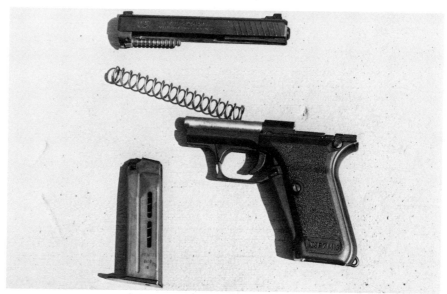

A view of the P7M13 after the grip has been removed. Some of the springs, particularly, have been reinforced since the earlier P7.

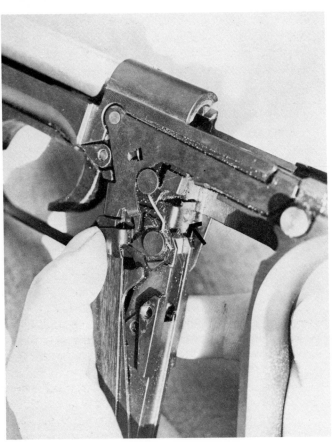

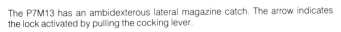

The P7M13 has an ambidexterous lateral magazine catch. The arrow indicates the lock activated by pulling the cocking lever.

(Below left) I rarely use the extended trigger-guard, except for long-range shooting. The P7M13 could be even more compact with a rounded guard.

(Below) A typical group obtained from the P7M13 at 12m, with moderately powerful ammunition.

Heckler & Koch P9S

Type: double action semi-automatic pistol.
Maker: Heckler & Koch GmbH, Oberndorf/Neckar, West Germany.
Calibre: 9mm Parabellum and ·45 ACP.
Overall length: 192mm, 7.56in.
Barrel length: 102mm, 4.00in.
Weight, empty: 790gm, 27.9oz.
Magazine capacity: 9+1 (·45 ACP, 7+1).
Construction: blued steel, fixed sights.

Until recently, European ·45 ACP pistols were rarely encountered, excepting Spanish copies of the Colt Government Model. As a result, I decided to test the P9S in ·45 ACP to compare it directly with the Government Model, a gun widely used in Europe by members of the IPSC and the combat-shooting fraternity.

Design work on the P9 began in 1966, the gun being marketed from 1969 onward. There were numerous innovations, including the distinctive delayed blowback action and extensive use of sophisticated production methods. The roller-lock, inspired by the German MG.42 and the Czech vz/52 pistol, permitted a 'semi-fixed' barrel to be used within the annular recoil spring. The polygonal rifling was also unusual in a modern pistol.

The P9 rapidly evolved into the P9S, the final product offering extremely attractive futuristic contours and low weight for its size. The well-shaped grip enhances pointability. Our ·45 ACP sample gun, with its seven-round magazine, is equivalent to the Colt Government Model with the advantage of a double-action trigger. Unfortunately for the combat shooter, the magazine catch is badly placed on the heel of the butt and handicaps reloading. The position of the magazine catch was dictated by the combination slide-stop/de-cocking lever, which lies just behind the trigger guard where cross-bolt magazine catches are often found on rival designs.

The de-cocking lever has several functions: when the slide is held in its rear position, a light pull frees it; when the hammer is cocked, a full pull on the lever returns the hammer to its half-cock notch, where accidental firing is impossible (though the gun can be fired by pulling the trigger); when the hammer is down, a full pull cocks the hammer. The system would have allowed the gun to be carried with a loaded chamber and cocked on the draw, had not the cocking-pull been so awkward.

Another interesting feature is the manual safety, rarely encountered on double action automatics and ever rarer on those with de-cocking systems. This allows the P9S to be carried cocked-and-locked ('Condition One' carry) or with the hammer down. When the hammer is cocked, a small bar protrudes from the back of the slide and can be felt in the dark; when a cartridge is chambered, the extractor protrudes far enough to act as an indicator.

The P9S is easy to field-strip. After the magazine has been removed and the chamber checked, the dismantling catch inside the trigger guard is pulled and the slide moved as far forward as possible. The slide can be lifted clear of the frame; the barrel pulled forward against the force of the spring, releasing it from the standing frame; and, finally, the rear of the barrel can be used to unlatch the bolt from the slide.

Though the trigger pull is long in both single and double action, it is quite light (about 1.5kg/3.3lb and a little less than 4kg/8.8lb respectively). As the P9S is quite light, recoil is quite noticeable and I would have appreciated an extension of the trigger guard to facilitate two-hand grip. Accuracy proved to be good, but not exceptional: surprisingly, the 9mm P9S shot better than the ·45 ACP type.

In ·45 ACP, the Heckler & Koch design has the same magazine capacity as the Government Model or the Llama 'Omni'. Unfortunately, the quirky positioning of the magazine catch is a great handicap and prevents the P9S being considered as a serious contender for combat use; in 9mm Parabellum, its magazine of only nine rounds is an insuperable handicap compared with the FN-Brownings, the Beretta 92 series or the Glock. Though the P9S was once a real breakthrough in modern automatic pistol design, it served largely to inspire H&K to more radical concepts.

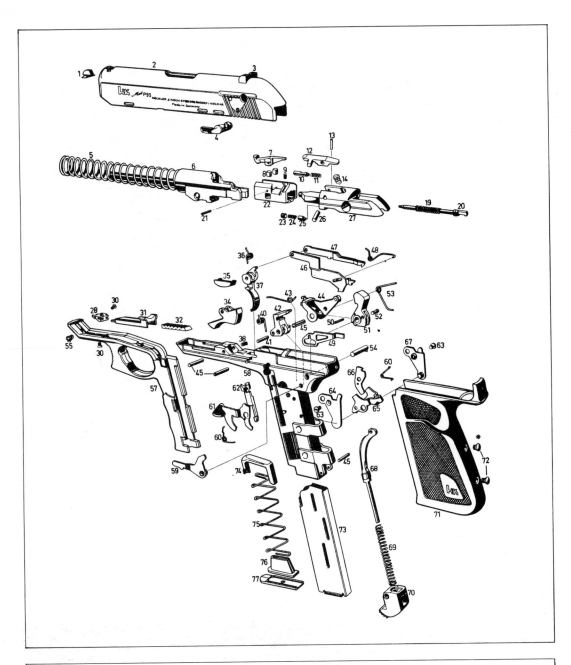

Key

1	Front sight	22	Bolt head	43	Spring for catch	62	Catch
2	Slide	23	Threaded pin	44	Disconnector	63	Countersunk screws
3	Rear sight	24	Compression spring	45	Cylindrical pin	64	Bearing plate, left
4	Safety catch	25	Catch bolt	46	Pull bar	65	Angle lever
5	Recoil spring	26	Cylindrical pin	47	Trigger lever	66	Intermediate lever
6	Barrel	27	Bolt head carrier	48	Spring for pull bar	67	Bearing plate, right
7	Extractor	28	Support	49	Indicator pin	68	Shank
8	Locking rollers	30	Raised head countersunk screw	50	Spiral pin	69	Compression spring
9	Compression spring	31	Buffer housing	51	Hammer	70	Magazine catch
10	Pressure pin	32	Plastic buffer	52	Stop pin	71	Grips
11	Compression spring for pressure pin	34	Barrel catch	53	Spring for disconnector	72	Raised-head countersunk screw
12	Locking catch	35	Insert piece	54	Axle for hammer	73	Magazine housing
13	Pin	36	Trigger spring	55	Threaded bush	74	Follower
14	Compression spring	37	Trigger	57	Trigger guard	75	Follower spring
19	Firing pin spring	38	Compression spring	58	Receiver	76	Support for follower spring
20	Firing pin	40	Elbow spring	59	Safety latch	77	Magazine floor plate
21	Spiral pin	41	Sleeve	60	Elbow spring		
		42	Catch lever	61	Cocking lever		

The P9S, showing its modernistic lines. (Courtesy of Heckler & Koch GmbH.)

The P9S as supplied in its cardboard box, accompanied by a solitary spare magazine.

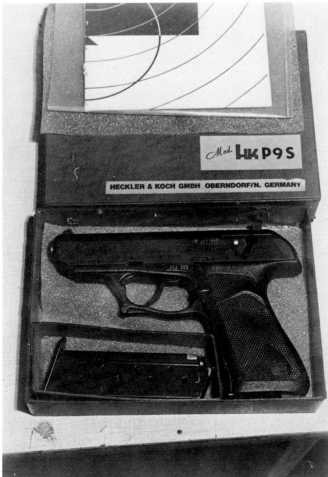

The unique P9S spiralling polygonal bore replaces conventional grooved rifling.

The P9S is not small, but its modern design (and the use of modern materials) keeps its weight down at the expense of appreciable recoil.

A typical nine-shot rapid-fire group (a full magazine plus one chambered round) obtained from the P9S at 15m. The Polygonal 'rifling' and the fixed barrel permit excellent shooting.

IMI Desert Eagle

Type: Magnum pistol, rotating bolt.
Maker: Israeli Military Industries (IMI).
Calibre: ·357 Magnum, ·44 Magnum conversion.
Overall length: 260mm, 10.2in.
Barrel length: 152mm, 6in.
Weight empty: 1760gm, 62oz.
Magazine capacity: 9 + 1.
Construction: steel frame, fixed sights (aluminium frame 1466gm).

At the beginning of 1983 news came of an innovative pistol being developed by Israel Military Industries, renowned for their conception and fabrication of military weapons such as the UZI machine pistol and GALIL assault rifle. IMI had never before conceived a handgun, and the fact that the new pistol was to be chambered in typical revolver calibres, ·357 Mag and ·44 Mag, was surprising. The concept of using this kind of ammo in a pistol rather than a revolver is often used only on prototypes and, commercially, the only known gun actually produced is the American Coonan. But the American origin of this design explains the choice of cartridges widely used in the States for both handgun hunting and silhouette shooting.

The 'Eagle', which was later to become the 'Desert Eagle', was shown for the first time in the Paris *Expo*, but the Eagle was not fired . . . because the pistol present was not fireable.

For some months, the specialised gun writers − including myself − asked the European importer for news of a sample gun to test but the Eagle was always in the process of improvement, and time passed.

At the end of 1985, articles began to be published in one or two American magazines and, finally, one sample pistol came into the author's hands.

Even with its standard 6in barrel, the Desert Eagle is a monster with its 1980 gm (steel frame and the 9 + 1 cartridges)!

One of the reasons for this extravagant weight is the choice of working principle necessitated by the very powerful ammunition. With a gun having mobile parts, like the automatic pistol, security cannot be achieved with a simple blowback and probably no more with the conventional locking. The choice of the Eagle is to use a gas-operated gun, with a fixed barrel and rotating positive locking . . . a system very similar to that used on many assault rifles, including the GALIL! Even if the Eagle is not the only auto pistol using those principles, their application here is original and deserves some comments.

The fixed barrel, one of the main elements of the system, is a massive tube with a big fore end. This tube is actually a sleeve containing the barrel itself and the gas conduct just beneath the former; a close examination of a cut-away view of the pistol shows that the small hole allowing the gas to leave the barrel is placed just ahead of the chamber: the gas is thus going forward, re-directed by a sloped part of the conduct to the rear and down, approximately beneath the muzzle.

The tube containing the barrel and the conduct is firmly fixed in three points: the massive fore part and the re-inforcement beneath the chamber are slided, and blocked by the axle of the disassembling lever. The slide has a massive block at its rear, comprising the rotating bolt, the firing pin and the manual safety; while its head is equipped with a fixed piston struck by the gas coming from the conduct. This forces the whole slide to go back, with the related consequences: unlocking, extraction, ejection, cocking of the hammer, and chambering of a new round.

The frame itself plays a major role in the operation of the gun: the two very strong recoil springs, around their long fixed guides, are placed into the frame beneath the fixed barrel. These two springs are linked together by a transversal bar on which pushes the fixed piston of the slide (see above) when moved by the gas.

The recoil compresses the two springs, allowing the return of the slide after gas pressure has dropped. Contrary to custom with this type of operation, the gas is not pushing on the piston inside a tube, but is delivered directly in the free space let under the barrel by the recoil of the slide. This is the reason why an initial high pressure is needed, since a high percentage is lost; which explains the position of the hole beneath the chamber.

The positive locking, which gives a complete safety, is provided by a rotating bolt whose head is equipped of three (3 × 120°) lugs, and a fourth that assures the rotating of the bolt when the lugs are penetrating in the mortice zone. The head of the bolt is equipped with a powerful extractor and a piston ejector; while the recess for the bottom of the cartridge has a central hole for the firing pin, acting as the bolt's axle. A powerful spring pushes the bolt forward, where it is locked by a piston, placed parallel to the bolt itself.

The bolt remains in the forward position until the piston is pulled back by the edge of the fixed barrel; which occurs when the slide is coming back from its rearward position, and allows the bolt to retract and to rotate; causing the locking of the system and the chambering of the cartridge. The reverse motion allows the unlocking and the extraction of the case.

The mechanism is based upon a stirrup. This system, common with a plain trigger, is unusual with the type used on the Eagle. With a plain trigger (like the one used on the Government or the early FN Brownings), when the trigger is pulled the stirrup pushes on the sear: here, when pulled, the trigger forces the stirrup forward and this pulls a hook that is the upper part of the sear. The stirrup itself is used to prevent the shooting of bursts. To engage the sear's hook the stirrup has to be in the upper position, and is pushed naturally in this position by its own spring, but each of the stirrup's arms has a vertical bar corresponding to a recess in the slide. When the latter is not completely closed, the stirrup is forced down and the gun cannot fire.

The moving of the slide, when the gun is fired, forces the stirrup down, separating rear bar from the sear's hook. The latter pivots and goes back, under pressure of its own spring, and the trigger has to be released to allow the stirrup to go rearwards to re-engage the sear's hook.

The ambidexterous manual safety is not placed on the frame but on the slide itself — an uncommon practice with single action auto pistols, but the gun, with its enormous slide surrounding the frame, leaves no place for a more common safety lever placed on the frame.

The safety chosen allows a very simple and efficient system. The axle of the safety has a spur which blocks the firing pin, two other spurs being simultaneously pushed down into the two recesses of the slide to the vertical bars of the stirrup. The advantage is that — the firing pin being blocked and the stirrup deactivated — all the manipulations of the slide, including the chambering of the first round or the unloading of the chambered cartridge, are possible: as the slide is not blocked as on most SA pistols when the safety is on. All of the dangerous manipulations are here perfectly safe: the drawback is that, with a safety lever not very accessible to the thumb, this is definitely a slow manipulation. The dimensions of the gun, however, make it a weapon unlikely to be carried concealed and, if used as a combat gun, it will probably be used by law enforcement agencies who have the opportunity to draw and unlock the safety before action occurs.

During the firing test a number of ballistics exercises were performed. The pistol compared to a S&W 6in revolver, and it was determined that the loss of power was marginal with the Eagle (Remington High Velocity FMJ, 364m/s with the Eagle compared to the 385m/s with the S&W; Winchester Lubaloy, 389m/s in place of 396m/s). Aguila ammunition was too weak to assure the proper cycling, the slide not moving completely and the head of the bolt not passing behind the upper cartridge of the magazine.

The trigger pull was not bad nor very good, with its 3kg. The practical test was restricted by the fact that only one magazine was available, and by the absence of any holster accepting the pistol, except for a very good Cordura external shoulder holster not made for quick draw but just for easy carrying of the pistol.

Shooting tests were made with numerous different ammos, with the — too weak — Aguila and handloaded cartridges occasioning numerous improper feedings.

You should be aware that, at the end of 1985, a semi-confidential document stated that the manufacturer would guarantee complete reliability with only four commercial loads: Remington R357 M2 or M3 158gn, Winchester X357 4P or 5P 158gn, Federal 357A or E, and CCI 3959 or 3960. Our tests allow us to add to this list the French SFM, the Winchester Lubaloy, the Norma SWC FMJ and the Sako.

All the manipulations required of the gun are easy . . . with not too tiny hands! The width of the grip is 65mm, compared to the 53mm of a High-Power or 55mm of a CZ . . . (A young girl had no problems mastering the Eagle, except for the manipulation of the slide stop. In the latter instance, even the strongest present at the test were unable to use the slide stop with only one thumb.)

Groups obtained are good, and the gun recovers very well after each shot due to its impressive weight.

Some questions arise concerning the combat use of this gun. The Eagle is cumbersome and is definitely not a 'standard' police or defence weapon (service in plain clothes is completely excluded, and even the average uniformed policeman would not be too happy to carry this on his belt for many hours a day). Furthermore, the Eagle will never be a fast gun to put into action: it is impossible to carry the gun safely with a chambered cartridge and without the inaccessible safety 'on'. But the Eagle could well be a winner for special units like SWAT or HRT, which always go into action with the gun already in their hand; while the fact that the ammo will be the same for both the SWAT men and the other police officers equipped with revolvers, could be appreciated by any official in charge of the supply . . .

The Desert Eagle field stripped, with its load of nine ·357 Magnum. A tenth round can be chambered, giving the pistol impressive fire power.

The manual safety, placed on the slide, has to push up for the fire position. This manoeuvre can be slow.

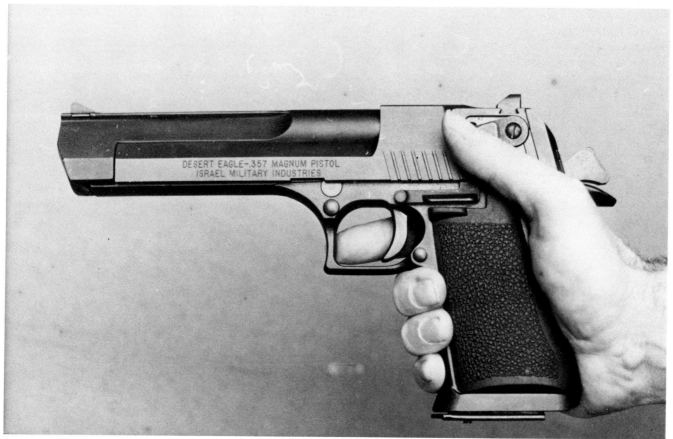

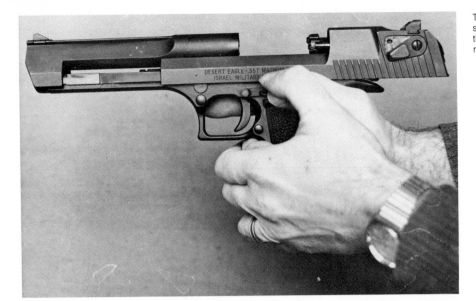

The Desert Eagle in the hands of René Smeets, showing the exceptional size of this pistol. Both thumbs are used to activate the slide stop. Note the rotating bolt, showing the lugs.

A typical group obtained with the Desert Eagle at 15 metres.

Korth Combat Magnum

Type: double-action revolver.
Maker: Waffenfabrik W. Korth, Ratzeburg/Holstein, West Germany.
Calibre: ·357 Magnum/·38 Special, or ·38 Special only.
Overall length: depends on model.
Barrel length: 75, 100 and 150mm (3-6in).
Weight, empty: not available.
Cylinder capacity: 6 (5 in older models).
Construction: blued or stainless steel, semi-adjustable (Combat) or fully adjustable (Sport) back sight.

An optional 9mm Parabellum variant is available. Blued guns have ventilated ribs; stainless guns, a plain sighting band above the barrel.

Handgun fans are often aware of the existence of the 'mythical' Korth revolvers, made by a constituent of the Dynamit Nobel Group, but very few have ever had the chance to shoot this veritable Rolls-Royce of revolvers. It is said that only five hundred are made each year, and that the fortunate customer has to wait some months for delivery.

However, the reward for the delay is worthwhile; the first sight of the gun is enough to convince the purchaser of the truly excellent manufacturing quality. Not only is the metal first class, but all the surfaces, including the internal parts, are highly polished to give an exceptionally smooth action.

The latest Korths are not unlike the Colt Python or L-Frame Smith & Wessons externally, and this aesthetic appeal is accompanied by excellent balance. The only originality that is immediately obvious is a cylinder release alongside the hammer on the right side. Pushed forward with the thumb of the firing hand to unlock the cylinder, this catch is badly placed and greatly inhibits rapid reloading. The quirky location is believed to result from the complexity of the internal mechanism (with more than seventy parts in all) leaving no room for a more conventional Colt or Smith & Wesson-style latch on the left side.

Closer examination reveals many more interesting features. Once the cylinder has been unlatched, for example, it can be removed simply by pressing the button on the right side of the frame above the trigger guard — simplifying cleaning or the substitution, without tools, of the optional 9mm Parabellum cylinder. The cylinder-locking system is also unique, the cylinder axle being pushed rearward by the spring-loaded ejector rod to force a stud into a recess on the shield. This gives a positive lock, while minimizing the gap between the front of the cylinder and the barrel (about 0.05mm) that would otherwise reduce velocity, power and accuracy.

The single-action trigger pull can be adjusted externally between 1 and 2.5kg (2.2-5.5lb) with a threaded bolt inside the trigger guard. The test gun was delivered with a factory-set pull weight of 1.4kg (3.1lb), which is excellent and not, in my opinion, in need of modification. The trigger travel is also adjustable externally, but requires simultaneous adjustment of two opposed threaded bolts and is better left to a qualified armourer.

Though many authors have written about the Korth, it is clear that few actually saw the inside of the gun, owing to the difficulty of removing the cover plate. This is not only fitted extremely tightly, but it requires a special tool (and the services of an expert gunsmith!) to remove it. Though such dismantling is rarely necessary once the trigger is properly adjusted, it is worthwhile to see not only the perfect polish of the internal parts but also the unique design of the trigger mechanism. The extraordinary smoothness of the double action results from the internal finish and the telescoping mainspring, giving a pull of 3.5kg (7.7lb). The trigger travel becomes progressively smoother, with no hard point to overcome nor any backlash. The Korth revolver is sold with five rollers of differing diameter, giving different progressive actions though — once again — replacement is best done by a competent gunsmith.

Needless to say, the Korth is exceptionally pleasant to fire, even in double-action mode and ·357 Magnum chambering. The grip is very good, and the gun easily controlled (helped, undeniably, by the 6in barrel of the test gun). The revolver is certainly not a European specialty; however, with guns such as the Manurhin MR 73 and the Korth, the Old World nevertheless has two products to compete with the best of the Americans.

The beautiful Korth stainless steel 'Sport' ·357 Magnum, with a 6in barrel. The unimpeachable manufacturing quality is clearly evident.

The cylinder, grips and side plate of this blued Korth have been removed. The side plate is particularly carefully fitted, and may need the services of a gunsmith to detach it; consequently, the working parts of Korth revolvers are rarely revealed. Note the unique telescoping mainspring shroud.

The cylinder of Korth revolvers may be removed in seconds, without tools, simply by pushing a button above the trigger guard on the right side of the frame once the cylinder has swung outward.

The handling and balance of this old-pattern Korth (note the half-length ejector) are perfect. The holstered gun is an H&K P7M13.

This impressive double-action group was obtained from the Korth at 25m.

MAB P15

Type: single-action semi-automatic pistol.
Maker: Manufacture d'Armes de Bayonne, Bayonne, France.
Calibre: 9mm Parabellum.
Overall length: 205mm, 8.07in.
Barrel length: 117mm, 4.61in.
Weight, empty: 1,105gm, 39.0oz.
Magazine capacity: 15+1.
Construction: all steel, fixed sights.

This was the only French 9mm pistol with a large-capacity magazine to be offered commercially in substantial numbers. However, despite some success in North America, the MAB P15 was never adopted by the military or police forces in its native country. This situation continually disrupted production until, in 1984, MAB went into liquidation. A rescue attempt was mounted in 1985, and a sample gun acquired for testing. At the time of writing, however, the future of the operation still looks uncertain.

The first impressions of the weapon are good: it is massive, well balanced and has one of the best grips I have ever handled. The all-steel construction gives confidence, and an empty weight of more than 1.1kg helps damp out recoil. When the MAB was developed in the 1960s, the FN-Browning High-Power was the archetypal 'modern' handgun and many of the improvements now regarded as commonplace were still unknown: how, then, would the MAB perform in the late 1980s?

A rotating barrel controls the slide/barrel lock, providing a system that seems to represent an intermediate stage between a delayed blowback and a true locked breech. The principle of the rotary lock is old, dating back to one of the patents sought by John Browning in 1897, and has been incorporated in guns such as the Savage, the Steyr-Hahn and the Czech CZ 24. The MAB barrel does not move back, but simply pivots laterally to release the slide to complete the conventional cycle of extraction, ejection, cocking and loading. The barrel has two lugs, the upper of which guides the slide while the lower one controls the pivoting of the barrel and its cradle.

Consequently, the barrel maintains its position, parallel to the slide and the direction of aim, in an attempt to improve accuracy. The barrel cradle extends into a long spring guide, fixed into the frame by the spindle of the slide stop, with its rear part acting as the feed ramp. The underside of the top of the slide has a long deep groove, curved to rotate and release the barrel and then straight to allow the slide to run back alone. The locking system is robust, combining the safety of a locked breech with the accuracy of a fixed barrel whose axis remains parallel with the slide.

Another point of originality is the complexity of the P15 mechanism, and the interaction of its many parts. A good example of this is provided by the bifurcated sear. When the trigger is pulled, the hooked trigger bar moves forward, pivoting the sear by means of the upper arm on the right side to release the hammer. The spindle of the manual safety lever blocks the lower (left) arm of the sear; unfortunately, if the trigger is pulled hard when the manual safety is applied, the axis pin of the sear can be twisted and may even break.

The trigger bar is returned to its upper position by a spring, reconnecting the sear after each shot. A mechanical safety is provided by the slide, which disconnects the sear and trigger bar after each shot and prevents the trigger bar rising into a corresponding slide recess (reconnecting the parts) until the action is completely forward. In addition, the spring of the magazine safety is strong enough to disconnect the sear and trigger bar when the magazine is removed. I do not like superfluous magazine safeties, and MAB's is particularly bad; contact with the magazine, deactivating the safety, relies on a tiny point of the safety lever resting near the the thin feed-lip of the magazine. If either of these parts wears badly or breaks, the gun immediately becomes unserviceable. Range trials soon showed the excellence of the grip design, which greatly facilitated sighting after a fast draw. The slide is difficult to move, owing to the design of the locking system, and weak people will have to use their strong hand – a bad point, as it necessitates changing the handgrip. The slide stop is easy to operate, but the manual safety lever is not: the thickness of the grip prevents easy manipulation by the thumb. The magazine catch is also difficult to operate, as it is necessary to pivot the pistol in the hand – an operation, familiar to the experienced IPSC shooter, which forces the forefinger out of the trigger guard and increases the reloading safety.

Field stripping is easy, the only trick being to remember to retract the slide far enough for it to be caught by the projection on the slide stop.

The magazine is a close copy of the High-Power pattern; the removable bottom inspires no confidence and the magazine lips are very sharp, making filling unpleasant though the fifteen rounds are retained satisfactorily. The front sight is too low, and its grooving creates more glare than it suppresses; the back sight notch is too small and is almost filled by the front sight in a two-hand stance, with very little spare light on either side. And, finally, the trigger travel is poor considering its reasonable pull of 2.5kg (5.5lb). The test gun shot too far to the left, which, with non-adjustable sights, demonstrates a lack of quality control in the factory. Differing ammunition, from hot FN to mild Hirtenberger loads, gave no trouble whatsoever though the poor trigger made accurate shooting difficult. Up to 15m, results were satisfactory for a defence weapon, but disappointing owing to the presence of a barrel/slide locking system specifically intended to promote good shooting.

It is a great pity that the MAB P15, conceived in the 1960s, was not revised to take advantage of the latest advances in handgun design before being re-introduced.

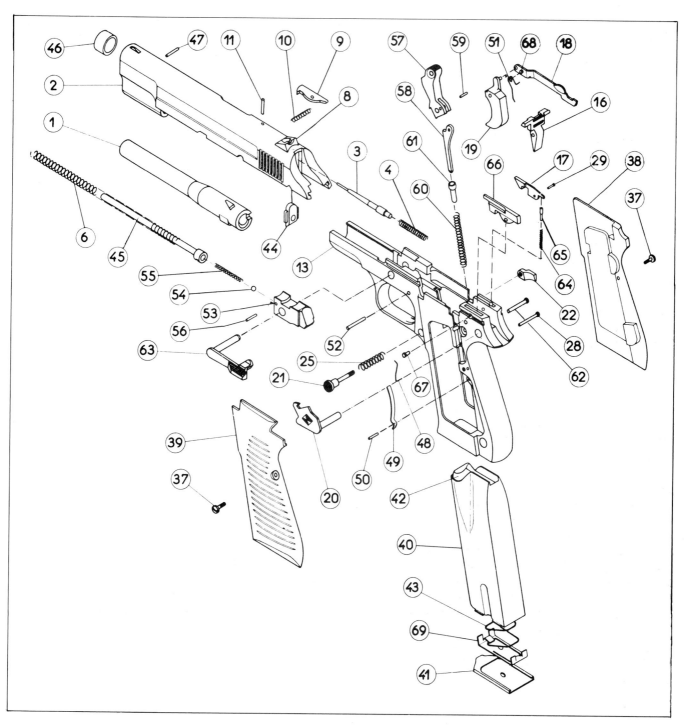

The P-15 is a robust all-steel pistol. Firing rapidly at 15m produced this group; adequate, but not particularly impressive and an adequate reflection of the poor trigger pull.

The MAB field-stripped.

The P-15 slide has been removed to show that the trigger bar must be released before it can return behind the sear arm, preventing a burst being fired.

The manual safety blocks the left arm of the sear. However, if the trigger is pulled with the safety applied, the sear spindle will be twisted and possibly even broken.

When a magazine is in place, the magazine safety is forced into its upper position and lies behind the sear arm. Unfortunately, contact between the safety and the magazine relies on the sharply-pointed safety-bar, which, if it breaks, will immobilise the gun.

The P-15 locks by rotating the barrel in its cradle, allowing the breech to pivot laterally without moving longtudinally.

Shooting the MAB P-15 without ear protectors is necessary in realistic training, though too much of it may damage the shooter's hearing.

126

Makarov

Type: double action semi-automatic pistol.
Maker: Russian, Polish, East German and Chinese arsenals.
Calibre: 9×18mm.
Overall length: 157mm, 6.18in.
Barrel length: 93mm, 3.66in.
Weight, empty: 700gm, 24.7oz.
Magazine capacity: 8+1.
Construction: all steel, fixed sights.

The Makarov pistol is still the most widely distributed military handgun in the Eastern Bloc, though recently superseded in Russian service by the 5.45mm PSM. Its distinctive cartridge − known in the West as the 9mm Makarov − has also been used in the obsolescent Soviet Stechkin selective-fire pistol (APS) and the current Polish wz/63 machine pistol.

Developed immediately after the Second World War had ended, possibly from the German 9mm Ultra prototype, the cartridge was intended to be less powerful than the then-current 7.62mm pattern used with the TT (Tokarev) pistols. Similar ammunition has been made in Europe under the Geco and Hirtenberg brandnames as the '9mm Police', for pistols such as the Walther PP Super and the SIG-Sauer P230. The Makarov pistols will usually fire 9mm Makarov, 9mm Police and even 9mm Short (·380 ACP) with reasonable accuracy.

The Makarov − by no means as large as it appears when photographed by itself − is, ultimately, a derivative of the Walther Polizei Pistole of 1929: a fixed barrel, double-action blowback, with the recoil spring concentric with the barrel, a trigger-guard lock controlling dismantling, and a safety placed on the slide. It is a simple design, containing (excepting the magazine) only 25 parts including the screws and springs. The manufacturing quality is quite good, with few tooling marks. The butt is an interesting design, with a squared skeleton and a one-piece plastic grip retained by a single screw through the backstrap. The general shape of the grip is very good, allowing a comfortable grasp.

The mechanism is classically double action, the sole concession to originality being the combination slide stop/ejector. As the slide stop does not double as a dismantling pin, it can share the trigger spindle to reduce the number of parts still more.

Light, well balanced and eminently concealable, the Makarov could have been a very good combat pistol. However, the cartridge is not very powerful − only marginally superior to the ·380 ACP − and would only provide adequate 'stopping power' if loaded with special bullets. The magazine capacity is also too small by contemporary standards. The major problem would have been the absence of original factory-loaded ammunition, had not the Makarov fired 9mm Police and 9mm Short without trouble. Accuracy was very good, even though the bullet diameter of 9mm Police/Short cartridges is slightly less than genuine 9mm Makarov; thus, the effect of the rifling is commensurately reduced and smaller than normal bullets tumbled into the target at 15m.

The manual safety allows the gun to be carried cocked-and-locked ('Condition One' carry). In the absence of an automatic de-cocking system, the hammer must be lowered manually by the thumb after the trigger has been pulled. (NB: the gun should be pointed in a safe direction!) No safety notch exists on the hammer base, but as the hammer − like that of the Walther PP − is securely held in the down position, there is no danger of accidental discharge. The trigger pull is good (2.5kg/5.5lb single action, and 5.5kg/12.2lb double action) with excellent travel.

It is unlikely that many people will have the opportunity of firing these little pistols; but, if 'Red Dawn' ever occurred, just remember that the Makarov can shoot 9mm Police or 9mm Short . . . but that Western guns chambering these cartridges *cannot* fire Soviet-type 9mm rounds.

A right-side view of a typical Soviet-made pistol, made in Tula in 1975. The position of the trigger within its guard betrays the existence of a double-action mechanism.

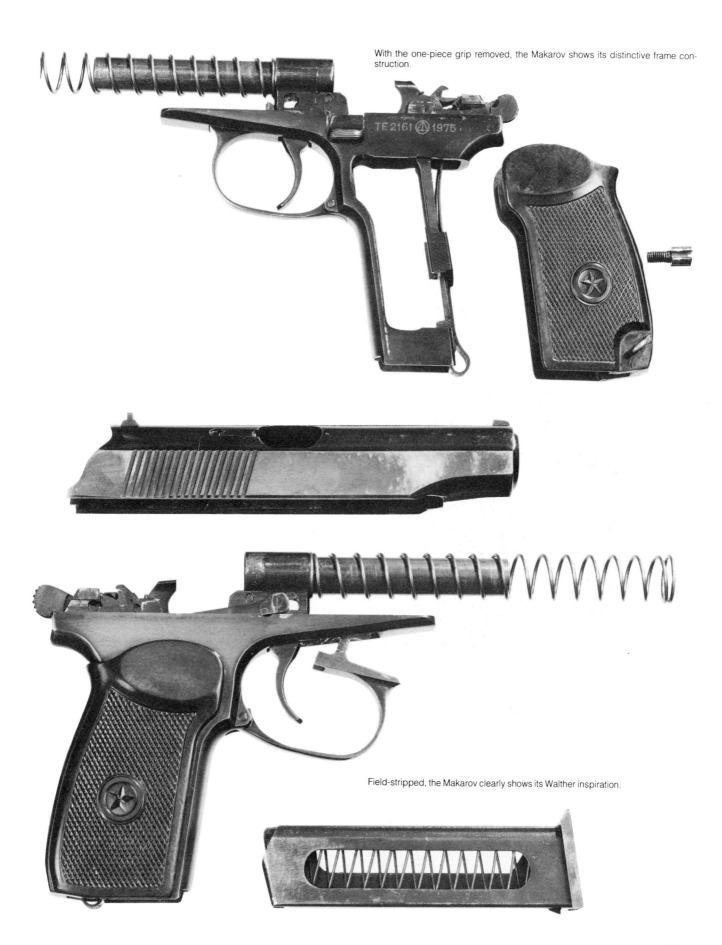

With the one-piece grip removed, the Makarov shows its distinctive frame construction.

Field-stripped, the Makarov clearly shows its Walther inspiration.

A two-hand grip emphasizes the Makarov's small size.

"ARMABEL"
DUMOULIN GERARD

Though the original 9mm Soviet cartridge gives the best accuracy, the Makarov will still shoot ammunition such as the 9mm Police or 9mm Short capably. The 'chest' group shown here was achieved with 9mm Short (·380 ACP) from a distance of 20m.

Manurhin MR 73

Type: double action revolver.
Maker: Manufacture de Machines du Haut-Rhin (Manurhin), Hendaye, France.
Calibre: ·357 Magnum/·38 Special or 9mm Parabellum.
Overall length, barrel length, empty weight: see notes.
Cylinder capacity: 6.
Construction: blued steel, various sights (see notes).

The MR 73 Défense, with fixed sights, is available with barrels measuring 63, 76 and 102mm (2.5-4in), giving an overall length of 195, 205 and 233mm (7.68-9.17in) and weights of 880, 890 and 950gm (31.0-33.5oz).
The MR 73 Constabulary has an adjustable back sight and five optional barrel lengths – 76, 102, 132, 152 and 203mm (3-8in). The overall lengths are 205, 233, 264, 283 and 334mm (8.07-13.15in) respectively, the weights being 890, 950, 1050, 1070 and 1170gm (31.4-41.3oz).
The MR 73 Sport has an adjustable back sight and a high squared front sight. Barrel options include 102, 132, 152 and 203mm (4-8in), the remaining data being identical with the Constabulary model.
Special Match Models exist in ·32 Long (152mm/6in barrel) and ·38 Special (145mm/5.71in), with specially honed trigger actions. The Long Range and Silhouette guns have 230mm (9.06in) and 275mm (10.83in) barrels respectively, the latter especially designed for metallic silhouette shooting. The GIGN, the special intervention group of the French national constabulary, uses a version of the 203mm-barrelled gun with a folding bipod.

France was the birthplace of many of the greatest European revolvers, such as the pinfire Lefaucheux, the 'Chamelot-Delvigne' and the excellent French Mle 1892 ('Lebel') service revolver. The Mle 1892, among the first small-calibre revolvers to be accepted for service, served the French Army until the mid 1930s. Though large numbers of foreign automatics had been purchased by the French during the First World War, and it had been admitted that the revolver's days were numbered as early as 1922, trials lasted almost until the outbreak of the Second World War. The two principal competing designs, the Mle 1935A and Mle 1935S, were ordered into limited production to facilitate field trials. Both were designed for the very weak 7.65mm Longue cartridge, the Mle 1935S ultimately evolving into the 9mm Parabellum MAC-50 (the current French service gun, unavailable on the commercial market) and the Mle 1935A into the SIG P 210. Both guns embodied the Petter system, named after the engineer responsible for the removable trigger system.

Not since 1892, therefore, has a single new revolver been created in France. During the 1960s, the success of the Sasia Method revived interest in such guns and so, in the early 1970s, Manurhin introduced the MR 73. The company had already made variants of the Walther P38, PP and PPK under licence.

One of the aims of the new gun was to embody the two main service calibres already adopted, ·38 Special/·357 Magnum and 9mm Parabellum. Using an automatic pistol cartridge in a revolver was not new – more than 300,000 ·45 ACP Colt and Smith & Wesson revolvers had been made during the First World War – and a 9mm Parabellum S&W copy had been made by Israeli Metal Industries in the 1950s. The Manurhin MR 73 and the comparatively unsuccessful FN 'Barracuda' have taken the concept still farther, providing exchangeable cylinders for the rimmed and rimless cartridges.

To an untrained eye, ·38 Special and 9mm Parabellum seem approximately the same size, and it is possible to shoot them both through the same barrel. However, as the average diameter of 9mm Parabellum bullets is about 0.355in, compared with 0.357-0.358in for ·38 Special and ·357 Magnum, it is evident that the rifling characteristics favour the bigger bullets.

The MR 73 is a splendid piece of machinery and, if the rare and expensive Korth revolver is the Rolls-Royce of European wheelguns, the Manurhin is at least the Cadillac. The quality and polishing of each part are excellent, the low-friction mechanism is highly sophisticated and the trigger pull is very smooth. The main component is a 'chariot', mounted on four wheels, which rolls inside the frame to transfer a pull on the trigger to the hammer. The system ensures a constant pull during the whole action. The cylinder moves anticlockwise, being released by a Smith & Wesson-style latch. The test gun was a Constabulary model, with a 102mm barrel, an exchangeable 9mm Parabellum cylinder, an adjustable back sight and a post-type front sight. Its trigger has an adjustable anti-backlash screw.

The handling qualities are excellent, the trigger pull being one of the best found on a revolver – the single and double actions measuring 1.9kg (4.2lb) and 3.5kg (7.7lb) on the sample gun. The use of ·38 Special in such a revolver gives the best results, while ·357 Magnum allows very precise single-action shots at long range combined with accurate double-action rapid-fire at distances up to 15m (using either Sasia's bowling draw and semi-crouch or the straight Cooper's draw and Weaver stance). Exchanging the cylinders is easy; the front screw on the removable side-plate is rotated until the cylinder axis-pin is released, then the whole assembly is removed and instantly replaced by the substitute unit.

One of the main problems encountered in using rimless automatic pistol cartridges in a revolver is retaining them in the cylinder. The usual method is to use full- or half-moon clips, which double as speedloaders, but Manurhin chose to be different and each chamber is provided with two circumferential springs that lock into the extraction groove of each cartridge.

I was not satisfied with the 9mm cylinder; not only were the small-diameter bullets less than accurate in an otherwise excellent revolver but the action also seized up after the first series, preventing the cylinder opening. The problem was caused by two of the chambers, in which the base of the 9mm Parabellum cartridges protruded fractionally farther than the others and consequently rubbed on the back of the frame. The gun worked satisfactorily when only the four remaining chambers were loaded, though ejection of 9mm Hirtenberg and Sellier & Bellot cartridges, particularly, caused additional difficulty. No problems were encountered in ·38 Special or ·357 Magnum.

The idea of supplying the exchangeable cylinders is probably none too practical, and mixing rimmed revolver with rimless pistol cartridges adds to the woes. Yet the Manurhin MR 73 is among the best of all the current revolvers, assuming price is not a deciding factor. (My favourite, the L-Frame Smith & Wesson Model 686, is appreciably cheaper.)

The main defect of the MR 73 is simply the lack of an adequate speedloader, the straight-line (2×3) Manurhin type being unworthy of the name.

The MR 73 'Constabulary' revolver, with a 4in barrel and an extra 9mm Parabellum cylinder.

The field-stripped MR-73 is revealed as one of the best-made of all the test guns, with an attention to detail absent from some of its rivals.

The adjustable 'backlash' or trigger-overtravel screw of the MR 73.

The MR 73 has a hammer with an independently pivoting firing pin, an adjustable back sight and a forward-moving cylinder latch.

The MR 73 was tested at medium ranges in accord with the Sasia Method: holster well back on the hip, a two-hand grip and a semi-crouched body position – efficient, but only perfected after extensive training.

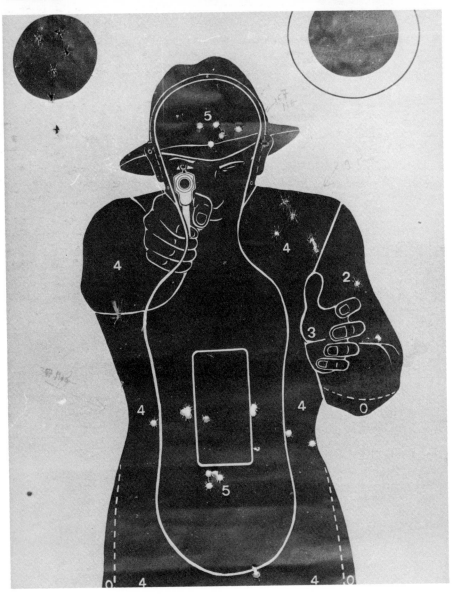

This typical Sasia Target has been peppered with the MR 73. On the black circle, upper left: six rounds of ·38 Special fired at 25m, one handed; in the 'head', six rounds of ·357 Magnum at 15m, single action, with a Weaver stance (note the sixth shot in the ear!); in the body, ultra rapid double-action fire with ·357 Magnum ammunition at 7m, after a fast draw; and, in the left shoulder, 6 rounds of 9mm Parabellum at 15m. Firing the Parabellum group occupied three minutes, as one of the chambers caused a potentially calamitous cylinder jam.

Manurhin MR 'Special Police F1'

Type: double action revolver.
Maker: Manufacture de Machines du Haut-Rhin (Manurhin), Hendaye, France.
Calibre: ·357 Magnum/·38 Special or 9mm Parabellum.
Overall length: 193, 206 and 231mm (7.6-9.1in).
Barrel length: 63, 76 and 102mm (2.5-4in).
Weight, empty: 918, 950 and 1000gm (32.4-35.3oz).
Cylinder capacity: 6.
Construction: blued (SP F1) or stainless (SP X1) steel, fixed sights.

In 1981, following a government-sponsored programme, Manurhin decided to produce a cheaper revolver than the excellent MR 73 (q.v.) – which was restricted to some elite units in the police and constabulary, including the GIGN ultra-specialized intervention group. As the French police had been involved with the Sasia Method since the 1960s, and as the MR 73 was the only revolver produced in France, the authorities had been forced to equip with foreign guns made by Colt, Llama, Ruger and Smith & Wesson (including an S&W Model 19 with a 75mm barrel, made to Raymond Sasia's specification as the '19/3 R.S.'). The special 'Presidential Hunting Service' was equipped with the Ruger Speed-Six, specially made for the national police in 9mm Parabellum with a cartridge collector patented by the Frenchman André Pilorget.

When the necessity arose for a less expensive gun, Manurhin associated with Ruger to produce a revolver combining the frame and action of the Speed-Six with a cylinder and barrel provided by Manurhin. The result was the RMR (Ruger-Manurhin-Revolver) 'Special Police', retaining the exchangeable cylinder concept but featuring half-moon clips and standard US-type speedloaders.

The Ruger mechanism is discussed in the relevant section. Dismantling is controlled by the trigger guard, while the cylinder latch is simply pushed in rather than forward (as in the S&W designs and the MR 73) or backward (as in the Colt or Uberti systems). The RMR was well made, though half the price of the MR 73 and obviously exhibiting rougher finish.

The cylinder – which rotated anticlockwise – was entirely new, having to match frames supplied by Ruger. The trigger lacked the smoothness of the MR 73, but the simple and efficient coil-type Ruger mainspring gave a very acceptable pull.

Problems with the royalties being paid to Ruger caused the RMR to be replaced in 1984 by the new 'Special Police F1', made entirely by Manurhin and its affiliates. However, apart from a few minor details, the gun remains exactly the same as the RMR; indeed, many of the parts will interchange.

One of the most important details is the reversion to a removable side-plate, rather than the unconventional Ruger system. By unscrewing the forward screw of this plate, the ·38 Special/·357 Magnum cylinder can be exchanged with the optional 9mm Parabellum unit. The 75mm-barrelled test gun had an exceptional trigger pull (2.5kg/5.5lb in single action, 5.2kg/11.5lb double action) which, though it did not compare with the honed excellence of the MR 73, was none the less more than acceptable in a service gun.

The gun was easily controllable, especially with its large grips, but the combination of ·357 Magnum and the short barrel is unpleasant in rapid fire: for this, the 10cm-barrelled option would be preferable. However, the ·38 Special was a dream to fire, with the more powerful '+P' loads giving maximum effectiveness. The fixed sights were very good, the flat front sight being developed specifically for the 'bowled draw' and isosceles semi-crouch Sasia Method. For instinctive shooting at ranges up to 15m, the MR F1 'Special Police' is a very good service and personal-defence gun.

The 9mm Parabellum was not tested, though some reports suggest it is a better dual-purpose gun than other revolvers sharing the same principles.

The MR F1 with its maker's 'speedloader' — which, however, is far from handy. The revolver is an obvious copy of the Ruger Security Six (q.v.) with a Manurhin-designed barrel and cylinder.

Despite its removable side plate (cf., dismantling the Security Six), the MR F1 reveals its Ruger-style lockwork. Removing the side plate is often difficult.

The action of the MR F1 is not as smooth as that of the MR 73. Though easily enough controlled with ·38 Special, firing ·357 Magnum may cause hand tremors.

136

Mini-Revolver

Type: single-action revolver.
Maker: North American Arms, Provo, Utah, USA.
Calibre: ·22 Long Rifle.
Overall length: 102mm, 4.0in.
Barrel length: 28mm, 1.1in.
Weight, empty: 140gm, 5oz.
Cylinder capacity: 5.
Construction: stainless steel, fixed sights.

I am sure there will be some readers who will disagree with my inclusion of the Mini-Revolver in this book. Their criticisms will be based on its lack of power or accuracy, but those scoffing at the Mini-Revolver will have missed an important point: to be effective, a combat handgun must be available when it is most needed, and the Mini-Revolver's diminutive size grants it great propinquity. It is, in fact, one of the most widely carried defensive weapons encountered in the United States. Many civilians or undercover police officers just cannot carry conventional revolvers or automatics without betraying that they are armed, while the Mini-Revolver can be carried unobtrusively under even minimal clothing. Compared to a Detonics MC-1 or a Smith & Wesson Model 38, the Mini-Revolver, though it may not seem like much, has many advantages compared to nothing.

As a combat round, the Long Rifle rimfire round is certainly not in the 'man-stopper' class, but many people have been killed by this cartridge and a well-placed ·22 Long Rifle bullet can still be very damaging. And, after all, no one wants to be shot with any cartridge; thus, the Mini-Revolver still offers a potential threat as a defensive weapon. Fired from a short barrel, the bullets tend to keyhole (or tumble) and can cause a messier, more massive wound than larger-diameter jacketed bullets such as the ·25 ACP.

The Mini-Revolver is obviously a very small weapon, and anyone with reasonably sized hands will have problems with the small bird's-head grip. This, which is normally precariously grasped with two fingers, makes even the mild recoil of the ·22 cartridge awkward to handle. Operation is even more difficult, as the Mini-Revolver has a single-action trigger. For any kind of rapid shooting, I find it quicker to cock the hammer with the non-firing thumb, though it is obviously possible to cock with the 'firing' thumb provided the necessity to change grasp is accepted. The spur trigger is small, but relatively easy to use. The hammer spur is enlarged to the point where it is easy to cock.

The sights are virtually useless, but the Mini-Revolver is really a belly gun (or, considering its size, a 'belly-button gun'!) for use at point blank range where sighting is irrelevant. The top strap and barrel-top have a matt finish, but glare is hardly likely to pose a real problem.

To load the Mini-Revolver, the cylinder pin must be removed by pressing a release button at the pin-tip. The cylinder can then be removed by pulling back slightly on the hammer and rolling the cylinder out of the frame. Since the Mini-Revolver is a single action, only four chambers should be loaded to leave a vacant chamber beneath the hammer for safety's sake. There is a half-cock notch, but it should not be relied upon. To eject empty cases, the cylinder pin serves as an ejector rod to punch the cases out of the chambers. Though reloading the Mini-Revolver is slow, the weapon is not likely to be used in a pitched barrel and the problem is insignificant. It is a close-range last-ditch weapon. However, because of the small and comparatively small bullet, attempts should always be made to score multiple hits to increase shocking power.

A hundred each of 37gn CCI-Speer and 38gn Federal hollow-point cartridges were used in the range tests, with much the same results. There were fourteen misfires, possibly owing to a light hammer fall. An accumulation of powder residue may also have contributed to these problems, as all occurred after a few cylinders-full had been fired. Unlike the other guns tested for this book, the Mini-Revolver was cleaned after fifty rounds owing to its small parts and, consequently, the magnified effect of fouling. The first few post-cleaning cylinders-full performed perfectly. Misfires occurred with both types of ammunition, but the cartridges all fired on the second or third attempt. At 5 yards, the diameter of 4-shot groups normally ran between 3 and 6in, which − though not very good for a larger gun − is quite acceptable in the Mini-Revolver. At the close ranges for which the Mini-Revolver is intended, it can still put its bullets into the torso or head where they will do the most damage. About one half of the bullets showed some tendency to keyhole (or tumble). Though not uncomfortable, recoil was noticeable as it turned the gun somewhat in the hand around the minuscule bird's-head grip. Combined with the single-action trigger system, this inhibits rapid follow-up shots.

The Mini-Revolver's performance certainly was not up to the standard of any other weapon in this work. The misfires were most distressing, and anyone choosing the gun should test it to ensure the mainspring is strong enough for sure ignition. The other shortcomings in the Mini-Revolver's performance are attributable to the need to sacrifice everything in pursuit of small size. Practice, especially in using the weak hand to cock the hammer, will undoubtedly improve close-range speed and accuracy.

I do not recommend the Mini-Revolver except for undercover police officers and civilians seeking an extremely concealable weapon − the only valid reason for choosing this weapon.

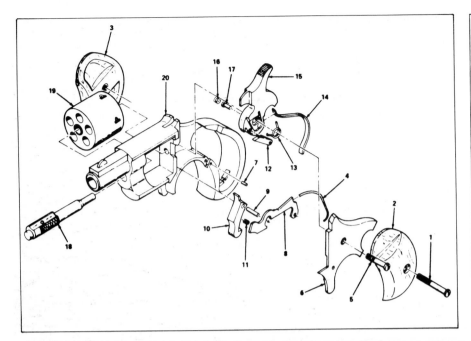

Key

1 Grip Screw
2 Grip Panel, L.H.
3 Grip Panel, R.H.
4 Latch Spring
5 Hammer Screw
6 Sideplate
7 Latch Pin
8 Cylinder Bolt
9 Trigger Pin
10 Trigger
11 Trigger Spring
12 Cylinder Hand
13 Hand Spring
14 Mainspring
15 Hammer
16 Index Spring
17 Index Pin
18 Cylinder Pin Assembly
19 Cylinder
20 Frame

The spur trigger and proportionately long cylinder for the ·22 LR rimfire cartridge are evident in this view of the Mini-Revolver.

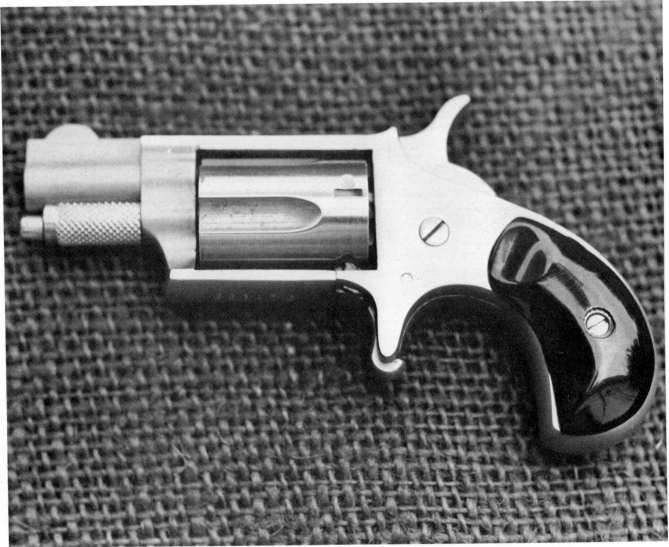

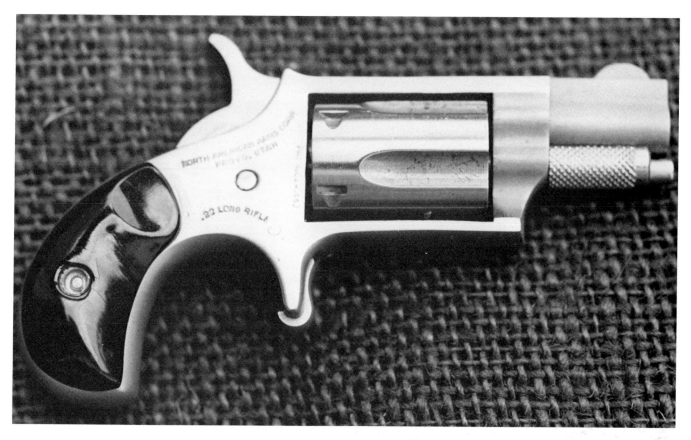

Note the bird's-head grip and single-action hammer.

The Mini-Revolver cylinder must be removed to facilitate ejection and reloading. The cylinder pin doubles as the ejector rod. Note the 'four-only' empties, as a round should never be chambered under the Mini-Revolver's hammer.

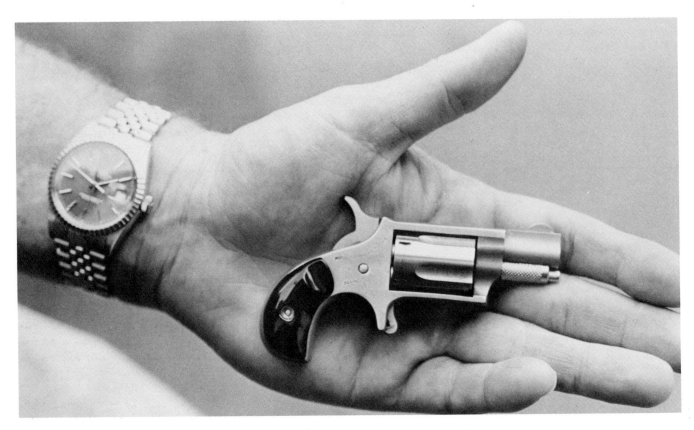

The primary recommendation of the Mini-Revolver is its small size.

Though only a ·22, grasping problems can make the Mini-Revolver difficult to control.

This 7-yard group shows that, at very close range, the Mini-Revolver is accurate enough to enable shots to be placed with reasonable confidence. Note that some rounds have a tendency to tumble on impact.

Peters Stahl Wechselsystem (PSW)

Type: semi-automatic pistol conversion unit.
Maker: Peters Stahl GmbH & Co. KG, Paderborn, West Germany.
Calibre: ·22 LR rimfire.
Overall length, barrel length, weight: dependent on the model.
Magazine capacity: generally 10 + 1.
Construction: steel slide, adjustable sights.

Training is an essential part of combat-handgun shooting, and while I am convinced of the necessity to train with full-power ammunition, I concede not only that this ammunition is expensive but also that there are times when less power is required.

An expedient is to use cheap cartridges such as the ·22 LR rimfire for initiation, familiarization or shooting on ranges where power is restricted. However, this is valueless if the weight, balance and handling characteristics of the training gun fail to duplicate those of the combat weapon. Until very recently, acceptable conversion kits were unobtainable for guns other than the Colt Government Model (for which the Ace Model or a factory conversion unit could be acquired). The numerous revolver accessories were usually complicated and often shot erratically; the only one that impressed me was the French Ferreti system proposed for some of the Smith & Wessons, but I have never encountered a ·22 speedloader without which, I feel, realistic combat-revolver shooting is impossible.

The situation has been changed by the Peters Stahl Wechselsystem (PSW), distributed in Britain by Parker-Hale Ltd and by Bar-Sto in the USA. At the time of writing, the PSW may be obtained for the SIG P240 (PSW I and P 210 (PSW II), the High-Power or its FÉG sibling (PSW III), the S&W Models 39 and 59 (PSW IV), the CZ 75 (PSW V), the Colt Government Model (PSW VI), the Colt Commander (PSW VII) and the Star 28M and 30M (PSW VIII). Some of these conversions can be obtained with long slides, but are more appropriate for target practice.

I tested the PSW III extensively on the High-Power and it performed extremely well. The conversion does not require a locked-breech and is a simple blowback, only the rear part of the 'slide' reciprocating after firing. The slide stop is useless when the 10-round magazine is empty and the breechblock is simply held back by the magazine follower; the slide stop is useful only as a dismantling pin when the PSW is in place.

The manual safety functions normally, though some High-Powers will not accept the PSW without some minor modifications. The adjustable sights are very good: better, in fact, than the sights of the original military pistol and comparable to those used on the HP 'Sport' model. Opinion of the PSW trigger pull depends on the degree of customization on the original gun, but is normally about 4kg (8.8lb) provided the superfluous magazine safety has been discarded.

The PSW shoots surprisingly pleasantly, once the firer has become accustomed to its minimal recoil and does not 'over control' the gun. Virtually all conventional combat-shooting techniques were practised, including 'double taps', and there were no feed problems. The conversion is very accurate, but the sights on the trial gun, presumably adjusted for a specific cartridge, shot high. The groups were very tight out to 20m, though a fast reload with the slide open is impossible owing to the hold-open system. Coincidentally, this feature emphasises to the trainee something every experienced combat shooter knows: always change the magazine before firing the last shot.

I cannot, of course, promise that all PSW conversions perform as well as the test example did in the High-Power. However, a friend's report of the PSW III in the P 210 is encouraging and I have no doubt that the Peters Stahl system gives many people the chance of practising with rimfire ammunition − even though the conversion is itself quite expensive, and rimfire training can never replace the real thing.

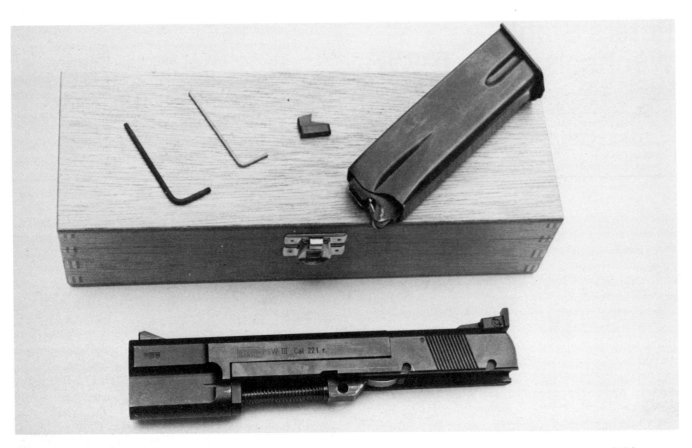

The PSW III conversion unit with its wood case, magazine, alternative sight and Allen keys.

The High-Power with the PSW III (top) and sub-calibre magazine (right).

The PSW III with its slide open, showing the major operating difference: the PSW is a blowback, only the lightweight slide reciprocating. The standard High-Power slide stop is useless when the PSW is fitted.

The performance of the 9mm High-Power (below) compared with results from the PSW (below right). The aiming point, in both cases, was the round sticker. The accuracy was comparable, though the conversion shot appreciably higher than the original full-power gun.

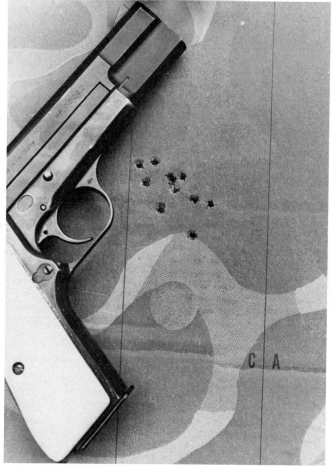

Ruger Security Six

Type: double-action revolver.
Maker: Sturm, Ruger Inc., Southport, Connecticut, USA.
Calibre: ·357 Magnum.
Overall length: 235mm, 9.25in.
Barrel length: 102mm, 4.0in.
Weight, empty: 950gm, 33.5oz.
Cylinder capacity: 6.
Construction: stainless steel, adjustable sights.

The Security Six was Ruger's first double-action revolver, and it has proven itself the equal of long-established designs from Colt and Smith & Wesson. In many ways, the Security Six is actually superior to its older competitors. Perhaps most noteworthy is its truly solid-frame construction, avoiding the side plate typifying Colts and Smith & Wessons. However, the Security Six can be field-stripped easily in a minute or less.

The Security Six also makes use entirely of coil springs. The firing pin, mounted in the frame, is spring loaded; a positive safety in the form of a transfer bar is interposed so that the hammer can only deliver a blow to the firing pin when the trigger is pulled virtually to the end of its rearward course.

Despite being lighter and more compact than competing ·357 Magnum revolvers, the Security Six is extremely strong. At the points receiving the most stress, the Security Six's frame has sufficient steel to provide extra strength. Cylinder wall thickness is also substantial, and the bolt cuts are offset so that they do not weaken the chambers. The cylinder locks at the rear and at the front of the ejector rod. The cylinder latch is depressed to release the cylinder, and though this may seem to run the risk of inadvertently releasing the cylinder, it is very secure in practice.

To prevent the back sight snagging, it is partially recessed in the top of the frame. On stainless guns, the sights can sometimes be difficult to pick up; on the Security Six, however, front and back sights are blackened. The top of the barrel is ribbed to restrict reflection, though the top strap is bright. This causes no problem in sighting, as the sights are raised far enough by the ramp to avoid glare.

The 4in barrel seems to be an ideal choice for the Security Six to provide proper balance. Combined with the rib atop the barrel and the ejector shroud, the Ruger barrel gives enough weight at the muzzle, though it is not as heavy as those of the Colt Python or Smith & Wesson 686.

I also found the chequered walnut semi-target style grips very comfortable, which, combined with excellent balance, made the Security Six easy to shoot. Single and double-action trigger pulls on the trial gun were both quite good. The double action pull was crisp and smooth, with no noticeable pressure build-up immediately before releasing the hammer. As a result, the Security Six is capable of very slick double-action shooting. The smooth trigger is an additional aid to rapid shooting. The hammer is a service rather than target type, but is entirely adequate for a combat revolver which will normally be fired double action.

Although the Security Six is available in blued and stainless steel, I prefer the latter for combat weapons — particularly those carried overtly and exposed to the elements. Unfortunately, the Security Six is polished when I would prefer the finish to be flatter and less reflective.

On the range, the test gun shot outstandingly and proved to be one of the most accurate tested for this book. At 15 yards, the diameter of rapid double-action groups often measured less than 2in; 3in groups were possible at 25 yards. 110gn Federal, 125gn Federal or Remington, and 158gn CCI-Speer jacketed hollow-point ammunition was used, with the 125gn loads giving the best performance by a slight margin. The Security Six handled very well and, despite its relatively light weight, recovery time was quite acceptable even with full-power ·357 Magnum loads.

The Ruger Security Six is one of the highest quality ·357 Magnum revolvers available, yet is quite reasonably priced. Its compactness offers great versatility. It represents an especially good choice for a uniformed police officer because, with a proper holster, it can double as a concealed-carry off-duty weapon. It is also ideal for a civilian seeking a gun for varied tasks. The ·357 Magnum round is powerful enough to serve for hunting, defence or survival, performing all such tasks more than adequately in a 4in barrel.

If I was restricted to a single handgun, the Security Six would receive serious consideration as that one gun. I recommend it highly, owing to its high quality, versatility and excellent value for money.

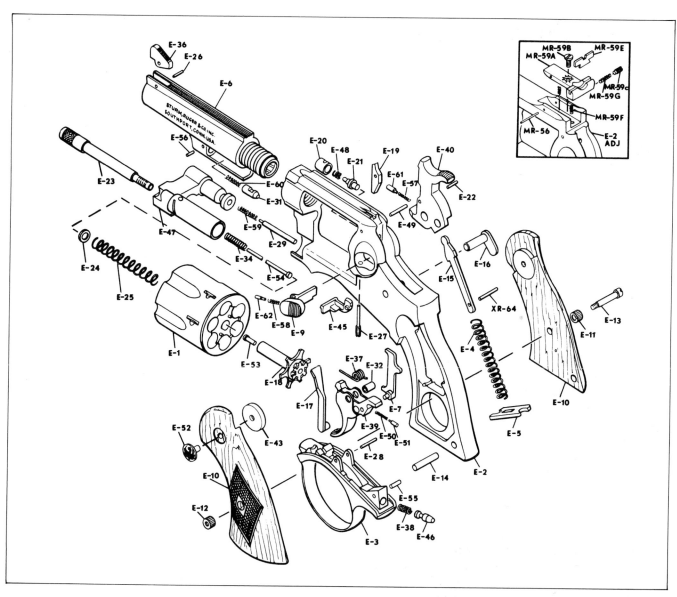

Key

E-6	Barrel (2¾", 4" or 6")	E-2 ADJ	Frame (Adj. Sight)
E-47	Crane/Crane Pivot Assembly	E-2R	Frame (Round Butt, Not
E-1	Cylinder		Shown)
KE-53	Cylinder Center Lock Pin	KE-31	Front Latch
KE-54	Cylinder Center Pin Rod	E-56	Front Latch Cross Pin
KE-34	Cylinder Center Pin Spring	KE-60	Front Latch Spring
KE-45	Cylinder Latch	E-36	Front Sight Blade
KE-29	Cylinder Latch Plunger	E-26	Front Sight Cross Pin
E-59	Cylinder Latch Spring	E-43	Grip Panel Boss
E-9	Cylinder Release Button	E-10L	Grip Panel (Left)
KE-27	Cylinder Release Pivot	E-12	Grip Panel (Left) Ferrule
KE-58	Cylinder Release Spring	E-10R	Grip Panel (Right)
KE-62	Cylinder Release Spring	E-11	Grip Panel (Right) Ferrule
	Plunger	KE-14	Grip Panel Dowel
XR-64	Disassembly Pin	E-13	Grip Panel Screw
E-18	Ejector	E-40AR	Hammer (Spurless) (Not
E-23	Ejector Rod		Shown)
KE-24	Ejector Rod Washer	E-40	Hammer (With Spur)
KE-25	Ejector Spring	KE-19	Hammer Dog
KE-21	Firing Pin	KE-22	Hammer Dog Pivot Pin
KE-48	Firing Pin Rebound Spring	KE-57	Hammer Dog Spring
E-2	Frame (Fixed Sight)	KE-61	Hammer Dog Spring Plunger

E-16	Hammer Pivot Assembly	KE-37	Trigger Spring
KE-15	Hammer Strut	E-3	Trigger Guard
KE-4	Mainspring	KE-46	Trigger Guard Plunger
KE-5	Mainspring Seat	KE-55	Trigger Guard Plunger Cross
E-52	Grip Medallion		Pin
KE-7	Pawl	KE-38	Trigger Guard Plunger
KE-51	Pawl Plunger		Spring
KE-50	Pawl Spring		
MR-59A	Rear Sight		
E-65	Rear Sight Blade		
MR-59B	Rear Sight Elevation Screw		
MR-59F	Rear Sight Elevation Screw		
MR-56	Rear Sight Pivot Pin		
MR-59C	Rear Sight Windage Screw		
MR-59G	Rear Sight Windage		
	Spring		
E-20	Recoil Plate		
E-49	Recoil Plate Cross Pin		
KE-17	Transfer Bar		
E-39	Trigger		
E-32	Trigger Bushing		
KE-28	Trigger Pivot Pin		

The distinctive Ruger cylinder latch is visible in this view. Note, additionally, the smooth and functional design of the frame and barrel.

The clean, compact lines of the Security Six make it a favourite gun on or off duty.

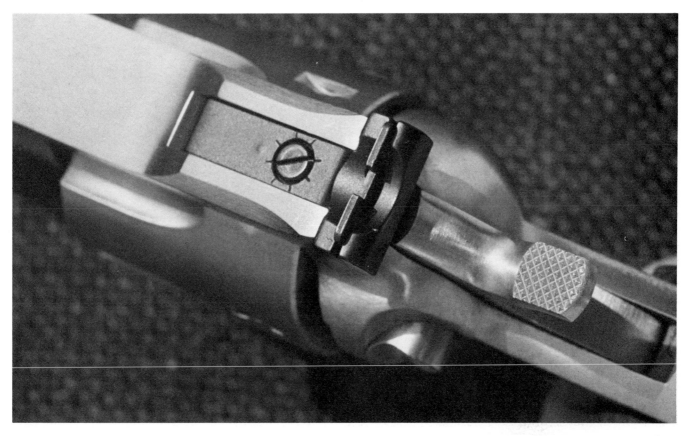

The back sight of the Security Six is recessed in the frame to keep the profile relatively snag-free, a bonus for concealed-carry purposes. The hammer is a service type.

I find the standard Security Six grips among the most comfortable on the market. They do not abrade the hand, even with full-power ·357 Magnum loads.

Though the Security Six is very sturdy, it is light enough to recoil appreciably with full-power Magnum loads.

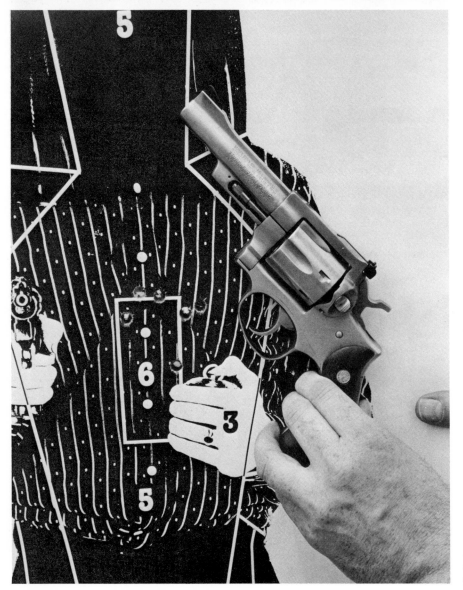

The Security Six was one of the most accurate revolvers tested for this book, as this 25 yard double-action group testifies.

Ruger Redhawk

Type: double-action revolver.
Maker: Sturm, Ruger Inc., Southport, Connecticut, USA.
Calibre: ·44 Magnum.
Overall length: 279mm, 11.0in.
Barrel length: 140mm, 5.5in.
Weight, empty: 1,415gm, 50oz.
Cylinder capacity: 6.
Construction: stainless steel, adjustable sights.

Anyone even casually examining the Redhawk will realize that it was intended not as a combat handgun, but as an outdoorsman's gun. It is being evaluated here, however, because (for example) rural police officers and game wardens often carry ·44 Magnum weapons for defence against predators — whether two or four-legged. These big holster guns may not be intended for use against human targets, but such use is possible.

The Redhawk is a massive weapon which is obviously capable of handling the ·44 Magnum round. The frame and cylinder are even more sturdy than those on the Smith & Wesson Models 29 and 629, which is normally viewed as the ultimate magnum.

The Redhawk's cylinder is especially noteworthy because of the substantial wall thickness and the fact that the bolt cuts are slightly offset. Both provide a considerable safety margin. The Redhawk's ejector rod does not help to lock the cylinder, as on Smith & Wesson guns; instead, the front cylinder lock is found on the crane. One thing I do not like much about this revolver is the lack of counter-bored chambers, though I realize that modern case heads rarely separate. The cylinder-release latch lies on the frame, in much the same position as the rival Colt and S&W types. The Ruger latch, however, is simply depressed to release the cylinder — unlike the pull/push versions associated with most competing revolvers. Although Ruger quality is generally very good, the cylinder needed to be closed very firmly on the test gun to ensure that the latch locked effectively. Since an engagement failure can disable the gun at a critical time, this possibility should be borne in mind.

Although the barrel of the Redhawk does not appear all that heavy, this is an illusion caused by the massive frame. The back sight is click-adjustable and has a white-outline blade. A particularly advantageous feature of the front sight is that the blade containing the coloured insert, retained by a plunger in its base, can be exchanged in a matter of seconds for one more appropriate to the conditions.

One innovation with the Redhawk is the use of only a single major spring to power the hammer and trigger. This is a real aid in achieving a good double-action trigger pull, particularly as the trigger has only to depress a single spring. However, this spring should only be altered by a competent gunsmith, as clipping a coil in an attempt to lighten the trigger pull can ruin the timing of the action. The Redhawk's smooth walnut service-type grip is large, but I find it (and the service stocks) quite comfortable. The only disadvantage I noticed is that, with my two-hand grip, the sharp edge of the butt sometimes cuts into my weak hand. Still, the Redhawk grip seems to be ideal for anyone with medium or large hands.

Being made of stainless steel, the Redhawk is well suited to its role as an outdoorsman's heavy holster gun. On the range, the test gun performed quite well, double-action group diameters at 25 yards running between 2 and 4in. 180gn Federal, 200gn CCI-Speer and 240gn Federal jacketed hollow-point rounds were used on the range, the 200gn CCI-Speer load performing the best. Despite the Redhawk's bulk and weight, recoil was very noticeable and recovery time was slow. Against a single adversary, however, a second fast shot will not normally be needed if the first round is well placed. There is also a theory that the noise and muzzle blast of a ·44 Magnum at close range has a disorientating effect on an assailant. However, without ear protection, it also has a similar effect on the shooter!

The best method of disconcerting an opponent in a gun-fight is with a well-placed heavy bullet, something the Redhawk is well capable of delivering. I would not count on the Magnum's reputation, though: a ·22 that hits the mark is more effective than a ·44 that misses. Too many of those who choose a ·44 Magnum for combat do so because of its 'macho reputation'. Anyone considering the Redhawk as a combat gun should be a very experienced shooter who is sufficiently practised enough with the gun to have overcome flinch. Powerful hands and forearms also facilitate control.

Although the Redhawk is useful as a combat arm in the specialized situations discussed earlier, I nevertheless prefer the 4in-barrelled Smith & Wesson Model 29 or 629 (q.v.) for such use. The Redhawk is primarily a handgun hunter's arm which doubles for self defence in an emergency. If it is the only gun someone owns, for example, it is a better defence than no handgun at all. After all, at least the Redhawk is powerful enough for the task.

The Redhawk is one of the sturdiest double-action ·44 Magnum revolvers on the market — and certainly looks the part. This 5in-barrelled version, the smallest option, is still massive. Note the smooth wood grips.

The Ruger ejector rod, unlike Smith & Wesson revolvers, plays no part in locking the cylinder.

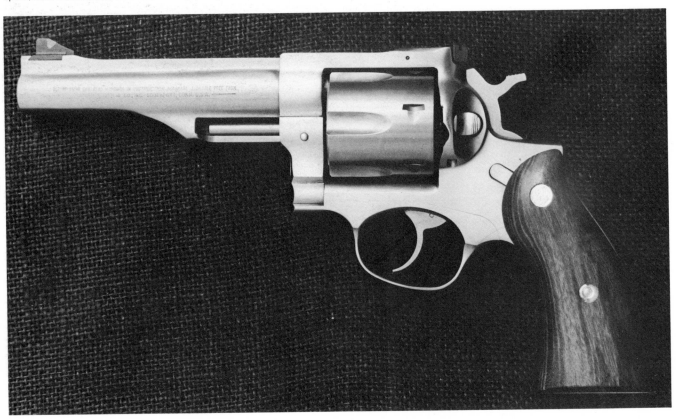

The massive Redhawk cylinder has sufficient wall thickness to give a good safety margin even with full-power ·44 Magnum loads.

Interchangeable front-sight blades enhance the Redhawk's versatility.

Though the Redhawk is a heavy, massive weapon, it still recoils appreciably with full-power ammunition.

The acceptable accuracy of the Ruger Redhawk, even with full-power ·44 Magnum loads, is shown by this double-action group obtained at 25 yards.

Seecamp LWS-25

Type: double-action semi-automatic pistol.
Maker: L.W. Seecamp Co., Milford, Connecticut, USA.
Calibre: ·25 ACP.
Overall length: 108mm, 4.25in.
Barrel length: 51mm, 2.0in.
Weight, empty: 370gm, 13oz.
Magazine capacity: 7+1.
Construction: stainless steel, no sights.

There are many who denigrate the ·25 automatic pistol as a combat arm, but, in some situations, a compact pistol in this calibre can be extremely useful. There is no doubt that the ·25 ACP lacks the stopping power of the 9×19 (9mm Parabellum), ·38 Special, ·357 Magnum and larger calibres; however, most ·25 pistols are highly concealable and can be carried in situations where a larger and more potent weapon cannot. The greatest combat handgun in the world is of no use if it cannot be available when required. The LWS-25 is so compact that it can be carried constantly, even under light summer clothing; and that is its greatest advantage.

There is a tendency to think of ·25 pistols as being cheaply-made weapons of dubious reliability. However, the finely crafted LWS-25 is a perfect example of the axiom that 'good things come in little packages'. Its manufacturer has a well established reputation in firearms design and innovation, a tradition continued with the LWS-25. Every aspect of the pistol shows the Seecamp attention to quality and detail. The result is the finest small automatic ever produced in the USA.

One of the first things one notices is the unusually clean profile. As the ·25 automatic is essentially a close-range weapon, the LWS-25 has no sights to catch while drawing it from a pocket. The hammer is also completely enclosed by the slide, eliminating another protrusion which could snag. Other highly efficient external features are the highly durable black Lexan grips and the trigger guard, which is large enough to allow easy access to the trigger. The magazine release lies at the base of the magazine well in European fashion. This is an advantage rather than a disadvantage on this gun, however, since it prevents the magazine being dropped by accident should a button on the frame be pressed inadvertently by a large finger wrapping around a small gun. As the LWS-25 has no single-action feature, external safety levers are unnecessary.

The use of double action only is one of the noteworthy features of the LWS-25, though by no means new. The normal ·25 automatic relies on a striker and cannot be entirely safe if kept ready for action with a round chambered, the striker cocked and the safety catch applied ('Condition One'). The safety can occasionally be reset by friction. If carried without a chambered round, the normal ·25 is not ready for action; the LWS-25, however, can be carried with a round chambered, yet remaining fully safe and instantly ready for action with a simple pull on the trigger. Unlike a standard double-action automatic, the LWS-25 hammer rides back down as the slide returns after chambering a new round. Each subsequent round must then be fired by the double-action trigger pull. Although this system takes some acclimatization, it is a logical and effectual combination of safety and simplicity with instant readiness.

Although the double-action system eliminates the need for normal locking safeties, the LWS-25 retains a magazine safety which locks both the hammer and slide when the magazine is removed. This safety prevents the LWS-25 from being fired even if a round remains chambered after the magazine has been removed, eliminating a common cause of accidents. It is necessary to drop the Seecamp magazine a fraction of an inch to remove a round without chambering a new one. Even with the magazine removed, the slide can be pulled back about 0.25in to check the state of loading. A slight cut in the top of the slide also acts as a loaded-chamber indicator by allowing a glimpse of a chambered cartridge.

Since the LWS-25 is intended to be carried close to the body, exposed to the effects of perspiration, the choice of stainless steel is sound. Aircraft-quality material is used to prevent fretting, finished in a flat grey to suppress reflection.

Since the LWS-25 is a close-range weapon, all testing was performed at 10 yards or less. Only full-jacketed factory loads were used, as ·25 ACP hollow points rarely expand properly. Federal, Remington and Winchester-Western ammunition was used, all performing equally. Reliability was excellent; there were no malfunctions. Most strings were fired very rapidly, since a small weapon such as the LWS-25 must depend upon multiple hits for effectiveness. Although there are no sights, it is possible to aim the Seecamp pistol by sighting down the top of the slide. Some groups were fired in this manner, while others were fired instinctively with one or two hands after drawing the gun from a pocket. Group diameters of 4in or smaller were normally obtainable at 7 yards. At the close ranges for which it is intended, the LWS-25 certainly showed acceptable accuracy.

It must be emphasized, of course, that the LWS-25 is a highly specialized close-quarters weapon intended for undercover use, particularly under light clothing. It is also a very useful back-up weapon for police officers whose holster gun is appreciably larger and more powerful. I would prefer a large-calibre gun for home-defence and personal protection, though the LWS-25 has safety and reliability conferring certain advantages. It is, in my opinion, the best 'hide-out' gun ever produced in the USA.

The magazine release on the butt-heel and the Lexan grips are obvious in this view, emphasizing the neat profile of the LWS-25 that helps make it an excellent pocket gun.

Note the full-size guard and obviously double-action trigger on the Seecamp pistol.

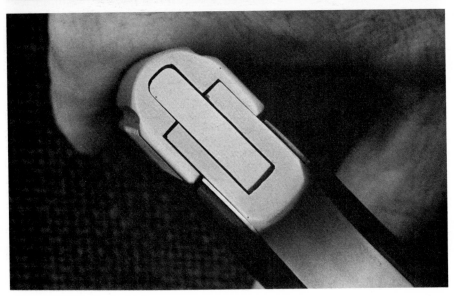

The LWS-25 hammer fits flush with the frame and will not snag clothing during the draw.

Omitting sights permits Seecamp to offer a smooth slide with the LWS-25. The semicircular cut-out acts as a visual loaded-chamber indicator.

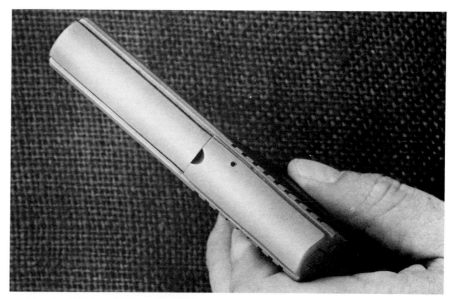

It is possible to 'sight' the LWS-25 at close range simply by looking along the top of the slide.

Multiple hits at 7 yards should be enough to down most attackers!

Sig P 210

Type: single-action semi-automatic pistol.
Maker: Schweizerische Industrie-Gesellschaft (SIG), Neuhausen, Switzerland.
Calibre: 7.65 or 9mm Parabellum.
Overall length: 215mm, 8.46in.
Barrel length: 120mm, 4.72in.
Weight, empty: 985gm, 34.8oz.
Magazine capacity: 8+1.
Construction: see notes.

There are several differing variants of the P 210. The **P 210-2**, the official service pistol of the Swiss army until replaced by the P 220 in 1975, has fixed sights. The **P 210-5** is a target-shooting derivative with a fully adjustable back sight and a 150mm (5.9in) barrel supporting the adjustable front sight. The **P 210-6** is similar to the P 210-2, but has an adjustable back sight, and there have been a number of luxury versions such as the superb 'Jubiläumsmodell' celebrating the 125th anniversary of SIG in 1978. A factory-made ·22in LR rimfire conversion is also obtainable.

Prior to 1949, the Swiss army was equipped with a collection of Parabellums and indigenous revolvers. During the early 1940s, however, trials were undertaken with the SIG-made pistols featuring 'packaged' lockwork developed by the French engineer Charles Petter. By 1944, SIG had made two series of prototypes — SP 44/8 and SP 44/16, with 8 and 16-round magazines respectively — and, after successfully negotiating comparative trials against the Pistole W+F Browning and Pistole W+F 47, the remarkable SIG-Petter was adopted as the Ordonnanzpistole 49 SIG. Shortly afterwards, the P 210, identical in all but name, appeared on the commercial market.

Very little of the P 210 was genuinely innovative, though many of the better elements of other designs were cleverly combined in one gun. Short recoil operation was preferred, with an enclosed cam-path used to drop the rear of the barrel in proven Browning fashion. The SIG recoil spring has a full-length guide rod to improve its smoothness, characteristic of the detailed attention paid to the evaluation of each part.

The full length of the slide is supported by guide-rails set inside the frame, offering longer than normal support. Together with the unusually long barrel and superb manufacturing quality, the immediate result is outstanding accuracy. Another advantage of this slide/frame construction is that the barrel lies appreciably lower in the hand to reduce the turning movement of the gun. The low profile necessitates raised retraction grooves at the rear of the slide.

Another interesting feature, borrowed from other guns but suitably modified for SIG's purposes, is the pleasantly chequered wraparound plastic grip, which combines excellent balance with ideal pointing qualities. The shaping of the upper front part of the grip facilitates manipulation of the safety lever (which, however, is not so easily replaced in its upper or 'safe' position).

The trigger acts on the sear through the classic Colt-Browning stirrup bar, which also acts as a mechanical safety. The system has an incredible smoothness, even 'straight from the box', as every detail has been carefully studied; for example, the relevant spring is placed directly under the trigger, rather than 'wrapped' as on so many other designs, and the slack is only about 3mm before the extremely sharp let-off point. The other excellent feature of the SIG trigger is its very compact removable 'packaged' mechanism, held in the frame behind the magazine by a single screw. This compact design allows a very long sear bar, actuated by the left upper portion of the stirrup and thereafter passing beneath the base of the hammer. The crispness of the trigger pull is partly due to the fact that the safety simply blocks the stirrup.

Any shooter using the P 210 cannot fail to be impressed by the quality of the trigger pull, by far the best found on an ex-factory pistol and far better than even some expensively customized guns. The SIG is simply typical of a country justly famed for its precision engineering. Once accustomed to muzzle-heavy balance, owing to the length of the barrel and slide, an owner is rarely anything other than delighted by the smoothness and accuracy of this extraordinary gun.

Accepting the disadvantages of the small calibre, the Swiss national team in IPSC competitions achieved outstanding performances with the P 210 for many years, before substituting ·45 ACP Colts customized by the German gunsmith Walter Ludwig. The greatest handicaps of the P 210, particularly considered as a combat pistol, are its small magazine capacity and the positioning of the magazine catch on the heel of the butt. It seems a pity that the experimental sixteen-shot SP 44/16 was not developed instead.

In addition, despite its legendary reliability, the P 210 was never cheap. Thus, it has been replaced by the SIG P 220 series.

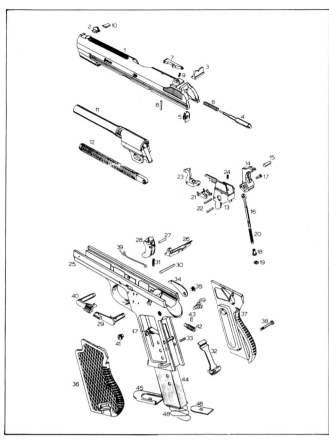

Key

1	Slide	26	Trigger rod
2	Front sight	27	Pin for trigger rod
3	Rear-Sight	28	Trigger
4	Firing pin	29	Safety lever
5	Firing pin plate	30	Trigger pin
6	Firing pin spring	31	Trigger spring
7	Extractor	32	Magazine holder
8	Bolt for extractor	33	Pin for magazine holder
9	Spring for extractor	34	Magazine safety
10	Cover for front sight groove	35	Screw for magazine safety device
11	Barrel	36	Grip plate left
12	Recoil spring	37	Grip plate right
13	Action casing	38	Screw for grip-plates
14	Hammer	39	Spring for slide stop
15	Hammer pin	40	Slide stop
16	Stirrup	41	Stop screw for action casing
17	Pin to stirrup	42	Pin (trigger pull)
18	Head of stirrup	43	Safety pin (trigger pull)
19	Lock-nut	44	Magazine box
20	Hammer spring	45	Base plate
21	Double-pull lever	46	Base plate inset
22	Pin for double-pull lever and sear	47	Feeder
23	Sear	48	Magazine spring
24	Sear spring	49	Feeder button
25	Frame		

This standard P 210-6 displays its adjustable back sight. The safety is easy to place on 'fire', as here, but appreciably more difficult to return to 'safe'.

The uncluttered right side of the P 210-6.

The P 210 magazine catch is poorly placed on the butt-heel; two hands are needed to release it, and the magazine is a very tight fit indeed.

The SP 210 field-stripped, showing the closed cam-path in the barrel depressor block and the full-length spring guide.

A view of the SP 210 frame with the slide removed. Note the tip of the stirrup-like trigger bar, part of which acts as the disconnector.

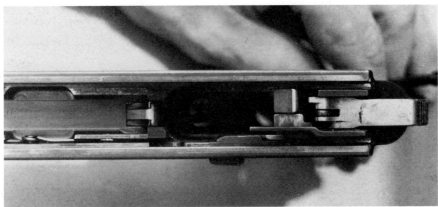

After a single screw has been removed, the complete trigger mechanism can be removed.

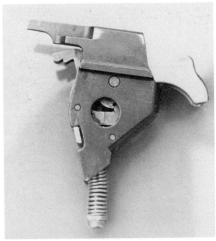

(Above) The SIG trigger system is very compact. Note the contact between the sear and the hammer, visible through the circular hole in the supporting bracket. The parts are in very close proximity, with the upper arm of the sear (top left, just below the ejector) needing only the smallest movement to release the hammer.

(Above left) The SIG P 210 is the best of the current low-magazine capacity combat handguns.

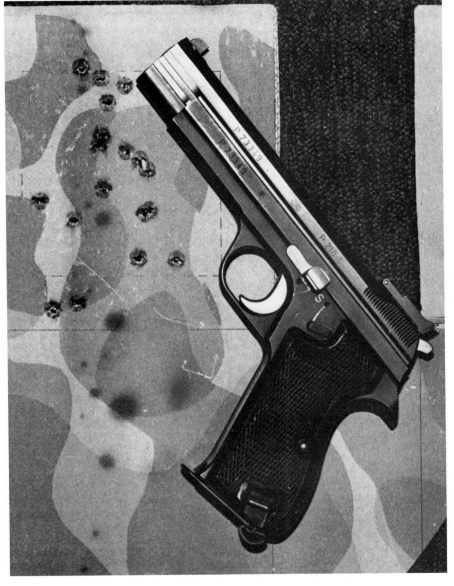

Two magazines — sixteen rounds, plus the chambered cartridge — to the head from 15 metres. No comment is necessary!

Sig P 226

Type: double-action semi-automatic pistol.
Maker: Schweizerische Industrie-Gesellschaft, Neuhausen am Rheinfalls, Switzerland
Calibre: 9mm Parabellum
Overall length: 195mm, 7.68in.
Barrel length: 110mm, 4.33in.
Weight, empty: 850gm, 30.0oz.
Magazine capacity: 15+1.
Construction: combination steel/alloy, fixed sights.

NB: owing to the quirks of Swiss firearms export laws, SIG market these pistols in partnership with J.P. Sauer & Son GmbH of Eckenforde, West Germany. They are, therefore, advertized as 'SIG-Sauers', though wholly SIG's design.

The P 226 is the latest in a series of SIG-made pistols, the first of which – the P 220 – was perfected in the early 1970s and subsequently adopted by the Swiss army as the 'Model 75'. The P 220 was replaced by the P 225 in time for the German police trials of 1975, the P 225 being appreciably more compact. The inefficient butt-heel magazine-catch of the P 220 was moved to the frame-side behind the trigger guard on the P 225.

The P 225 was accepted by the German authorities as the 'Pistole 6' (P6) and issued, together with the Walther P5 and the Heckler & Koch P7, to units of the state police. The P 226 appeared in 1983 to satisfy the US JSSAP requirements, which included a reversible magazine catch and a large-capacity magazine.

The guns all embody an interesting variation of the locking system embodied in the FN-Browning High-Power, though the perfected SIG version owes something to light machine-gun practice. Instead of the conventional locking lugs engaging recesses in the top inner surface of the slide, the SIGs feature a massive squared barrel-block that rises into the ejection port in the slide. Unlike most other pistols featuring Colt-Browning locking systems, the engagement of the SIG block is visible externally.

The P 226 is a conventional-looking gun, with a profusion of levers and catches on the frame-side. The reversible magazine release lies immediately behind the trigger guard; the dismantling catch, which may be obtained for right- or left-handed firers, appears above the trigger; the slide stop protrudes above the grip; and a de-cocking lever will be found ahead of the left grip in front of the slide stop. The de-cocking lever breaks contact between the sear and a cocked hammer to drop the latter into the intercepting or 'safety' notch. This notch provides the rest position of the hammer; should it fail, however, the firing pin is locked by an angular vertical firing-pin lock until the final stages of the trigger travel. This allows the P 226 to be carried safely with a loaded chamber.

The pistol has an anodised alloy frame and slide, with an excellent matt finish, though the barrel, locking system and many of the trigger components are steel. The workmanship of parts such as the multi-strand recoil spring is typical of SIG, as is the P 210-like construction, with the slide carried on rails inside the frame. This feature is most obvious when the slide is retracted to its limit, where the additional support offered by the SIG system compared with (for example) the FN-Browning High-Power is most obvious.

The SIG handles pleasantly, though, like most guns with large-capacity magazines, there is a perceptible shift in balance – an increasing muzzle-heaviness – as cartridges are fired. The P 226 points adequately, and has an eminently controllable recoil. The well-chequered black plastic grips and backstrap improve grasp, and minimize hand-slip. The slide is held open after the last round has been fired and ejected, whereupon the magazine catch can be pressed, the magazine dropped and replaced – though practised firers will reload before the last shot is fired. A push on the slide stop allows the action to close, feeding a fresh round into the chamber. Pressing down on the de-cocking lever drops the hammer safely and the gun can be holstered with confidence, though the de-cocking system does not double as a manual safety catch and springs back to its upper position.

The SIG P 226 functioned flawlessly with a variety of cartridges, ranging from weak commercial loadings to notoriously vicious British 9mm Mark 2Z cartridges. Like all guns, it is necessary to experiment with differing loadings to find the optimum – which, with the trial pistol, proved to be 4in-diameter groups at 25 yards. There was, however, a marked difference between the trigger pull necessary to fire the first (double-action) shot, about 6.4kg or 14.1lb, and the crisp 2.3kg (5.1lb) single-action operation thereafter. The single-action pull was excellent, with a mere 6mm travel and a crisp break-point, though the double-action travel of nearer 15mm was less satisfactory. The 'average diameter' of the groups is rather misleading, as attenuation was often twice as great vertically as horizontally. The weakest of the loadings, such as Finnish Lapua, was only just capable of moving the slide back to the limit of its travel and could, perhaps, prove troublesome in some individual guns.

The fixed sights – a blade and an open notch – are sturdy, and unlikely to catch on the draw even though the edges are best rounded-off after purchase. Though there may seem little possibility of changing the sights to adjust to the point of impact, SIG not only offers sight-adjusting tools to move the sights in their dovetails but also replacement sights of differing height.

Not only does the P 226 rank among the world's best combat pistols but it is also a worthy descendant of the P 210. Whether its alloy frame and slide are as durable as those of its more traditionally-made predecessor may be disputed, though, apparently, all but one of the guns submitted to the US JSSAP XM9 pistol trials passed the mandatory 5,000-round endurance test.

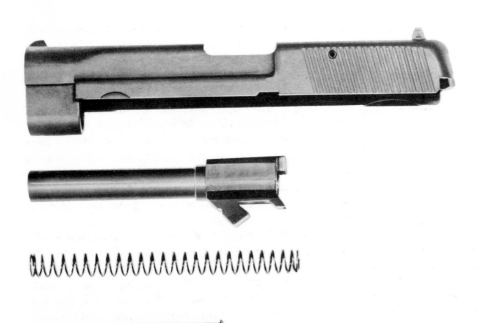

The SIG P 220, shown here field-stripped, is a sturdy modern combat hand-gun – particularly in its latest modification, the P 226. Locking is effected by lifting the barrel block into the ejection port. (Courtesy of SIG).

(Right) The P 220 locking block rises into the slide by way of the ejection port, as shown here. (Courtesy of SIG).

Smith & Wesson Model 10

Type: double-action revolver.
Maker: Smith & Wesson, Springfield, Massachusetts, USA.
Calibre: ·38 Special.
Overall length: 210mm, 8.25in.
Barrel length: 76mm, 3.0in (heavy pattern).
Weight, empty: 905gm, 32oz.
Cylinder capacity: 6.
Construction: blued steel, fixed sights.

The Model 10, 'Military and Police', dates from 1899; since its introduction, the M&P has been Smith & Wesson's best-selling gun and has established itself as the most popular duty revolver serving US police departments. It has also achieved wide distribution among police agencies in Europe and Asia.

The large number of variations of the Model 10 add to its versatility. It is available with round or square butts, and barrels of 2-6in. Alloy or stainless steel frames (Models 12 and 64 respectively) allow even more choice — though the most popular police version is probably the steel framed, 4in heavy-barrelled square-butt gun. For testing, however, I have chosen the 3in-barrel/round butt combination as an acceptable compromise between concealability and performance.

The Model 10 is a basic, functional design. Although it lacks frills, it is still a high-quality reliable weapon. Built on Smith & Wesson's medium ('K') frame, the Model 10 is sturdy enough to handle '+P' ·38 Special loads in perfect safety. The same frame is, in fact, used for the ·357 Magnum Models 19 and 66.

Although the square butt is more popular on the longer barrelled Model 10s, I prefer the round butt on the 2in- and 3in-barrelled models since it aids concealment. Even in 'snub' form, however, the Model 10 is a relatively bulky weapon better suited to a holster than a pocket. The 3in barrel is as convenient in a holster as the shorter type, and still clears leather and clothing fairly quickly. The sturdy heavy barrel not only adds ruggedness, but also helps to damp muzzle flip during rapid double-action shooting. Unlike the K-, L-, or N-Frame magnums, the Model 10 does not have an ejector shroud. It does, however, have a lug beneath the barrel which protects the front of the ejector rod.

Although the sights are not sophisticated, they are entirely satisfactory. Fixed sights have two advantages over the adjustable types in combat: they have fewer protrusions to catch during the draw and are less likely to be knocked out of alignment. Although they are not the fastest sights to acquire, I have some affection for the Model 10's. The top strap and the flat top of the barrel have a matt non-reflecting finish.

The Model 10 cylinder release lies on the left side of the frame, in traditional Smith & Wesson fashion, and must be pushed forward. The cylinder-wall thickness is sufficient to handle factory-loaded ·38 Special ammunition, including '+P' types. Another advantage of the longer barrel is that the ejector rod allows full-length extraction of spent cases, though it is still advisable to raise the muzzle so that the cases will fall clear.

The hammer and trigger are the standard narrow types. Both single- and double-action pulls on the test gun were good, the latter being especially smooth and crisp. This allowed very effective double-action shooting: at 15 yards, 3in-diameter 6-shot groups were virtually standard. Firing three 'double taps' with 125gn Remington '+P' jacketed hollow-point loads showed that recovery time, balance and 'pointability' were all above average. Although the best groups were obtained with the 125gn Remington bullets, 110gn CCI-Speer and Federal jacketed hollow-points and 158gn Federal semi-wadcutters also performed acceptably.

The design of the Model 10 has been well proven by time and experience. Its simplicity and lack of gimmicks make it an excellent choice for home or business defence, police or security units, or almost any task where the firepower of the autoloader or the power of a magnum is not required. Though ·38 Special is not the optimum combat round, it is at least acceptable — particularly with '+P' or good standard semi-wadcutter loads. The Model 10 is one of Smith & Wesson's least expensive revolvers and thus offers a very cost-effective choice of combat arms. It is an excellent weapon and would still be good value at a higher price.

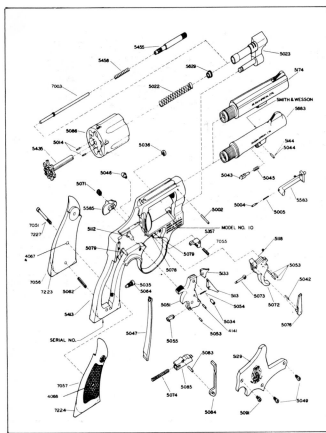

The Model 10 has the functional look to be expected of one of the world's most popular duty weapons.

Round butt and fixed sights help make the 3in-barrelled Model 10 a good compromise between performance and concealment.

One advantage the 3in-barrelled Model 10 has over its 2in barrel variant is full-length extraction.

The heavy barrel on the Model 10 helps control muzzle flip, aiding accurate shooting.

The Model 10 is easily controlled, even in rapid double-action fire with full-power loads.

The S&W Model 10 displayed good accuracy, as this 15 yard double-action group attests.

Smith & Wesson Model 25-5

Type: double-action revolver.
Maker: Smith & Wesson, Springfield, Massachusetts, USA.
Calibre: ·45 Colt.
Overall length: 238mm, 9.38in.
Barrel length: 102mm, 4.0in.
Weight, empty: 1,245gm, 44oz.
Cylinder capacity: 6.
Construction: blued steel, adjustable sights.

Throughout the twentieth century, to special order, Smith & Wesson occasionally chambered an N-Frame revolver – normally the Model 25 – for the ·45 Colt cartridge. In 1977, to celebrate the company's 125th anniversary, a commemorative ·45 Colt revolver was produced in limited numbers. The management was surprised, however, at the interest in this revolver as a shooter's rather than collector's item, and the Model 25-5 subsequently became a standard product.

Built on the large N-Frame, the Smith & Wesson Model 25-5 is an ideal heavy-duty police weapon – my personal 'top choice' as a holster arm, its only disadvantage being weight. The bulk of the 25-5 is more than compensated by the effectiveness of the ·45 Colt cartridge. The heavy bullet of this round offers excellent stopping power, particularly when a semi-wadcutter is used. Unlike magnum cartridges such as the ·357, ·41 or ·44, which get their stopping power from high velocity, the ·45 Colt does not over-penetrate. Even in an urban environment, a standard velocity ·45 Colt bullet is much safer for police use, being less likely to pass through a target and hit an innocent bystander than its high-velocity rivals. Additionally, the ·45 Colt bullet is more likely to stay inside an attacker, thus delivering more of its power to the target than a small-calibre jacketed bullet that passes straight through. For the uniformed police officer, stopping power without excessive penetration is the optimum combination: the ·45 Colt meets the criteria perfectly.

A more subtle advantage of the Smith & Wesson Model 25-5 as a combat handgun is its impressiveness when viewed from the muzzle. The sight of that huge bore may well take the resistance out of an assailant and prevent the necessity for lethal force – though, of course, no-one should rely on a firearm as just a threat.

The 25-5 is an extremely high quality product, typical of all Smith & Wesson N-Frame guns. It is well-fitted, well finished and nicely blued. The N-Frame is S&W's sturdiest pattern and is heavy enough to handle even the powerful ·44 Magnum. Owing to the large diameter of the ·45 Colt case,

however, the cylinder walls are relatively thin. Consequently, though the 25-5 has a good safety margin with factory loads (or reasonable handloads), 'hot' ammunition should be avoided: in this calibre, high velocity is not necessary.

The gun comes with a target hammer and a target trigger. The trigger pull is quite good, especially in single-action mode. Both single- and double-action are crisp and comfortable. In common with the other N-Frames (and the Models 19 and 66), the ejector rod is housed in an under-barrel shroud so identifiable with Smith & Wesson. To restrict glare and assist sighting, the top strap and the top of the barrel are ribbed. The large chequered-head cylinder-release latch must be pushed forward to unlatch the cylinder yoke.

Though Smith & Wesson's N-Frame full-bore and magnum handguns are excellent, I have never liked the large Goncalo Alves target grips supplied by the factory. These I normally replace with Pachmayr neoprene grips as soon as possible. The Pachmayrs not only fit my hand better, but cushion recoil more effectively and aid control during rapid double-action shooting.

The 25-5 performed excellently on the range. All testing was undertaken with Federal's 225gn semi-wadcutter hollow-point factory loads, which I knew to perform well in these guns. At 25 yards, diameter of 6-round double-action groups averaged about 4in. When I moved in to 15 yards, groups of 3in or better were possible. The serrated ramp-type front sight, with its red insert, and the adjustable white-outlined blade back sight performed well enough, though perhaps not to everyone's tastes.

The gun proved highly controllable, even during rapid fire. The combination of the weight of the 25-5 and the medium velocity of the ·45 Colt cartridge kept recoil and muzzle flip at a reasonable level. I believe that most shooters would find the combination of the 25-5 and Federal factory loads easier to shoot than, for example, the S&W Model 19 with full-power ·357 Magnum cartridges.

I think so highly of the 25-5 for defensive use that the gun next to my bed is a 25-5, with the barrel cut to 2.5in and the butt rounded by custom pistolsmith Curt Hardcastle. Had I not owned this gun, I would probably have kept a 4in-barrel 25-5 instead. I chose the Smith & Wesson to defend my person because I respect its quality and the stopping power of the ·45 Colt cartridge; I know the combination will do its job without endangering my neighbours. For the same reason, I rate the 25-5 as an ideal duty weapon for uniformed police and even for use by plain clothesmen in a shoulder holster under a heavy jacket. The Smith & Wesson Model 25-5 is, in my opinion, the best of the heavy full-bore combat revolvers, though its bulk inhibits concealment.

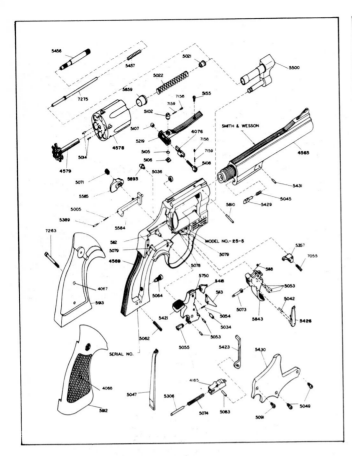

As with all S&W N-Frame guns, the 25-5 is very impressive — particularly when viewed from the wrong end.

I do not normally retain these target-type factory-fitted grips, replacing them with the Pachmayr neoprene variety.

Though its cylinder is large, the Model 25-5 does not have the thick chamber walls of the Models 29 and 57.

The 4in-barrelled S&W Model 25-5 offers a ramp-mounted front sight with a high-visibility coloured insert, a boon in aligning the sights.

The 25-5's weight and the mildness of the ·45 Colt cartridge make the combination very comfortable to shoot.

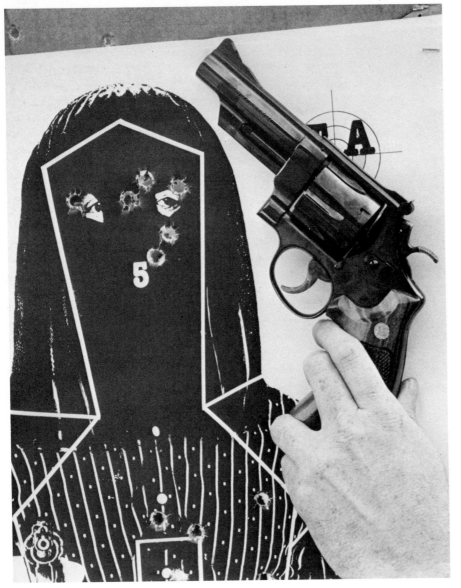

The Smith & Wesson Model 25-5 is very accurate, as this 15 yard double-action group illustrates.

Smith & Wesson Model 38

> **Type:** double-action revolver.
> **Maker:** Smith & Wesson, Springfield, Massachusetts, USA.
> **Calibre:** ·38 Special.
> **Overall length:** 162mm, 6.38in.
> **Barrel length:** 51mm, 2.0in.
> **Weight, empty:** 410gm, 14.5oz.
> **Cylinder capacity:** 5.
> **Construction:** blued steel, fixed sights.

This short-barrelled design is a true 'pocket revolver', which can not only be carried in a pocket but also, in a emergency, fired through it. The combination of the alloy frame with a shrouded hammer provides one of the most convenient of all 'concealed-carry' firearms.

Alloy frames have always been somewhat controversial, many people judging them less durable than steel types. Continuous use with high-pressure loads may strain alloy frames, but their advantages more than outweigh their deficiencies. The alloy frame is at its best on a gun such as the Model 38, which is intended to be carried constantly; the alloy frame results in a gun so light that its presence is hardly noticed. I do not normally use '+P' loads in my Model 38, though I have known people chamber such loads in airweight Smith & Wessons. I prefer to use a medium velocity load with a heavy semi-wadcutter bullet in my 'snubs'. I normally fire about 500 rounds a year through my Model 38, and it has certainly stood up well so far. It is important to remember that these guns are carried far more than they are fired and, though they must perform well when needed, compactness and low weight are of prime importance.

The integral Model 38 hammer shroud gives it a 'camel's hump' on top of the frame, but facilitates a quick draw from beneath clothing without snagging the hammer spur. The shroud even allows the gun to fired in the pocket in an emergency, an advantage that should not be underrated in undercover work. For those who want to cock the Model 38 for single-action fire − for which I see little use − a small spur protrudes above the shroud.

Apart from the hammer shroud and the alloy frame, the Model 38 is similar to the other J-Frame Smith & Wessons with a light 2in barrel and a five-round cylinder. The round butt has a slightly different feel, owing to the shroud hump, but is otherwise conventionally S&W.

The sight radius is short, and the ramp and notch sights are certainly not exceptional. At close range, however, they are good enough for reasonable accuracy. I normally find the sights of the Model 38 take a little longer to acquire because of the hump, but the difference is minimal and soon overcome by practice.

For the range testing, I used 158gn CCI-Speer, Federal and Remington lead semi-wadcutters, plus 158gn Federal round-nose loads. The best groups were obtained with the round-nose bullets, but the more destructive semi-wadcutters are a better choice for combat. At 10 yards, the diameters of rapid double-action groups averaged 3-4in, with a few sub-3in groups obtained with the round-nose loads.

As one must expect with such a small lightweight gun, muzzle flip was noticeable even with the standard-velocity service loads. However, neither flip nor recoil was at all uncomfortable. However, practice is necessary to haul the Model 38 back on target for a second shot. Many shooters find the small J-Frame S&W grips extremely uncomfortable when shooting, especially with airweight guns such as the Model 38. I actually like the tiny round butt, though, and it is undeniably an aid to concealment − even in a shallow trouser-pocket.

The Model 38 is plainly and simply a 'carry gun', intended to be concealed comfortably and discreetly. Its ·38 Special chambering gives it acceptable power for its size. For the civilian or police officer, I give the Model 38 a very strong recommendation. Unlike many other 'snubs', the S&W is light enough to be carried without a holster in a pocket or purse. For this reason, it is popular with women.

Airweight and 'snub' revolvers inevitably require more time to master than heavier, longer-barrelled patterns. Their effective use, therefore, is largely dependent on assiduous practice. The Model 38 remains my favourite ·38 'snub', though there are more suitable weapons for carrying openly in a holster or home defence.

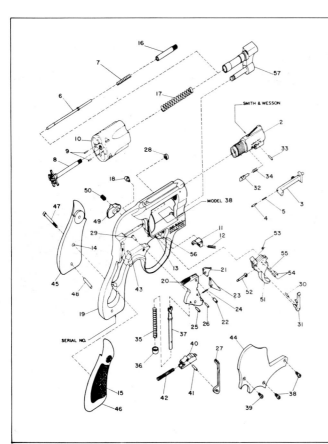

Key

1	Barrel Pin	30	Hand Pin
2	Barrel, 2"	31	Hand
3	Bolt	32	Locking Bolt
4	Bolt Plunger	33	Locking Bolt Pin
5	Bolt Plunger Spring	34	Locking Bolt Spring
6	Center Pin	35	Mainspring
7	Center Pin Spring	36	Mainspring Rod Swivel
8	Extractor Assembly	37	Mainspring Stirrup
9	Extractor Pin	38	Plate Screw, Crowned
10	Cylinder	39	Plate Screw, Flat Head
11	Cylinder Stop	40	Rebound Slide
12	Cylinder Stop Spring	41	Rebound Slide Pin
13	Cylinder Stop Stud	42	Rebound Slide Spring
14	Escutcheon	43	Rebound Slide Stud
15	Escutcheon Nut	44	Side Plate
16	Extractor Rod	45	Stock, Left
17	Extractor Spring	46	Stock, Right
18	Frame Lug	47	Stock Screw
19	Frame with Stud, Bushing & Lug	48	Stock Pin
20	Hammer	49	Thumbpiece
21	Hammer Nose	50	Thumbpiece Nut
22	Hammer Nose Rivet	51	Trigger
23	Sear	52	Trigger Lever
24	Sear Spring	53	Hand Torsion Spring
25	Stirrup Pin	54	Trigger Lever Pin
26	Sear Pin	55	Hand Torsion Spring Pin
27	Hammer Block	56	Trigger Stud
28	Hammer Nose Bushing	57	Yoke
29	Hammer Stud		

The shrouded hammer of the S&W Model 38 makes it a true pocket revolver.

Incorporating a hammer shroud in the frame design gives the Model 38 a different feel to other J-Frame Smith & Wessons.

The most distinctive feature of the Model 38 is its humped back and inset hammer spur.

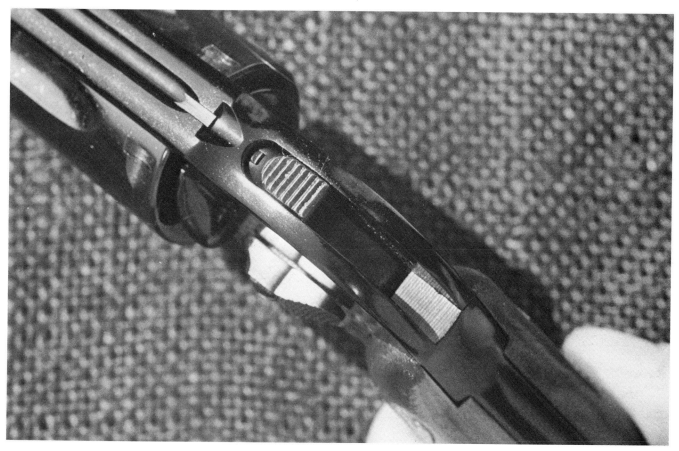

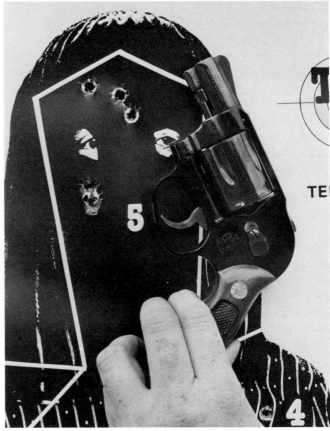

The Model 38, in common with other J-Frame S&W .38s, has a five-shot cylinder with offset bolt cuts. This contributes greatly to its cylinder strength.

10-yard accuracy with the Model 38 is acceptable, despite its light weight and short barrel.

The light frame of the Model 38 makes it jump a little with full-power loads, but shooting is surprisingly comfortable.

Smith & Wesson Model 60

Type: double-action revolver.
Maker: Smith & Wesson, Springfield, Massachusetts, USA.
Calibre: ·38 Special.
Overall length: 165mm, 6.5in.
Barrel length: 51mm, 2.0in.
Weight, empty: 540gm, 19oz.
Cylinder capacity: 5.
Construction: stainless steel, fixed sights.

The Model 60, a variant of the Smith & Wesson Chief's Special, was S&W's first stainless steel handgun and, therefore, introduced one of the most important handgun developments of all time. Although disadvantageously brighter and more noticeable than blued steel, the ability of stainless steel to resist corrosion while enduring humidity, salt water and other harsh conditions has made it invaluable in the production of combat handguns.

I bought my first Model 60 in 1967 and took it to Southeast Asia, where it performed above all expectations. It rode constantly in a cargo pocket when I was on operations and in a shoulder holster next to my perspiring body at other times, yet it never showed the slightest sign of rust. Since then, I have remained a true believer in the Model 60 and it is still one of my favourite weapons.

Like the Models 36 and 37 Chief's Specials, the Model 60 was designed to give greater compactness while still chambering the ·38 Special cartridge. The reduction is achieved by using a small frame with a slim round butt, and reducing the cylinder capacity to five rounds. Trading one shot to obtain the small cylinder seems a reasonable way of achieving a more concealable gun. The Model 60 is one of the few 'snubs' on the market which is a genuine 'pocket revolver' and can be carried without a holster. This is a real advantage in a covert-carry weapon, as the bulk of a holster often draws unwanted attention to the gun.

Although Smith & Wesson does not recommend '+P' ammunition in the Model 60, the five-round cylinder has certain advantages; for example, the bolt cuts are not located over the chambers, where they would reduce cylinder strength. Consequently, the Chief's Special has a stronger cylinder than many larger-framed six-shot guns, though '+P' loads can loosen a J-Frame S&W if used regularly. I prefer standard velocity semi-wadcutters rather than '+P' loads, the heavier bullet giving reasonable stopping power without heavy recoil or pressure.

The sights of the Model 60 are rudimentary, though more than adequate at close range. The combination of these minimal sights and the 60's small butt can make shooting it difficult to master. Another problem is that the small size of the Chief's Special makes the ejector rod too short to extract the cases completely. Thus, the gun must be tipped muzzle-up to allow the cases to fall free. The hammer and trigger are both narrow standard service types, though anything else would be too bulky for a such a small gun.

I have often found that trigger pulls on stainless-steel guns are smoother than on comparable blued ones, though the sample Model 60 does not have one of the better pulls of its type. However, like most Smith & Wessons, the pull is still crisp and tolerable – even though a little heavy – and will probably 'shoot in' after a few hundred rounds.

Range tests were undertaken at 10 and 15 yards, using 158gn Federal semi-wadcutter, 125gn Federal Nyclad 'Chief's Special' hollow point semi-wadcutter and 158gn Remington round-nose loads; 150 rounds were fired, exclusively double-action, the 158gn Federal bullet performing best. Group diameters at 10 yards were normally under 4in, with some staying below 3in. At 15 yards, the groups were not very different. Accuracy certainly wasn't pinpoint, but all five rounds stayed in the chest cavity on human-figure targets. Even with medium-velocity loads, the Model 60 jumps appreciably and has a noticeable muzzle blast. With practice, however, the firer learns to haul the gun back on target instinctively.

The Model 60 is one of the best concealed-carry revolvers on the market, and is particularly suited to humid conditions where perspiration can affect a weapon carried close to the body. However, selecting the Model 60 inevitably involves compromise; a larger-frame gun with a larger grip would be easier to shoot, but it would also be more difficult to conceal. For anyone who carries a gun more than he shoots with it, the Model 60 is an ideal choice. Constant practice to master its idiosyncrasies is essential, as the Model 60, though accurate enough to score hits, is less forgiving to beginners. A favourite solution is to put oversize combat grips on the J-Frame 'snubs', but this increases their bulk unnecessarily. If one seeks the compactness of the Model 60 or comparable designs, frequent practice is the best answer.

For those willing to take time to master it, the Model 60 – together with the Smith & Wesson Model 38 – is the best compact revolver in the world. I personally rate the Model 60 highly, and recommend it for concealed carry. It is also a good choice for anyone who must keep a defensive weapon in a moist environment. However, since such guns are often stored in a drawer or on a shelf, a larger and more powerful stainless-steel revolver (e.g., Smith & Wesson Models 66 and 686, or the Colt Python) may be more effective. The Model 60 is primarily a 'carry gun', its forte simply being reasonable power in a minimal package.

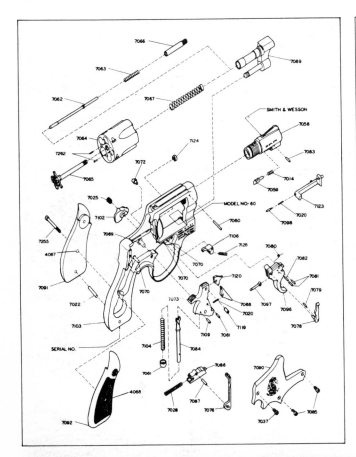

Key

4067	Escutcheon	7080	Hand Spring
4068	Escutcheon Nut	7081	Hand Spring Torsion Pin
7014	Locking Bolt Spring	7081	Sear Pin
7020	Bolt Plunger Spring	7081	Trigger Lever Pin
7020	Sear Spring	7082	Hand Spring Pin
7022	Stock Pin	7083	Locking Bolt Pin
7025	Thumbpiece Nut	7084	Stirrup
7028	Rebound Slide Spring	7085	Plate Screw, Crowned
7037	Plate Screw, Flat Head	7086	Rebound Slide
7058	Barrel	7087	Rebound Slide Pin
7059	Locking Bolt	7088	Sear
7060	Barrel Pin	7089	Yoke
7061	Mainspring Swivel	7090	Sideplate
7062	Center Pin	7091	Stock, Round Butt, Left
7063	Center Pin Spring	7092	Stock, Round Butt, Right
7064	Cylinder with Extractor and Pins	7096	Trigger
		7097	Trigger Lever
7065	Extractor	7098	Bolt Plunger
7066	Extractor Rod	7102	Thumbpiece
7067	Extractor Spring	7103	Frame, Round Butt
7069	Hammer Stud	7104	Mainspring
7070	Cylinder Stop Stud	7106	Cylinder Stop
7070	Rebound Slide Stud	7109	Stirrup Pin
7070	Trigger Stud	7120	Hammer Nose
7072	Frame Lug	7123	Bolt
7073	Hammer	7124	Hammer Nose Bushing
7076	Hammer Lock	7128	Cylinder Stop
7078	Hand	7255	Stock Screw
7079	Hand Pin	7262	Extractor Pin

The Model 60 was the first of Smith & Wesson's stainless steel handguns, and remains amongst the best. Excepting material, it looks just like any other Chief's Special.

The Model 60's small round butt and short barrel make it harder to shoot, but easier to conceal.

The short barrel of the Model 60 is still effective enough. Note the ramp-mounted front sight.

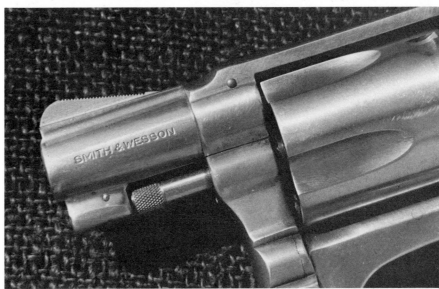

The tiny, round butt on the Model 60 frustrates many large-handed shooters, though I like it greatly.

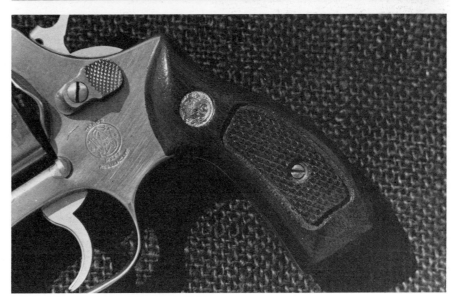

Despite its small size, I find the Model 60 a joy to shoot.

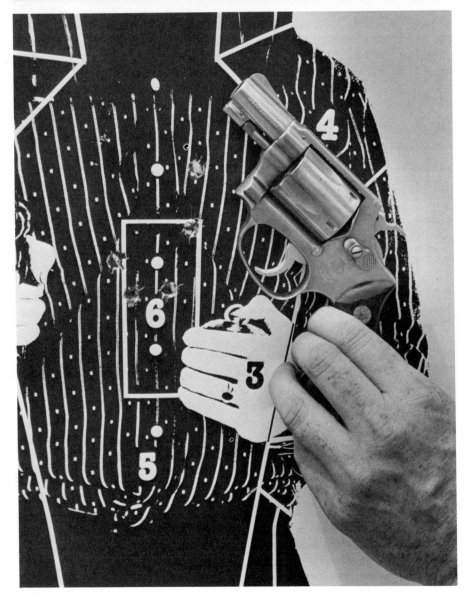

This 10 yard double-action group obtained with the Model 60 shows that is more than capable of doing its job.

Smith & Wesson Model 65

Type: double-action revolver.
Maker: Smith & Wesson, Springfield, Massachusetts, USA.
Calibre: ·357 Magnum.
Overall length: 210mm, 8.25in.
Barrel length: 76mm, 3.0in.
Weight, empty: 935gm, 33oz.
Cylinder capacity: 6.
Construction: stainless steel, fixed sights.

This K-Frame magnum is the stainless version of the revolver issued by the FBI and is an extremely effective combat arm. The Model 65 is, in simple terms, a 'no-frills' version of the Model 66. However, the omission of the latter's adjustable sights proves advantageous in snap shooting. In addition, the clean lines of the Model 65 make it an especially formidable-looking weapon.

Smith & Wesson's K-Frame has proven sturdy enough for the ·357 Magnum round although, supposedly, a steady diet of full-power loads will eventually loosen the gun and erode the firing cone. However, I normally shoot such loads in my Models 19, 65 and 66, and have never noticed problems — though the maker's caveat should be borne in mind by those who do a lot of full-power shooting with these revolvers. Theoretically, the K-Frame magnums were intended to be used with ·38 Special for practice and ·357 Magnum loads for duty, but I have two strong objections to this procedure: first, I believe that one should practice with the same round selected for duty and, secondly, I do not like to use the ·38 Special in ·357 Magnum chambers as the hot gases may cause excessive erosion.

Though the Model 65 is not particularly light, it is comfortably carried in any compact holster/wide belt combination for long periods. This is the great advantage of the K-Frame magnums over larger guns: they are reasonably compact while acceptably powerful.

The combination of a round butt and a 3in heavy barrel is especially good, as the gun remains relatively concealable while offering enough barrel length not only to provide an effectual sight radius but also counter muzzle flip. The barrel lacks the ejector shroud of the Models 19 and 66, though a protecting lug receives the catch on the ejector rod. The weight of the barrel contributes to the desirable muzzle heaviness of the Model 65. The fixed sights are surprisingly easy to acquire rapidly, and are acceptable out to at least 25 yards. The top strap and the top of the barrel have a matt finish, which facilitates sighting.

The cylinder of the 65 is the same as that of the Models 19 and 66, but lacks counter-bored chambers. This is really little disadvantage, though I admit I prefer the security of counter-boring; however, the savings in cost are undoubtedly passed on to the consumer. The chamber walls are sufficiently strong to handle factory-loaded ·357 Magnum cartridges, but are by no means as thick as those on the big Models 27 and 28 or, for that matter, the 586/686 series. Consequently, factory ammunition or factory-equivalent handloads should be considered the most powerful permissible in this gun. An added advantage of the 3in barrel is that the ejector rod is long enough for complete extraction.

I have always found Smith & Wesson's round-butt K-Frame guns very comfortable to hold, and the Model 65 is no exception. The sharply chequered service stocks may cut into the hand when full-power magnum loads are fired continuously, but I still like them. On my 2.5in-barrelled 66, however, I use a compact Pachmayr grip that I would recommend to anyone who finds the standard Model 65 stocks uncomfortable. Any oversize grip will naturally detract from the concealability of the Model 65 'snub'.

The trigger pull on the test gun is quite good, especially in double-action mode. The trigger is the smooth combat type, and the hammer is simply the standard service version. Both are simple, functional items that are perfectly suited to this highly functional magnum revolver.

The Model 13 is the blued version of the Model 65, darker and less reflective, with advantages in concealment. However, for anyone working in humid condition, where the gun is carried next to a perspiring body, stainless steel is preferable — particularly as it is possible to have stainless weapons specially blued.

The 65 was one of the most enjoyable of all the test guns to shoot on the range. Despite its noticeable recoil with full-power loads, I felt no discomfort even after firing two hundred rounds of factory-loaded ·357 Magnum ammunition in two hours. Loads included 110gn CCI-Speer, 125gn Federal and 140gn CCI-Speer jacketed hollow-points, plus some 125gn Remington semi-jacketed hollow-point loads. The heavier CCI-Speer bullets seemed to give the best results, though the others performed satisfactorily. The diameter of the 15-yard groups averaged 2-3in, opening to 4in (or a little more) at 25 yards.

There are so many good ·357 Magnum revolvers on the market that it is difficult to rate one as the best. For concealed carry, though, the 3in-barrelled Smith & Wesson Model 65 is one of the front runners. I also approve it for home defence, assuming good expanding-bullet loads are used, as it is a particularly versatile combination of power and small size. The reasonable price is another point in the S&W 65's favour.

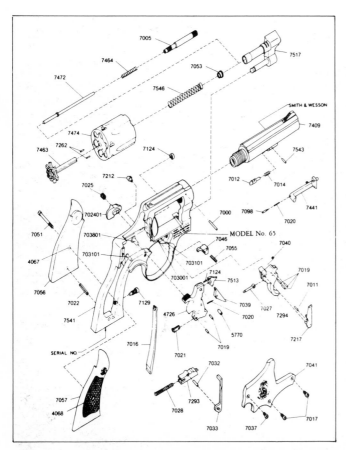

Key

4067	Escutcheon	703101	Cylinder Stop Stud
4068	Escutcheon Nut	7032	Rebound Slide Pin
5770	Hammer Nose Rivet	7033	Hammer Block
7000	Barrel Pin	7293	Rebound Slide Assembly
7098	Bolt Plunger	7037	Flat Head Plate Screw
7020	Bolt Plunger Spring	703801	Hammer Stud
7472	Center Pin for over 2″ bbl	7039	Sear
7464	Center Pin Spring	7040	Hand Torsion Spring
7005	Extractor Rod for over 2″ bbl	7041	Side Plate
7546	Extractor Spring	7046	Cylinder Stop
7517	Yoke	7051	Stock Screw Square Butt
7011	Hand Pin	7441	Bolt
7012	Locking Bolt for over 2″ bbl.	7053	Extractor Rod Collar
7014	Locking Bolt Spring	7055	Cylinder Stop Spring
7016	Mainspring	7056	Stock, Service, Left Side, Square Butt
7017	Plate Screw, Crowned		
7019	Hand Spring Pin	7057	Stock, Service, Right Side, Square Butt
7019	Hand Spring Torsion Pin		
7019	Sear Pin	7124	Hammer Nose Bushing
7019	Stirrup Pin	7129	Frame Lug
7019	Trigger Lever Pin	7513	Hammer Nose
7020	Sear Spring	7474	Cylinder with Extractor Pins & Gas Ring
7021	Stirrup		
7022	Stock Pin	7212	Frame Lug
702401	Thumbpiece	7543	Locking Bolt Pin (heavy bbl)
7025	Thumbpiece Nut	7262	Extractor Pin
7294	Trigger Assembly	7463	Extractor
7027	Trigger Lever	7217	Hand
7028	Rebound Slide Spring	7124	Hammer Nose Spring
703001	Trigger Stud	7409	Barrel, 4″ (Heavy)
703101	Rebound Slide Stud	7541	Frame for heavy barrel only

The combination of the 3in barrel and round butt offers a good balance between concealment and performance.

The Model 65 offers a ramp-mounted front sight and a back sight groove integral with the frame.

The top-strap of the Model 65 is unusually clean, without adjustable sights, and allows a very rapid snag-free draw.

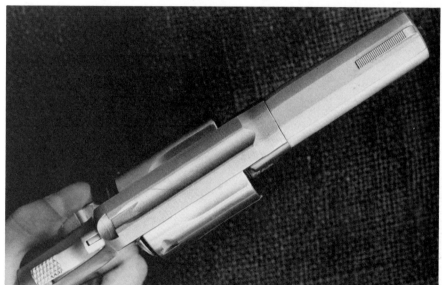

Recoil under full-power ·357 Magnum loads is quite noticeable, yet the Model 65 is eminently controllable.

In rapid double-action strings, the Model 65 performed beautifully at 15 yards.

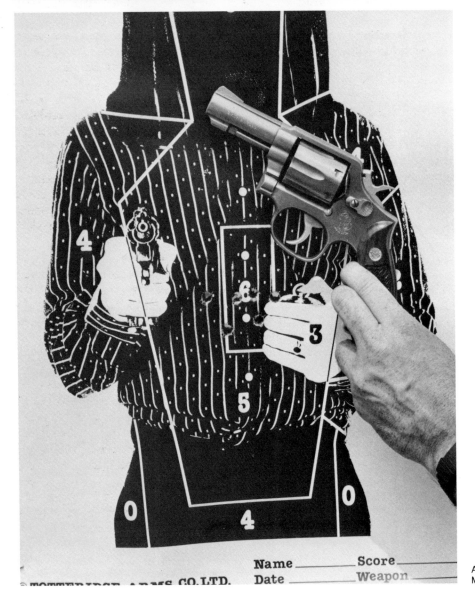

A typical double-action group achieved with the Model 65 from 15 yards.

Smith & Wesson Model 66

> **Type:** double-action revolver.
> **Maker:** Smith & Wesson, Springfield, Massachusetts, USA.
> **Calibre:** ·357 Magnum.
> **Overall length:** 190mm, 7.5in.
> **Barrel length:** 63mm, 2.5in.
> **Weight, empty:** 880gm, 31oz.
> **Cylinder capacity:** 6.
> **Construction:** stainless steel, adjustable sights.

When Smith & Wesson introduced the Model 19 'Combat Magnum' in 1955, it was soon labelled the 'peace officer's dream gun' owing to its combination of ·357 Magnum power with the relatively light K-Frame. As the years have passed, the Model 19 and its stainless-steel counterpart — the Model 66 — have retained their popularity for duty use, though, during the last few years, their ability to withstand arduous service with full-power ·357 loads has been questioned. Under normal conditions, however, the Models 19 and 66 offer an excellent compromise between power and weight. Although 4in-barrelled guns are by far the most common, I have chosen to evaluate the 2.5in barrel version favoured as a plain-clothes or undercover weapon.

The 'snub' 66 is still a good-sized gun, and is actually larger than most automatics with 4-5in barrels. It has very sleek lines, though, and is one of the most handsome of all combat revolvers. The combination of the quick-draw front sight with the stubby barrel and ejector shroud results in a formidable-looking weapon which clears leather reasonably well. Unfortunately, even the short-barrel Model 66 is too large to be used as a pocket revolver. Though its back sight has sharp edges that could snag on a lining (I normally have the blade edges rounded), the round-butted 'snub 66' conceals and draws well under business clothing.

The cylinder of the Model 66 is the normal S&W K-Frame magnum type, and thus lacks excessive wall thickness. It is safe enough with standard factory ammunition or equivalent handloads. The chambers on my test gun are counter-bored, though S&W has been discontinuing counter-boring on magnum revolvers. With the 2.5in barrel, the ejector does not have quite enough travel to fully extract spent cases so it is important to invert the gun to complete extraction.

The top of the barrel and the top strap have a matt non-reflecting finish, and combine with the ramp-mounted Baughmann quick-draw front and click-adjustable back sights to facilitate accurate shooting despite the minimal sight radius. The Model 66 is extremely good for fast instinctive pointing, as the short barrel seems to balance the gun quite well.

The 2.5in-barrelled 66 has a smooth combat trigger and a semi-combat hammer, a good combination on a gun intended for rapid double-action fire at close range. The trigger pull, especially in double action, is quite good in my gun — typical of most stainless-steel S&W revolvers.

I liked the round butt, with its service-style stocks, though the chequering can be abrasive when full-power loads are fired. Currently, I have a set of Pachmayr neoprene grips on my revolver, owing to the number of full-power ·357 Magnum loads I have been firing, but I have tested many comparable guns with factory stocks and found them all entirely adequate. The Pachmayrs are among the best substitute grips as they do not affect concealability adversely; I do not like oversize grips on a gun designed expressly for concealment.

The stainless steel variant is preferable, owing to its corrosion resistance, but the blued Model 19 is also available with a 2.5in barrel.

The exclusively double-action shooting tests were undertaken at 15 and 25 yards, the gun proving particularly accurate despite its short barrel. Loads included 125gn Federal, 140gn and 158gn CCI-Speer jacketed hollow-points, the lighter Speer bullet performing best. Group diameters at 15 yards were often as tight as 2-3in, opening to about 4in at 25 yards. Despite appreciable nuzzle blast and flip, the 66 can be hauled back on target quite quickly for follow-up shots. Recoil is noticeable, but not intolerable. I fired a few strings of 12 rounds, necessitating a reload in the middle of a string. For some reason, I have always found the short-barrel Model 66 exceptionally suited to speedloaders, perhaps because of the small non-target grips. This session, using the Safariland Comp II loader, was no exception.

Like all short-barrel magnums, the 2.5in Model 66 should be avoided by inexperienced shooters and others who are likely to flinch from excessive muzzle blast. I like the 66 'snub' a great deal, and consider it a lot of fun on the range — though, perhaps, not as practical as many other concealment revolvers. The 4in-barrelled option can be concealed almost as easily and is a more effectual weapon. Many police officers who choose the 2.5in-barrelled Models 19 or 66 for off-duty purposes end up carrying them in an inaccessible ankle holster. For home-defence the Model 66 is certainly appropriate, though there are better choices. With the 4in or 6in barrels, the 66 is a nice outdoorsman's revolver that can double for home defence. The 4in-barrelled Models 19 and 66 are at their best, however, when carried openly in a service holster. For this purpose, they are among the best revolvers on the market. I like the looks of the 2.5in-barrelled gun, and the way it shoots, but for nine out of ten shooters the 4in barrel is more practical.

The short version of the stainless steel Model 66 'Combat Magnum' is a formidable-looking weapon.

Though the round butt and short barrel aid concealment, the adjustable sights on the Model 66 may snag clothing during the draw.

Note that the back sight and base-rib are blackened, helping rapid alignment of the sights.

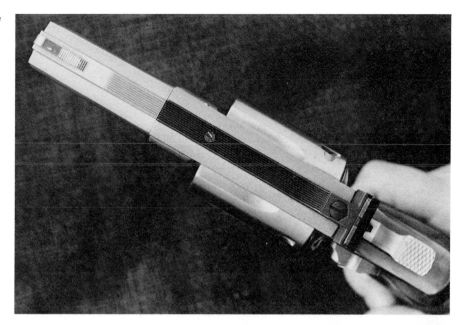

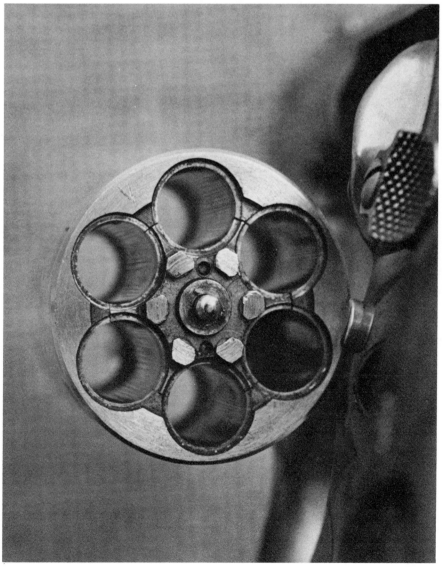

The S&W Model 66 is built on the medium K-Frame; thus, its cylinder wall thickness is insufficient to handle ammunition developing in excess of 'factory' pressure and care should be taken not to strain the gun.

Though it shows substantial muzzle blast, muzzle flip and recoil with full-power loads, the Model 66 is comfortable to shoot once it has been mastered.

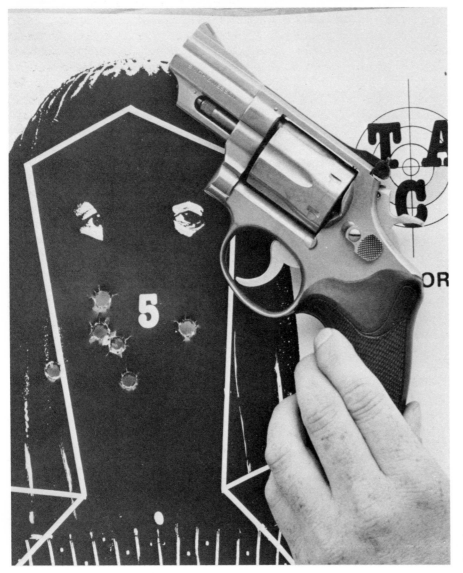

The 2½in-barrelled Model 66 is capable of very accurate shooting at any combat range, as this 15-yard group indicates.

Smith & Wesson Model 469

Type: double-action semi-automatic pistol.
Maker: Smith & Wesson, Springfield, Massachusetts, USA.
Calibre: 9mm Parabellum.
Overall length: 175mm, 6.88in.
Barrel length: 89mm, 3.5in.
Weight, empty: 765gm, 27oz.
Magazine capacity: 12+1.
Construction: blued steel, fixed sights.

Although Smith & Wesson's Models 439 and 459 have established a good reputation for quality, custom gunsmiths have enjoyed a steady business 'improving' 9mm S&W automatics. The most popular conversions have involved shortening a full-size 439 or 459 to make it more concealable. The 'ASP' is the best known of such transformations. In 1983, Smith & Wesson introduced its own compact 9mm pistol, the Model 469.

The 469 is much more than just a 'cut down' 459, as it has been designed specifically to offer substantial firepower in a small package. The resulting gun offers so many advantages over the 439 and 459 that it has already been accepted by many experts as the company's best 9mm automatic.

The Model 469 was designed with concealment in mind, and every effort has been made to remove protrusions. The small serrated-ramp front sight and the fixed back sight are suitably compact; and the hammer is bobbed to eliminate the spur. The top of the hammer is grooved to permit thumb-cocking once pressure on the trigger has been used to move the hammer back a short distance. Whether single action is necessary in a concealed-carry gun, of course, may be debated.

The de-cocking lever rotates a steel plate over the firing pin before safely dropping the hammer, and is also as small as practicable. A persistent criticism of the 459 has always been the thick grip necessitated by the double-row magazine. The 469, however, uses thin pebbled Delrin grips to aid concealment and improve handling.

The only features of the 469 I consider to be disadvantageous for concealment or rapid fire are the bulky finger-rest extension on the base of the magazine and the hooked trigger guard. Although the magazine spur does give the little finger a comfortable rest when firing, it adds unnecessary bulk. Perhaps magazines could be offered without the extension, to allow for personal preference! The squared, chequered trigger guard is copied from some of the customized S&W automatics, but is not as useful as it seems: few shooters hook their fingers over the guard, preferring a two-hand grip on the butt.

The overall impression of the Smith & Wesson Model 469 is that of a businesslike weapon, and it lives up to its appearance. The combination of the matt blued finish and the black grips aids concealment, as the gun is less likely to be spotted should a jacket fall open.

The 469 is mechanically similar to the 439 and 459, with purely minor differences. It uses the same locked-breech system with the recoil-spring guide resting on a flat near the barrel. Like the larger S&W 9mm pistols, the 469 barrel has only one locking lug. A primary difference between the 469 and the 439/459 series is the omission of a barrel bushing. The barrel cut-out in the slide acts as its own bushing and mates with a slightly keg-shaped muzzle. As every 469 I have fired has been quite accurate, the system seems to work effectively. Dismantling and assembly is virtually the same as the procedure adopted with the larger guns.

Even though the sights are fixed, I found them attractive. The combination of the vertical yellow front bar and the white-outlined rear notch made target acquisition easy even under poor light. The fact that the back sight base and blade are radiussed not only eliminates an edge which might snag, but also leads the eye into the proper sighting position.

The 469 incorporates the double-action trigger system pioneered by its predecessors. Normally, the gun will be carried with a round chambered and the hammer down ready for a pull through on the trigger to bring the gun into action. Subsequent rounds will then be fired in single-action mode, as the slide cocks the hammer during its cycle. In common with other double-action systems incorporating a de-cocking system, I recommend that the safety be applied before chambering the first round so that the hammer will follow the slide back down when the round is chambered. The safety can then be pivoted into the 'fire' position once the pistol is loaded. I do not believe that a double-action automatic should be carried with the safety applied, since the instant first shot is this type of weapon's great advantage. Although both single- and double-action pulls show a certain amount of creep and imprecision typical of these Smith & Wessons, I still find them acceptable.

The magazine release button on the 469 is in the normal Colt-Browning/S&W position behind the trigger-guard on the frame, and does not protrude too far. In practice, it is necessary to press the thumb firmly over the button to depress it far enough to release the magazine. The magazines are normally kicked out with sufficient force to drop free from the gun. Since the 469 is fitted with a magazine safety, it cannot be fired with the magazine removed and is immobilized during the changeover. Two magazines are supplied with each gun.

The 469 performed outstandingly on the range. At 15 yards, firing the first round double-action, the diameters of quick 12 or 13-round groups were normally below 3in. At 25 yards, under identical conditions, 4-5in groups were about the maximum. The pistol was comfortable to shoot, handled excellently and functioned flawlessly. My 469 has now fired more than 500 shots — mostly jacketed hollow-points — without a malfunction. I shoot so well with the

Model 469 that I won third place in a local IPSC match against dozens of highly customized ·45 automatics, despite firing all first rounds double-action and using an inside-waistband holster.

I am extremely enthusiastic about the 469. It is not only the best US-made 9mm automatic, but I also believe it to be the best US factory-made combat autoloader. It is one of my own favourite guns, and my standards are very high for guns I choose for combat use. The outstanding 469 is suited to almost any 'off duty' combat, plain-clothes, undercover, personal protection, home-defence, military back-up or survival needs.

The Model 469 is designed for concealment and, as this photograph shows, there is little to catch during a draw other than the magazine extension.

Thin grips, an easily accessible magazine-release catch and the slide-mounted de-cocking lever are all shown to perfection in this left-side view of the 469.

The S&W Model 469 has the fashionable hooked and chequered trigger guard, a legacy from shortened 'custom' Smith & Wesson automatics. I do not believe that this guard is much of an advantage, and would prefer the extra concealability possible with a conventional rounded guard.

Note the bobbed hammer and rounded back sight, which aid rapid draws from beneath clothing.

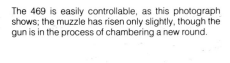

The 469 is easily controllable, as this photograph shows; the muzzle has risen only slightly, though the gun is in the process of chambering a new round.

At 15 yards, the Model 469 shows exceptional accuracy.

Smith & Wesson Model 629

Type: double-action revolver.
Maker: Smith & Wesson, Springfield, Massachusetts, USA.
Calibre: ·44 Magnum.
Overall length: 238mm, 9.38in.
Barrel length: 102mm, 4.0in.
Weight, empty: 1,220gm, 43oz.
Cylinder capacity: 6.
Construction: stainless steel, adjustable sights.

The idea of the S&W ·44 Magnum being suitable for combat use did not originate with Dirty Harry, but those Clint Eastwood films certainly popularized the N-Frame as a fighting handgun. Casting myth aside, the Models 29 and 629 present problems in combat. They are big and bulky; hard to handle for anyone not skilled with them; overly powerful for urban and most rural use; and relatively expensive to own and shoot. However, despite these drawbacks, I do consider the 29/629 to be the best of the ·44 Magnum 'combat' revolvers, though, unlike Harry Callahan, I use one with a 4in barrel rather than 6.5! (6in barrels are standard on current guns.) I do think Eastwood has the right idea for anyone wanting to carry a 29 or 629 concealed; a shoulder holster is ideal. When carried openly, a broad belt and heavy holster help to distribute the gun weight.

With the 4in barrel, the 29/629 is bulky, but not so much so that it cannot be carried by someone who really needs its power. The big magnums are probably best left in the hands of rural police and park rangers, who have to deal with dangerous game in addition to criminals. Civilians living in rural areas may have a similar need for such a powerful gun, but the 29/629 is of little use in the hands of the average police officer or, worse still, an inexperienced civilian.

The Smith & Wesson Model 629 is a very impressive looking weapon, at least part of its mystique coming from its powerful appearance. The N-Frame is suitably sturdy, though its heavy-duty cylinder is not as massive as that of the Ruger Redhawk (q.v.). Wall thickness is still sufficient for any factory loads or reasonable handload. The chambers are counter-bored, as I prefer to see on magnum revolvers, but – unfortunately – S&W has been producing such guns without counter-boring during the last couple of years.

The 629's adjustable sights are what one expects from top-line S&W revolvers. The front ramp contains a red insert, while the back sight is 'micro' click-adjustable and incorporates a white outline blade. Since the ·44 Magnum is designed for long-range use, these sights are a real advantage and are compact enough that they don't really inhibit a rapid draw. The matt-finished top of the barrel and the top strap inhibit glare.

In common with most N-Frame Smith & Wessons, the 629 is supplied with Goncalo Alves target stocks, which I dislike. Not only do I find the grip uncomfortable, but also that it is almost impossible to position the gun correctly in the hand: the butt is simply too thick. My first task with these guns is always to fit new Pachmayr neoprene grips!

The 629 – the stainless version of the blued Model 29 – was one of the most eagerly awaited guns in firearms history. The combination of stainless steel and the ·44 Magnum round makes the anticipation worthwhile, too, as the Model 629 is an outstanding amalgam of power and durability. Since most 629s will be carried outdoors, in an open belt holster, the stainless construction is a real bonus.

The single- and double-action trigger pulls are both normally quite good, and the test gun was no exception. The double-action pull was smooth and crisp, allowing jerk-free shooting. The 629 has the smooth combat trigger rather than the serrated pattern on the Model 29. Either seemed acceptable, and I have no definite preference. The S&W target-type hammer is of some use in long-range single-action shooting, but makes no difference in double action.

For range testing, I used 180gn Federal and 200gn CCI-Speer jacketed hollow-points, 240gn CCI-Speer jacketed soft-points and medium velocity 240gn Remington lead round-nose loads. I especially like the less powerful Remington load, since it is more comfortable to shoot and allows rapid recovery in fast double-action strings. The diameter of double-action groups at 25 yards was normally 4-5in with the Remington ammunition. The heavier loads were about as accurate, but were slower owing to greater recoil and consequent recovery problems. But I did not find the 629 impossible to tame. However, anyone planning to master the gun for combat must acclimatize to it gradually, by starting with light loads and working up to full power. A flinch can affect accuracy adversely, nullifying the power of the ·44 Magnum.

Although I do not recommend the Smith & Wesson Model 629 for most combat uses, the guns are ideal for anyone who has a valid need for the power or simply a liking for big bores. Under a heavy jacket, with a proper holster, the 29/629 series can even be concealed adequately. It is a lot of gun, but promises a mighty deterrent.

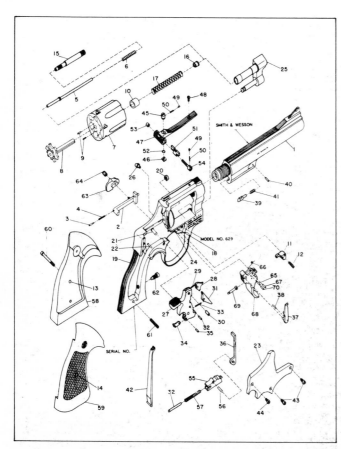

Key

1	Barrel	26	Frame Lug	51	Rear Sight Slide, W.O.
2	Bolt	27	Hammer	52	Rear Sight Spring Clip
3	Bolt Plunger	28	Hammer Nose	53	Rear Sight Windage Nut
4	Bolt Plunger Spring	29	Hammer Nose Spring	54	Rear Sight Windage Screw
5	Center Pin	30	Hammer Nose Rivet	51	Rear Sight Slide 8⅜" W.O.
6	Center Pin Spring	31	Sear	55	Rebound Slide
7	Cylinder	32	Sear Pin	56	Rebound Slide Pin
8	Extractor	33	Sear Spring	57	Rebound Slide Spring
9	Extractor Pin	34	Stirrup	58	Stock, Left
10	Gas Ring	35	Stirrup Pin	59	Stock, Right
11	Cylinder Stop	36	Hammer Block	60	Stock Screw
12	Cylinder Stop Spring	37	Hand	61	Stock Pin
13	Escutcheon	38	Hand Pin	62	Strain Screw
14	Escutcheon Nut	39	Locking Bolt	63	Thumbpiece
15	Extractor Rod	40	Locking Bolt Pin	64	Thumbpiece Nut
16	Extractor Rod Collar	41	Locking Bolt Spring	65	Hand Spring Pin
17	Extractor Spring	42	Mainspring	66	Hand Torsion Spring
18	Cylinder Stop Stud	43	Plate Screw, Crowned	67	Hand Spring Torsion Pin
19	Frame	44	Plate Screw, Flat Head	68	Trigger
20	Hammer Nose Bushing	45	Rear Sight Elevation Nut	69	Trigger Lever
21	Hammer Stud	46	Rear Sight Elevation Stud	70	Trigger Lever Pin
22	Rebound Slide Stud	47	Rear Sight Leaf	68	Trigger
23	Sideplate	48	Rear Sight Leaf Screw	71	Trigger Stop Rod
24	Trigger Stud	49	Rear Sight Plunger		
25	Yoke	50	Rear Sight Plunger Spring		

The massive symmetry of the Model 629 is evident in this view. Its target grips have a distinctive speedloader cut-out.

Though the stainless steel finish on the Model 629 is somewhat reflective, it is well suited to a revolver which will spend most of its time in a belt holster.

A bad guy's view of the S&W 629 shows one of its greatest advantages. It's a great discourager.

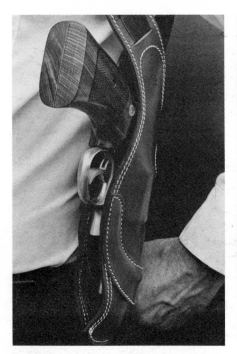

I believe that the best way to carry the 629 is concealed in a shoulder holster such as this, made in England by Horseshoe Leather.

With full-power ·44 Magnum loads, there's little doubt that you are firing a very powerful gun.

The Smith & Wesson Model 629 not only packs great power, but is also very accurate. This group double-action, achieved from 15 yards, presents mute testimony.

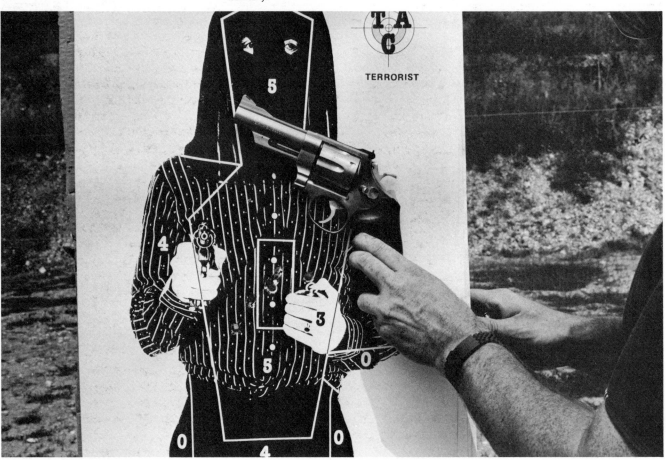

Smith & Wesson Model 639

Type: double-action semi-automatic pistol.
Maker: Smith & Wesson, Springfield, Massachusetts, USA.
Calibre: 9mm Parabellum.
Overall length: 190mm, 7.44in.
Barrel length: 102mm, 4.0in.
Weight, empty: 1,020gm, 36oz.
Magazine capacity: 8+1.
Construction: stainless steel, adjustable sights.

Smith & Wesson introduced its first 9mm automatic, the Model 39, in 1956. This ancestor of the 639 had been developed in the late 1940s with the US military market in mind, but the decision to adopt a 9mm pistol was not forthcoming and production of the Model 39 was deferred. It subsequently reappeared on the civilian and police markets, encountering such success that – during the first fifteen years – it was difficult to find a Model 39, so rapid were its sales. A small number of Model 39s had been acquired by foreign and US military authorities, and a special stainless steel variant (the Mark 22 Model O) had been developed for the US Navy SEAL teams. Generally, however, Smith & Wesson has relied on commercial sales of the pistols and a 14-shot version, the Model 59, appeared in 1971.

During the 1980s, new US military trials – the JSSAP – encouraged Smith & Wesson to improve its products, primarily in safety, sights and general reliability. Finally, in 1982, two new pistols were introduced in stainless steel.

Despite the obvious advantages of the 659's large-capacity magazine, I have chosen to evaluate the standard Model 639 owing to its superior handling qualities – and because the large-capacity S&W I rate most highly, the Model 469, is evaluated elsewhere in this book. I chose the stainless steel Model 639 rather than the aluminium-frame 439, believing that the corrosion resistance of the former has considerable advantages in a holster gun.

The stainless finish on the Model 639 is not really bright, though still somewhat reflective. The top of the slide is sandblasted to restrict glare and facilitate sighting. The impression is of a handsome and durable-looking weapon. The walnut grip-panels are chequered and, combined with the chequering on the backstrap, prevent even a wet 639 slipping around in the hand. The pistol lies well in the hand, balancing well and sighting instinctively. Anyone who has fired the Model 39 or 439 will immediately notice the extra weight of the 639, its frame being stainless steel rather than a light alloy. The added weight is a real advantage in handling recoil and gives the Model 639 a rapid recovery time. On the debit side, it is not as comfortable to carry on long trips as its alloy-frame cousins.

One of the improvements on the 639 is the fully-adjustable back sight, protected by prominent lateral ears. For military or police use, these ears increase ruggedness appreciably; however, they are a positive disadvantage in concealment, as they are likely to snag clothing during the draw. The back sight is blackened and easily seen, but the bright front sight is sometimes difficult to locate. An orange insert of the type found on many S&W revolvers would be a great improvement.

One real appeal of the 639 for police use is the multiplicity of safeties. There is a slide-mounted de-cocking lever, which blocks the firing pin while the hammer is lowered; a trigger-actuated firing-pin lock; and an additional safety that prevents the weapon being fired when the magazine is removed. The magazine safety is a mixed blessing, as it disables the gun during magazine changes to leave the firer vulnerable – a possible fault in a combat pistol. The de-cocking system is most useful when loading. I normally engage the safety before chambering the first round, so that the hammer safely rides down as the slide returns to its locked position. Simply pushing the safety up to its 'fire' position enables the pistol to be fired by a pull through on the trigger.

The double-action automatic has always attracted controversy in the USA, largely as the double-action pull required for the first shot is normally much heavier than the subsequent single-action pull. I have found that it is relatively easy to adjust to two different trigger pulls with a little practice. Generally, though, the 'out-of-the-box' triggers of most double-action pistols are rather heavy and normally benefit from the services of a competent gunsmith. Care must be taken that safety or reliability is not sacrificed for a smoother trigger pull. The most important advantage of the double-action automatic for police or home-defence use is that its trigger action offers greater safety under stress with instant readiness for action. I do not subscribe to the commonly held American view that the double-action pistol is 'the solution to a non-existent problem'.

The magazine release on the Model 639 lies on the frame, behind the trigger guard. The 639 magazine kicks out reliably when the button is depressed, thus facilitating magazine changes. The magazine is made of stainless steel, two being supplied with each gun. A fixed lanyard ring lies at the base of the magazine well. In addition to the obvious advantages of preventing loss, a lanyard can also be used to brace the weapon in the manner of a rifle sling. On the negative side, it can be used as a garotte in a hand-to-hand struggle.

Dismantling the Model 639 is straightforward. After removing the magazine, and checking that the chamber is empty, the slide is retracted until the slide-stop cut is level with the front of the slide stop; the stop can then be pushed laterally out of the frame. The slide, barrel and recoil spring can then be removed from the frame, and the barrel and spring lifted out for further maintenance. When assembling the gun, there is a knack in getting the recoil spring properly positioned against its small retaining cut in the frame, but few other problems will be encountered.

Testing the Model 639 showed that it is extremely reliable and very accurate. More than 200 rounds were fired with a selection of hollow-point ammunition, without a misfire. Accuracy was excellent, 8-round group diameters normally averaging 2-3in at 15 yards and staying around 3-4in at 25 yards. All groups were fired with an initial double-action shot, the remainder being single action. A few groups were also fired as eight individual double-action rounds from the draw. The most accurate load proved to be the 115gn Federal jacketed hollow-point.

Stainless-steel construction, reliability and accuracy are greatly on the Model 639's favour. I consider it especially suitable as a military/police holster gun, or for home defence. It is unsuitable, however, for concealed carry.

The lines of the Model 639 are good, despite the unnecessarily bulky sights, and its grip is comfortable.

Most shooters find the 639 is more comfortable than the thicker-gripped Models 59, 459, and 659.

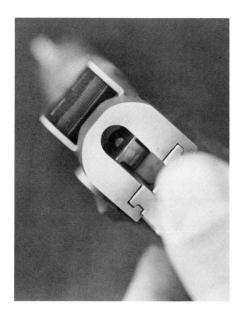

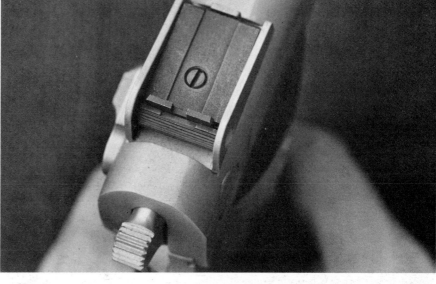

(Above) As an added safety, a steel bar is rotated between the hammer and the firing pin when the decocking system is operated.

(Above right) Though the Model 639 back sight is quite good, I do not like the bulky 'eared' protectors, which inhibit concealment and can snag clothing on the draw.

An ejected case is still in the air, but the 639 slide has already returned to battery. The muzzle climb has been minimal.

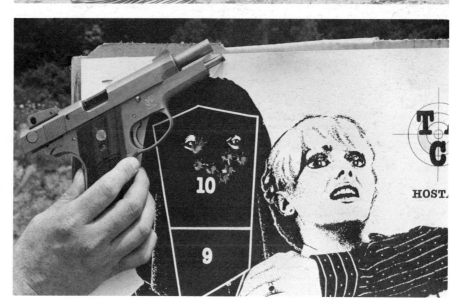

Accuracy is beyond question where the Model 639 is concerned, as this 15-yard group illustrates.

Smith & Wesson Model 686

Type: double-action revolver.
Maker: Smith & Wesson, Springfield, Massachusetts, USA.
Calibre: ·357 Magnum.
Overall length: 248mm, 9.75in.
Barrel length: 102mm, 4.0in.
Weight, empty: 1,190gm, 42oz.
Cylinder capacity: 6.
Construction: stainless steel, adjustable sights.

Although the medium K-Frame Smith & Wesson Combat Magnum has been extremely popular since its introduction in 1955, these ·357 Magnums have received a steady diet of increasingly powerful loads as ammunition evolved and hotter-burning powders appeared. Although most shooters of K-Frame S&W magnums practised principally with ·38 Special, keeping ·357 Magnum loads for duty, there were some who believed — as I do — that one should always practice with the 'duty' round.

As the K-Frame magnums began to show erosion, particularly around the forcing cone, Smith & Wesson introduced the first L-Frame gun in 1981. This gave shooters a gun sturdy enough to fire full-power ·357 Magnum loads regularly, yet was not as large as the N-Frame ·357 Models 27 and 28. The L-Frame magnums incorporated many other features, the sum being an excellent duty weapon. The cylinder and the portion of the frame containing the cylinder and barrel are both much heavier than those on the K-Frame guns. The cylinder cut-out in the frame is almost as large as on S&W's massive N-Frame revolvers. The front of the frame, enclosing the strengthened forcing cone, is especially sturdy, as is the top strap and the base of the frame. The grip and the trigger guard, however, remain those of the smaller K-Frame.

The barrel, with a massive under-lug/ejector-rod shroud based on the Colt Python pattern, is another noteworthy feature of the L-Frame ·357 Smith & Wessons. The weight of this lug, together with the heavy barrel, helps dampen recoil and muzzle flip while allowing faster recovery during double-action shooting. The L-Frame barrel is shrink-fitted, thus eliminating the barrel pin found on other S&W revolvers and reducing labour costs. The top of the barrel and frame are longitudinally grooved and matt finished to reduce glare. The heavy-duty front sight contains a red insert, facilitating sighting, while the blackened fully-adjustable back sight is a standard S&W feature.

The cylinder — released in standard S&W manner — is more massive than those of the K-Frame guns, the additio-

nal wall thickness allowing a good margin of safety with all current ·357 Magnum loads. Unlike most earlier S&W ·357 Magnums, the cylinder is not counter-bored; with modern ammunition, however, there is very little chance of the head separating from the case. Smith & Wesson now seems to be eliminating counter-boring on all its magnum revolvers, a practice I consider unsatisfactory. Two very useful features of the Model 686 are its 'semi-target' hammer, wider than the service pattern but not as broad (or as cumbersome) as the target type, and the similar intermediate trigger. The 686's trigger is also smooth, much to my liking.

The back of the grip is grooved to prevent slipping in the hand. Although I find the K-Frame target stocks used on the L-Frame guns more comfortable than the N-Frame type, I still dislike them sufficiently to replace them with Pachmayr neoprene grips as soon as possible. The factory-fitted target stocks have sharp chequering common to most S&W types, and incorporate a speedloader cut-out to facilitate reloading. The chequering cuts into the shooter's hand if full-power loads are used.

Although all shooting with my 686 has been double action, I have dry-fired it to test the single-action trigger pull (which is light and smooth). The double-action pull is relatively heavy, but it is crisp and shows no tendency for the pull to increase immediately before let-off. This is a boon to fast double-action shooting. Although the test gun did not prove to be as accurate as some of the rival ·357s, its performance at 15 and 25 yards was still good. The diameter of double-action groups at 15 yards averaged 3-4in; and at 25 yards, it measured 3.5-5in. The Remington 125gn semi-jacketed hollow-point load performed especially well, giving groups of 2in or less at 15 yards.

The 686 handles exceptionally well, its massive barrel and under-lug making a notable difference in controllability. The gun points well and balances nicely in the hand, especially with the 4in barrel. Although the same basic gun is available in blued steel, as the Model 586 (or, with fixed sights, as the 581 and 681), I prefer the 686 for its corrosion-resistant properties.

The Model 686 is sufficiently hefty to be best suited to a suitable belt-holster, where the stainless steel will protect the exposed gun from the elements. Here, too, the adjustable sights will not interfere with a draw as they can from beneath a coat. One advantage of such sights is that — apart from aiding accuracy — they can be adjusted to a variety of different loads, the trajectories of which are rarely the same.

The Smith & Wesson Model 686 is at its best as a duty gun for uniformed police or for protecting the home. It is also ideal for rural areas, where a handgun is carried openly for defence or hunting. I would prefer a ·44 Magnum were I to encounter dangerous game; otherwise, the 686 is a good compromise for the outdoorsman.

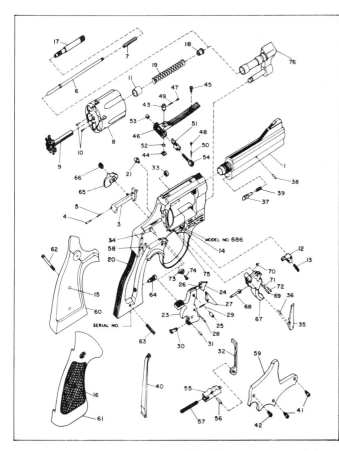

Key

#		#		#	
1	Barrel	27	Sear	52	R. S. Spring Clip
3	Bolt	28	Sear Pin	53	R. S. Windage Nut
4	Bolt Plunger	29	Sear Spring	54	R. S. Windage Screw
5	Bolt Plunger Spring	30	Stirrup	55	Rebound Slide
6	Center Pin	31	Stirrup Pin	56	Rebound Slide Pin
7	Center Pin Spring	32	Hammer Block	57	Rebound Slide Spring
8	Cylinder	33	Hammer Nose Bushing	58	Rebound Slide Stud
9	Extractor	34	Hammer Stud	59	Side Plate
10	Extractor Pin	35	Hand	60	Stock, Left
11	Gas Ring	36	Hand Pin	61	Stock, Right
12	Cylinder Stop	37	Locking Bolt	62	Stock Screw
13	Cylinder Stop Spring	38	Locking Bolt Pin	63	Stock Pin
14	Cylinder Stop Stud	39	Locking Bolt Spring	64	Strain Screw
15	Escutcheon	40	Mainspring	65	Thumbpiece
16	Escutcheon Nut	41	Plate Screw, Crowned Hd.	66	Thumbpiece Nut
17	Extractor Rod	42	Plate Screw, Flat Hd.	67	Trigger
18	Extractor Rod Collar	43	R. S. Elevation Nut	68	Trigger Lever
19	Extractor Spring	44	R. S. Elevation Stud	69	Trigger Lever Pin
20	Frame	45	R. S. Leaf Screw	70	Hand Torsion Spring
21	Frame Lug	46	R. S. Leaf	71	Hand Spring Pin
22	Front Sight Blade, Patridge,	47	R. S. Plunger	72	Hand Spring Torsion Pin
23	Hammer	48	R. S. Plunger	73	Trigger Stop
24	Hammer Nose	49	R. S. Plunger Spring	74	Trigger Stop Screw
25	Hammer Nose Rivet	50	R. S. Plunger Spring	75	Trigger Stud
26	Hammer Nose Spring	51	R. S. Slide	76	Yoke

The Model 686 has the cylinder and barrel of a heavy gun, yet retains the K-Frame and grip.

The 686 is very sturdily built, particularly at the juncture of the frame and barrel.

The cylinder of the S&W 686 is sturdier than those of the K-Frame magnums, such as the Model 19 or 66.

The most distinctive feature of the Smith & Wesson Model 686 is its massive barrel and underlug.

Massive barrel and heavyweight construction help to minimize recoil, even with full-power loads.

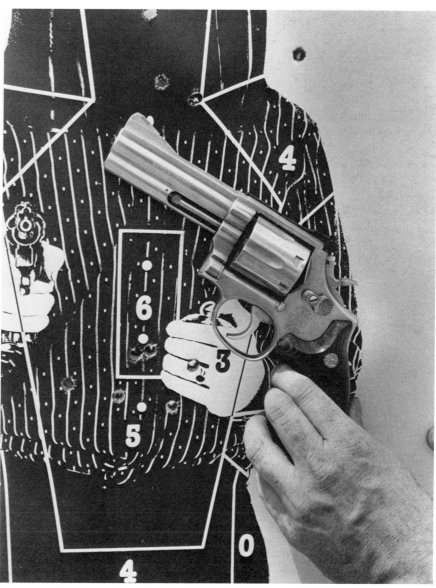

The accuracy of the Model 686; a 25 yard double-action group.

Steyr GB-80

Type: double-action semi-automatic pistol.
Maker: Steyr-Daimler-Puch AG, Steyr, Austria.
Calibre: 9mm Parabellum.
Overall length: 216mm, 8.50in.
Barrel length: 136mm, 5.35in.
Weight, empty: 960gm, 33.9oz.
Magazine capacity: 18+1.
Construction: steel (with some synthetic parts), fixed sights.

The GB is an interesting delayed blowback design, apparently dating from 1969-72. A few guns were distributed in the USA in the 1970s, as the 'Rogak P-18', but performance was so poor that the pistol was soon labelled the 'Jammatic'. Subsequently, Steyr-Daimler-Puch became involved and — after extensive modification — the much heralded, long-awaited GB-80 reappeared on the civilian market in 1982.

Delivered in a cardboard box with only a single magazine, the GB-80 is a big gun. Its action incorporates a delayed blowback, necessary to handle the high pressures generated by the 9mm Parabellum round. The system also embodies a fixed barrel, like the Heckler & Koch pistols, and should promote above average accuracy. The delay is obtained by a specially chambered muzzle bushing, into which gas bleeds through two ports drilled through the barrel into the bore. When the GB-80 is fired, a portion of the propellant gases vents through the ports into the chamber and prevents the slide recoiling until the residual pressure drops to a safe level. The gas chamber is locked to the inside of the slide by lugs. The slide does not begin to move until the bullet has left the barrel, after which it completes the classic cycle of extraction, ejection, cocking, chambering and locking.

The GB-80 offers a conventional double-action trigger system, which includes a de-cocking lever in which a spindle is interposed between the hammer and the firing pin to prevent accidental discharge when the hammer is dropped. The GB-80 de-cocking lever, automatically returned to its uppermost position by a spring, does not double as a safety catch.

Dismantling is straightforward. Once the magazine has been removed and the chamber checked, the dismantling lever (on the right side of the frame), is pushed downward. The muzzle bushing can then be rotated to the left and removed, and the recoil-spring and guide rod may be pulled off the front of the frame. The slide is then pulled backward, upward and off the frame.

The eighteen-shot magazine has the largest capacity of all modern pistol designs, apart from the rarely encountered Soviet APS (Stechkin) — though a 20-round auxiliary magazine can be acquired for the High-Power, or 'machine pistols' such as the Mini- and Micro-Uzi.

Despite the excellent reputation of Steyr's AUG and SSG rifles, the GB-80 was overlooked by an Austrian army preferring to take the Glock (q.v.). It seems strange that the product of a tiny independent company should be taken instead of one backed by a renowned manufacturer of well-proven military equipment. However, range tests suggest that the GB-80 is not a success. Its trigger travel is excessive and, though the pull-weights are acceptable (2.5kg/5.5lb and 6.3kg/13.9lb in single and double action respectively), the let-off point is surprisingly sudden and the gun exhibits a marked tendency to roll into the hand unless held very firmly. The test gun also appeared to shoot to the left, though a very firm two-hand grip was subsequently found to centre the shots effectively. Compared with the smooth shooting of the Glock, the handling of the GB-80 came as an unpleasant surprise.

During range tests, I encountered some puzzling problems. There were some feed failures — including one 'stove-piped' cartridge, which supposedly happens only with empty cases — and three misfires, each with the first double-action shot after exchanging magazines. All three cartridges fired with a second pull, suggesting that the factory-regulated striker blow was only marginally effectual.

Failures apart, the GB-80 proved to be very accurate indeed. However, the extensive advertising campaigns in Europe and the USA are, in my opinion, very misleading; the handling qualities of the big Steyr pistol not only negate its accuracy but also reduce its value as a combat weapon.

GB80 loaded and safe

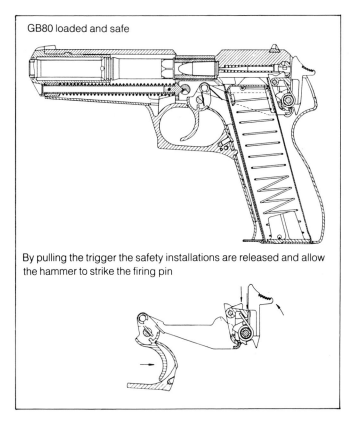

By pulling the trigger the safety installations are released and allow the hammer to strike the firing pin

Steyr GB80, reloading.

GB80 cocked, loaded and safe, trigger system on single action

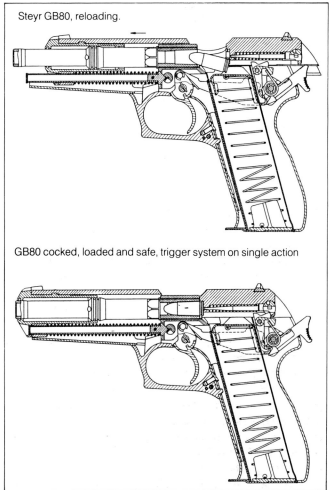

The right side of the bulky GB, with the hammer cocked.

(Above) The left side of the GB, in its cardboard box. Note that there is only one additional magazine.

(Above left) This view shows the enormous size of the Steyr pistol, the magazine capacity of eighteen rounds (plus another in the chamber) being the greatest found in a combat handgun.

If gripped carefully, the GB can be very accurate; however, it is not particularly pleasant to shoot.

Tokarev TT-33

Type: single-action semi-automatic pistol.
Maker: Tula Ordnance Factory, USSR, and others (see notes).
Calibre: 7.62x25mm.
Overall length: 185mm, 7.28in.
Barrel length: 115mm, 4.53in.
Weight, empty: 780gm, 27.5oz.
Magazine capacity: 8+1.
Construction: blued steel, fixed sights.

The Tokarev has been made in the USSR and many satellite countries, including Poland (FB-monogrammed grips), the People's Republic of China (Types 51 and 54), Hungary (Pisztoly 48M) and Yugolavia (M57). Modified guns have been made in North Korea, as the T68, and in Hungary ('Tokagypt') and Yugoslavia in 9mm Parabellum (M65 and M70). The 'Tokagypt' was made for the Egyptian army.

Until 1930, the Red Army was still equipped with the gas-seal revolver designed by the Belgian Nagant brothers and adopted in 1895. However, as the Mauser C/96 pistols were also common in Russia, the decision was taken to adopt an automatic pistol. The engineer Fedor Tokarev based his work on two existing guns — the M1911 US Army Colt Government Model, from which he took the locking system, and the older Mle 1903 FN-Browning that provided the general overall shape. The cartridge was a minor adaptation of the 7.63mm Mauser type. The Tokarev was initially disliked, and several important changes were made to the design. In fact, had not war intervened, it is probable that the Tokarev would have been replaced in the early 1940s. During the war, however, such large quantities of the gun were made — probably because tooling already existed —that production continued in the post-war period until the advent of the Makarov (q.v.).

The TT is rugged and surprisingly well balanced. It incorporates the Colt-Browning short-recoil action, with the barrel locked to the slide by two transverse ribs, and the characteristic link sharing the slide-stop spindle. The guns also feature a removable barrel bushing, a stirrup-type trigger, a short recoil-spring guide, and a Colt-type magazine. Several changes were made to simplify production, including entirely circumferential locking ribs and a strengthened muzzle bushing. The recoil-spring plug has been replaced by a simple disc, blocked by the base of the muzzle bushing, and a clever 'packaged' trigger unit facilitates dismantling.

This sub-group contains the hammer, the sear, the disconnector and the mainspring, and can simply be pulled out of the frame for maintenance. The tiny assembly, flawlessly made, has two prolongations serving as the cartridge guides and — in the case of the left bar — the ejector.

The principal novelty in the trigger system is the mainspring, which lies inside the hammer. When the hammer is cocked, compressing the spring, a pull on the trigger presses the stirrup to disconnect the sear spring from the hammer. The hammer then flies forward under the pressure of its own spring, strikes the firing pin running through the breechblock and fires the gun; recoil then causes the slide/barrel group, locked together, to run back until the actuating link pulls the breech downward, disengaging the locking lugs and allowing the slide to reciprocate alone.

The Tokarev is extremely easy to dismantle, being essentially similar to the Colt Government Model apart from the omission of the recoil spring and the locking of the slide stop with a simple spring-clip. This clip must be pulled backward to free the slide-stop pin. The grips are retained by a novel, if inconvenient rotary locking bar inside the butt.

Like many Soviet firearms (cf., PPSh submachine-gun), the Tokarev places a premium on simplicity, reliability and simple operation. It is a typical military weapon, not intended for modern combat shooting techniques, and its protruding bobbed hammer will invariably snag clothing during a concealed-carry draw. The simplification of its design is even carried to a point where there is no manual safety at all! The Tokarev must be carried with an empty chamber or with the hammer carefully lowered to half-cock on a loaded chamber, the latter being potentially dangerous and particularly ill-advised.

The magazine catch, like the slide stop, is crude but efficient; and the sights are not among the best, being too thin and too low. However, the Tokarev is easy to fire and very accurate. Though the 7.62mm Tokarev ammunition is rarely encountered in the West, the test gun fired Fiocchi-made 7.63mm Mauser cartridges flawlessly. The trigger pull on the test pistol measured just 3.1kg (6.8lb), its operation being good but unexceptional.

The Tokarev is a rough, reliable gun: one of the classics from the 'other side'. Among the best of the variants, however, are the Hungarian 48M, the Yugoslav M57 and the essentially similar 9mm Tokagypt.

205

The left side view shows the clean lines of the Tokarev, with a plain trigger . . . and no manual safety catch. The five-shot group is typical of this gun, which is easily handled.

The right side of the Tokarev displays the flat clip retaining the combined slide stop/dismantling pin. The protruding bobbed hammer has to be thumb-cocked on the draw.

Field-stripped, the Tokarev shows some interesting features, including the removable annular bushing — not cut or slotted, like most other Browning-type guns — and the tiny 'packaged' trigger mechanism. The locking lugs are milled entirely around the barrel to simplify production.

The sights of the Tokarev are far better than those of many classic military pistols, though too thin and a little low.

Uberti Inspector

Type: double-action revolver.
Maker: Aldo Uberti & C. SaS, Ponte Zanano (Brescia), Italy.
Calibre: ·38 Special (·32 S&W Long also available).
Overall length, barrel length and unladen weight: see notes
Cylinder capacity: 6.
Construction: see notes.

The Inspector can be obtained with barrels measuring 55, 65, 75, 100 and 150mm (2.2-5.9in). The sights are generally fixed, though a ventilated rib and adjustable back-sight can be obtained on 'Inspector Target' guns fitted with 100 or 150mm barrels. The finish is blue or matt chrome.

Two basic models of this revolver were tested, one with a 75mm barrel and fixed sights and the other with the optional 100mm ventilated-rib barrel and adjustable back sight. Both guns resemble Colts (the Agent and Diamond-back respectively), which is probably hardly surprising: Uberti is well known as a manufacturer of replica revolvers, including black-powder Colts, as well as many of the parts for the 'Mauser' and 'Trident' revolvers marketed by Ranato Gamba. The cylinder latch, trigger system, clockwise-rotating cylinder, floating firing pin, off-set locking-bolt notches and removable side-plate are all very typically Colt. The 75mm-barrelled Inspector can be considered as a typical 'back up' gun, weighing just 700gm (24.7oz), easily concealed and chambering a typical dual-purpose service/defence cartridge. The ·38 Special does not offer particularly good stopping power, except with soft- or hollow-point bullets — or the very special proprietary cartridges favoured by police in Europe and the USA alike. The '+P' loads are not recommended for regular use in the lightweight Uberti frame, though the few used in testing caused no problems other than accelerated heating.

The short-barrel Inspector is easy to handle, its wide trigger allowing an excellent opportunity to maintain the trigger-finger position in single- or double-action mode. Both pulls were acceptably light (1.5kg/3.3lb and about 4kg/8.8lb respectively) and extremely smooth. By comparison, the action of the 100mm-barrelled gun was disappointing, with an inferior single-action travel and a heavy double action with appreciable backlash. It is probable that the action of Uberti revolvers varies from gun to gun, though the attention of a gunsmith is usually enough to restore smoothness.

The manufacturing quality and finish of both guns — internally and externally — were good. The hammer has a long, wide spur and is easily cocked, but may snag clothing during a concealed draw.

The sights on the 'police' model are excellent, and the front sight, mounted on its lengthy ramp, comes rapidly into the notch of the back sight. Combined with the unusually good double-action pull on the trial gun, the sights promoted impressive accuracy at distances between 3 and 15 metres. Results at 25 metres were also praise-worthy, though the point of impact was a little low.

Field-stripping the Inspector is not particularly easy, as access to the mechanism is only possible after first the cylinder latch and then the side-plate have been removed. The Smith & Wesson system, rather than one based on Colt's, would have made life far easier.

The competitively priced Inspector is particularly suited to firers with small hands and, as ·38 Special generally has little recoil, the revolver is recommended for women, inexperienced marksmen and 'off duty' police use. The accuracy of the 'Inspector Target' test gun proved to be disappointing, the advantages of its adjustable back sight being negated by the poor trigger pull. On the basis of my experience on the range, I can only suggest that the purchaser tries the Uberti trigger before buying a gun.

The short-barrelled Uberti revolver shows its obvious Colt inspiration. Mounting the cylinder latch on the removable side-plate is an interesting, if unsatisfactory departure from normal practice.

The 4in-barrelled 'Inspector Target' proved to be a disappointment on the range. (Courtesy of John Walter.)

The Inspector, atop its cardboard box.

Short-barrelled Uberti Inspectors are not only very handsome, but also easy to shoot.

Walther PPK

Type: double-action semi-automatic pistol.
Maker: Carl Walther GmbH, Ulm/Donau, West Germany.
Calibre: 7.65mm Auto (·32 ACP) and 9mm Short (·380 ACP).
Overall length: 155mm, 6.10in.
Barrel length: 83mm, 3.27in.
Weight, empty: 560gm, 19.8oz.
Magazine capacity: 7+1.
Construction: blued steel, fixed sights.

The Walther PP/PPK series has been made in many differing guises. The basic PP (8-shot magazine) and the smaller PPK (7 shots) were made prior to 1945 by Waffenfabrik Walther of Zella-Mehlis. Production was licensed to Manurhin of Mulhouse-Bourtzwiller, France, in 1955, though many of the guns were shipped back to the new Walther factory in Ulm, marked and proved in Germany. Production began again in Germany in the 1970s. The PPK/S — a PPK with a PP slide — was made for the US market, the dimensions of the standard PPK failing to meet the US Gun Control Act of 1968. The PPK/S has been made by Manurhin and, under licence, for Interarms. A ·22 LR rimfire variant of the PP/PPK has also been made, along with a 'PP Super' chambering the more powerful 9mm Police cartridge.

The original Polizei-Pistole ('PP') was patented in Germany in 1929, production beginning in 1930. Rapid commercial success encouraged the introduction of a similar, but smaller gun intended for undercover work. Not only did the success of the Walthers inspire a legion of rivals, such as the Mauser HSc and the Sauer 38H, but many hundreds of thousands were made for the commercial, paramilitary and military markets prior to the end of the Second World War.

Being robust, reliable and concealable, offering many technical innovations when it was introduced, the PP/PPK series was highly prized as a war souvenir and rightly regarded as a landmark in the history of automatic pistol design. After postwar production had been licensed to Manurhin, Walther being prevented from making handguns in Germany until 1956/7, the little pistols once again established themselves in personal-defence roles. The 'use' of a PPK by the fictional British MI6 agent, James Bond, contributed greatly to its popularity.

The PPK has been included as a representative of the numerous double action personal-defence pistols made by many companies, sometimes in calibres as small as ·22 LR. The test gun was a new Ulm-made 9mm Short PPK, the principal differences from the basic PP being the smaller grip, frame and slide, and one less cartridge in the standard magazine (the PP magazine can be used, but it protrudes below the butt).

The PPK is a blowback, with a double-action trigger system and a distinctive dismantling procedure based on a pivoting trigger guard. One of the most original features is the de-cocking/safety mechanism, which inspired many copies; the spindle of the de-cocking lever simultaneously disconnects the hammer from the sear and blocks the firing pin as the hammer descends. The de-cocking lever is not spring-loaded, and can act as a safety catch until reset manually. There is also a firing-pin safety in the form of a small block, which is only raised when the trigger is pulled. In single-action mode, movement of the trigger simply pivots the sear by way of the trigger bar, releasing the hammer; in double action, however, the pivoting sear rotates, releases and then rises past the hammer.

There is no external slide-stop (or 'hold-open') lever, the internal combination ejector/stop unit, raised by the magazine follower, retaining the slide after the last round has been fired and ejected. The only way to release the slide is to retract it slightly, allowing a spring to lower the ejector/stop into the frame-well. In common with most fixed barrel pistols, particularly those chambering low-powered ammunition, the Walther PPK is surprisingly accurate. The travel and pull-weight (2.5kg, 5.5lb) in single-action mode were very good on the test gun, though the double action was heavy (7.2kg, 15.9lb) and somewhat imprecise.

The sights are tiny, if easily located, but the PPK is not intended for long-distance shooting. I experienced problems firing at metal plates placed 15-20 metres away, as I could not distinguish the sight picture against the dark background; otherwise, the little PPK gave good groups. Easily concealed, pleasant to carry and nice to fire, the PP/PPK series can still provide a good 'back up' when used in conjunction with hollow-point loads.

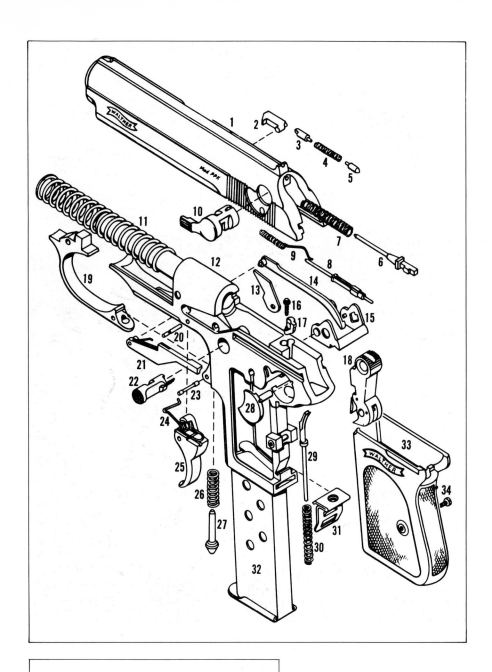

Key

1 Slide
2 Extractor
3 Extractor Plunger
4 Extractor Spring
5 Safety Catch Plunger
6 Firing Pin
7 Firing Pin Spring
8 Cartridge Indicator
9 Indicator Spring
10 Safety Catch
11 Recoil Spring
12 Frame and Barrel
13 Hammer Release
14 Trigger Bar
15 Cocking Piece
16 Hammer Block Plunger and
   Spring
17 Hammer Block

18 Hammer
19 Trigger Guard
20 Trigger Pin
21 Ejector and Spring
22 Magazine Catch
23 Trigger Guard Pin
24 Trigger Spring
25 Trigger
26 Trigger Guard Spring
27 Trigger Guard Plunger
28 Hammer Pin
29 Hammer Strut
30 Hammer Spring
31 Lanyard Loop/Mainspring
   Retaining Bar
32 Magazine
33 Grip
34 Grip Screw

The left side of the PPK shows the combination safety catch/de-cocking lever on the slide. The seven-shot group was made at 12m.

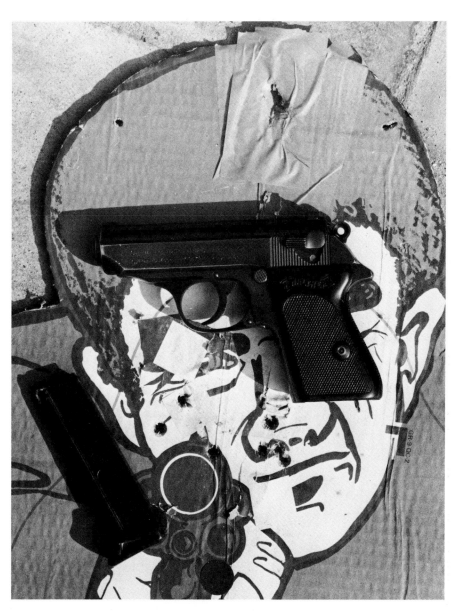

The dismantling method pioneered by the Walther PP has been copied by numerous other guns, including the Soviet Makarov. The slide can be removed after the trigger guard is pulled downward.

The Walther PPK, field-stripped. Note the fixed barrel and annular recoil spring, typical of most blow-backs.

The PPK with its grip removed to show the parts of the trigger mechanism and the construction of the frame. The magazine has been provided by a larger PP, containing one more round than the PPK pattern, but will fit provided the firer accepts that it will protrude beneath the butt.

Walther P5

Type: double-action semi-automatic pistol.
Maker: Carl Walther GmbH, Ulm/Donau, West Germany.
Calibre: 9mm Parabellum (see note).
Overall length: 180mm, 7.09in.
Barrel length: 90mm, 3.54in.
Weight, empty: 900gm, 31.8oz.
Magazine capacity: 8+1.
Construction: blued steel slide with an alloy frame, partly adjustable sights.

Variants of the P5 have been proposed in ·22 LR rimfire, 7.65mm Auto (·32 ACP), 7.65mm Parabellum, 9mm Short (·380 ACP) and 9mm Police/9mm Ultra.

The P5 was developed for the German police trials of 1975, in which it competed with the Heckler & Koch PSP (P7) and the SIG-Sauer P225 (P6).

Walther was the first manufacturer to perfect a double-action trigger system robust enough for military service, the P.38 being adopted by the German army in 1940 and re-adopted by the Bundeswehr in 1957. Postwar production then began again in the new Ulm/Donau factory, the gun being renamed 'Pistole 1' in 1963. Thus, it is not surprising that Walther should simply have based the P5 on the P1 — particularly as two short variants, the P38K and the P4, had appeared before work on the police gun commenced.

Many of the P5 components are shared with the P1, though the two guns are radically different externally. The locking system, the twin recoil springs, the general design of the frame, the magazine catch, the enveloping slide and the magazine are all common to both guns, and the Walther engineers even went so far as to place the ejection port on the left of the gun (a most unusual position) simply to retain the ejecting rod of the P38/P1 on the right!

The P5 is much more compact than its predecessor, with vastly improved sights and a superior glare-suppressing band atop the slide. The trigger guard has been extended, allowing the Walther to be fired with a gloved finger, and some cosmetic improvements are also evident in the slide/frame construction.

The P5 incorporates the traditional Walther short-recoil system, movement of the slide/barrel lock being controlled by a floating actuator striking the standing frame during the initial recoil movement. This highly efficient unit has been copied by Beretta, and is described more fully in the section devoted to the Beretta 92SB. One advantage is the linear barrel movement, promoting better than average accuracy.

The P5 exhibits several interesting features, including the combined slide stop/de-cocking lever, and the unusual firing-pin safety. This consists of a tipping firing pin and a transverse locking bar; when the trigger is pulled, an actuator simultaneously raises the firing pin into the path of the hammer (in the 'down' position, the firing-pin head lies opposite a recess in the hammer body) and disconnects the

locking bar. After the last round has been fired and ejected, the magazine follower holds the P5 slide open. Pressing the de-cocking lever initially allows the slide to run forward, chambering a fresh cartridge, without releasing the hammer; a second push is then needed to operate the de-cocking system by breaking the contact between hammer and sear. The safety is absolute, as the firing pin remains in its lower position where it cannot be struck should the safety notch on the sear fail to intercept the hammer.

Having no manual safety, the P5 cannot be carried safely with a cartridge chambered and the hammer cocked. In common with virtually all modern automatic pistols, a disconnector ensures that the gun cannot fire until the slide is securely locked to the barrel. The P5 is easily field stripped. Once the magazine has been removed and the chamber checked, the slide is pulled back to allow the dismantling latch to be turned down, the slide is removed, the barrel-lock pressed and the barrel released from the slide. The handling qualities of the P5 are greatly appreciated by German and Dutch police units, though there are some problems. The magazine catch lies under the butt, preventing fast reloading as both hands are required to release the magazine. In addition, the magazine falls inevitably into the weak hand, making immediate presentation of a new magazine difficult unless well practised. Additionally, the voluminous grip makes releasing the slide difficult while maintaining aim — particularly unfortunate, as the 'double action' slide-stop/de-cocking lever is easy to use, and much more convenient than other modern designs. The slide stop cannot be inserted in the slide notch externally, being actuated solely by the (internal) magazine follower — preventing the firer rectifying double feeding by locking the slide back before removing the magazine. Though double-feeds are rare with factory-loaded 9mm Parabellum ammunition, the problem, if it arises, could be fatal for the firer.

The Walther P5 can only be carried in a few appropriate holsters, owing to its shape and the extended trigger guard. The draw is easy; the handling characteristics are generally good, if unexceptional. The front sight has an obtrusive white dot, placed too far down the blade and contributing to a tendency to shoot high in rapid fire.

The sample gun had a trigger pull of 6.1kg (13.5lb), with a long regular travel, and virtually no backlash as let-off occurs just as the trigger stops against the back of the trigger guard. The single-action pull is a short, sharp 2kg (4.4lb). The gun is pleasant to shoot. However, I feel that the P5 is an obsolescent design, with too limited a magazine capacity and a badly placed magazine catch. Walther may concur, developing the new P88 to supplement the P5 until such time as the comparative sales potential of the two can be assessed. The P88 is a new ambidexterous pistol, with a fifteen-round magazine, but favours the Browning-type cam-finger actuated lock rather than the traditional Walther system. Whether this will prove as effectual as the latter remains to be seen, but it is undeniably easier to make.

This group — the nine shots to the left of the gun — was obtained with the P5 from 15m. In adverse light, the 'improved' sights point low.

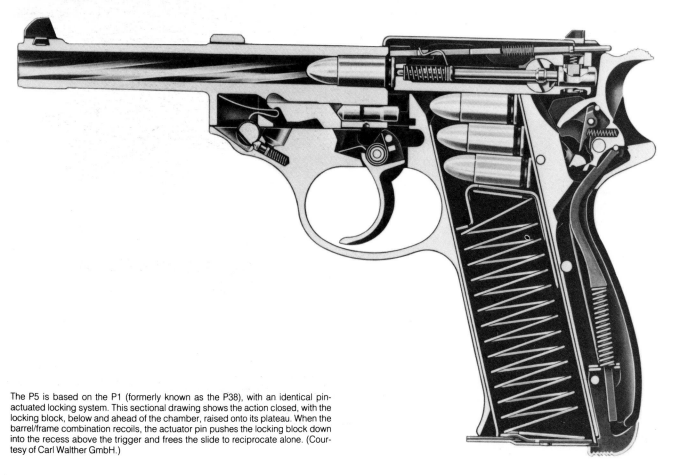

The P5 is based on the P1 (formerly known as the P38), with an identical pin-actuated locking system. This sectional drawing shows the action closed, with the locking block, below and ahead of the chamber, raised onto its plateau. When the barrel/frame combination recoils, the actuator pin pushes the locking block down into the recess above the trigger and frees the slide to reciprocate alone. (Courtesy of Carl Walther GmbH.)

A comparison of the P5 and the P1, showing the differences in size and the absence of an ejection port on the right side of the P5 slide. The magazines are interchangeable.

(Right) The slide-tops of the P1 (top) and P5 (bottom).

(Bottom right) The P5 barrel, although much shorter than the P1's, gives excellent accuracy. Note the slight differences in the locking blocks, and the absence of a front sight on the newer gun (its sight being carried on the slide).

(Below) The P5 balances well, but I rarely use the extended trigger guard to facilitate a two-hand grip.

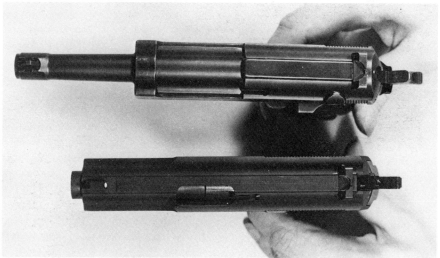

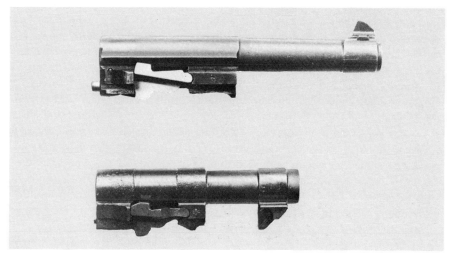

217

Dan Wesson Model 15

Type: double-action revolver.
Maker: Dan Wesson Company, Monson, Massachusetts, USA.
Calibre: ·357 Magnum.
Overall length: 305mm, 12.0in.
Barrel length: 152mm, 6.0in.
Weight, empty: 1,245gm, 44oz.
Cylinder capacity: 6.
Construction: blued steel, adjustable sights.

The Dan Wesson ·357 Magnum has two primary re-commendations as a combat handgun: it is versatile and accurate. Its versatility comes from the rapidly exchange-able barrels, adjusting length from 2in to 8.5in or more. For combat use, 2in, 3in and 6in barrels are really the only practicable choices. Grips can also be interchanged to con-vert the Dan Wesson from a round-butt combat stock to a square-butt target pattern.

The barrel and its shroud are removed with a special tool, and simply replaced with the length desired. A feeler gauge ensures the proper cylinder/barrel gap. It is normally necessary to re-sight the gun after changing barrels, since each barrel will have a different point of impact. However, experience usually teaches the firer where each of his barrels will shoot and he can often adjust the sights almost automa-tically.

The quality of Dan Wesson revolvers is normally quite high, and the guns have a good solid feel. Their lines are clean, with little clutter, and the 'light switch' cylinder release lies on the yoke in front of the cylinder rather than in the more traditional position on the rear of the frame. The Dan Wesson system seems to lock the cylinder securely, though rapid reloading takes some practice. Once mastered, the Dan Wesson can be loaded about as quickly as its rear-latching rivals. I can probably reload Smith & Wesson revolvers more quickly than others, but this is doubtless a personal preference. The Dan Wesson cylinder is heavy enough to handle ·357 Magnum loads without problems. Extraction is smooth and efficient. The ejector rod is housed in a full Colt Python-type under-barrel lug, though, unlike the Python's, the Wesson type is squared off. This lug puts substantial weight under the barrel, where it helps to dampen recoil and hold the sights on target. The rib along the barrel provides another superficial similarity to the Python.

Concealability naturally depends on which of the barrels is fitted, though I do not feel that the 15-2 (2in barrel) is as good a concealed-carry gun as the Smith & Wesson Models 13, 19, 65 and 66 with 2in barrels. The 15-2 is bulky, even with the shortest barrel in place. I would choose the 4in or 6in versions carried in an open holster.

The 15-2 sights are quite good, with a red insert in the front ramp and a click-adjustable square back-sight notch

wide enough to facilitate reasonably rapid target acquisi-tion. A small Allen key is needed to adjust the back sight, one being incorporated in the barrel-changing tool. The sight radius with the 6in barrel is, of course, appreciably better than the short-barrelled options.

The semi-target type hammer is easily cocked with the thumb, though I am more interested in the gun's double action performance. The trigger is also a semi-target pat-tern, but is smooth rather than ribbed. Internal safeties include a transfer bar and a rebounding frame-mounted firing pin. This combination prevents the Dan Wesson firing unless the trigger is pulled. The trigger pull on the test gun was smooth and crisp, an adjustable Allen screw behind the trigger acting as a stop to minimize backlash.

The interchangeable grips allow the firer to choose his favourite for specific applications. Since the Dan Wesson revolvers have a central post projecting below the frame (thus omitting a conventional backstrap) an unusually com-prehensive selection of grips is available. I find the smooth walnut grips supplied with the sample gun very comfortable indeed. Recoil is virtually imperceptible with them, and they proved ideal during rapid double-action shooting. I find that the target grips supplied with Colt or Smith & Wesson revolvers fit my hand very poorly, yet those on the Dan Wesson are much better.

The bright blue finish on the Model 15 is very attractive, though a stainless steel ·357 Magnum is also made for those seeking corrosion resistance.

I have had far less experience shooting Dan Wessons than the products of the other major US revolver manufacturers and, as a result, I am always amazed at their accuracy. The test gun was no exception; at 15 yards, double-action group diameters of 2.5in were not uncommon, while some 25 yard groups ran as tight as 3in (though the average was nearer 3.5-4in). The 6in barrel and underlug helped keep muzzle flip to a minimum, and recovery time in two- or three-shot 'bursts' was very good. The most accurate load proved to be the 158gn Federal jacketed soft-point, though 125gn CCI-Speer jacketed soft-point, 110gn Federal and 158gn CCI-Speer jacketed hollow-points all performed adequately.

The Dan Wesson Model 15 is a very accurate and versa-tile weapon, though it is somewhat bulky to be concealed. However, with the 2in or 4in barrel, it could be covertly carried in suitable circumstances. For normal police duties – or home defence – the 4in barrel is probably the best. The 6in barrel on the test gun certainly aided accuracy, but would undoubtedly slow the draw. Another point to re-member about long barrels is that they may be used as a lever by an assailant attempting to disarm the shooter.

The Dan Wesson's accuracy makes it popular with sil-houette shooters and handgun hunters alike, for some of whom it doubles as a defence weapon. The Dan Wesson is at its best in areas where restrictive legislation prevents owning several differing guns. A Model 15 owner, in effect, already owns several guns in a single package.

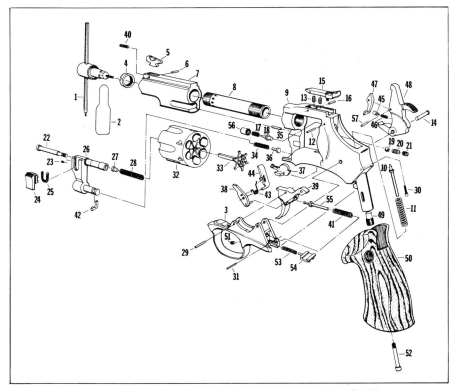

This shows a short-barrelled version of the Dan Wesson Model 44 revolver. Dan Wesson produce or have produced a model 11, 12, 14 & 15 (.357 Magnum only) , a Model 8/9 (.38 Special), a Model 22 (.22 LR or .22 Magnum), a Model 41 (.41 Magnum) and a Model 44 (.44 Magnum).

The Dan Wesson is a handsome gun, with good lines.

The heavy ribbed barrel and smooth combat grips are noteworthy in this view of the Model 15.

This not only shows the heavy barrel shroud of the Dan Wesson revolver, but also the nut securing the interchangeable barrels.

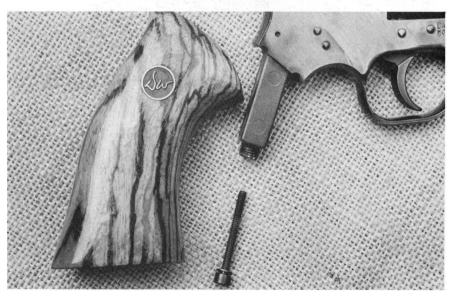

Dan Wesson's efficient bar-type attachment allows grips to be selected for individual tasks.

A long barrel and moderately heavy frame help damp the recoil of the Dan Wesson Model 15, even with full-power ·357 Magnum loads.

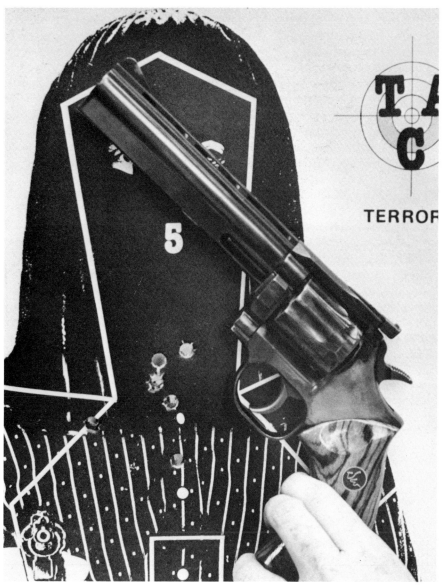

The Dan Wesson revolver displayed excellent accuracy, as this 25 yard double-action group illustrates.

Appendix One
A personal choice

RENE SMEETS

My personal gun was selected some years ago, when the choice was not as vast as it is today, and no-one likes to put a tried and tested possession aside. When I chose my gun, many of the newest designs were experiencing teething troubles, some had magazines that were too small (such as the Heckler & Koch PSP), the spares for others were difficult to obtain, and guns such as the Beretta 92SB, Glock or Star M30 did not exist.

Being a civilian, I had a completely free choice; I simply had to remember lessons given by the great combat hand-gunners and martial arts instructors of the time, and that my gun would be carried concealed under normal clothes. A slide holster on the strong hip, a shoulder holster or a cross-draw were all possibilities.

I immediately rejected the revolver, owing to its numerous restrictions − not least of which is the unnatural angle of the grip compared with most automatic pistols and the bulk of the cylinder. I did not select a double-action automatic, as I was convinced by Jeff Cooper's arguments and no regulations forced me to carry a gun with the hammer down on an empty chamber. I am convinced that if you have to draw, you must be able to fire as quickly as possible and that this is best achieved by proper training. Finally, I felt I was restricted to just two guns: the Colt Government Model and the FN-Browning High-Power, both universally battle tested and known for their reliability.

Finally, I rejected the ·45 ACP, which was too large and restricted magazine capacity too greatly − though the Colt is certainly as reliable as the High-Power and, in fact, more robust. I know that police statistics indicate that 90 per cent of all actions involve fewer than three shots, and that if I have to defend myself, it seems, it will be in or near my car against two or three aggressors. However, the '7+1' of the Colt seemed too small; why risk being caught with an empty gun, or without a spare magazine, when I could have 13+1? I regarded 9mm Parabellum as the most versatile combat cartridge, offering good stopping power, excellent penetration with full metal-jacket bullets, and an ability to pass through light 'armour' such as car doors and many supposedly bullet-proof vests. Though it was once true that the choice of 9mm Parabellum bullets was restricted, this is no longer so: soft- and hollow-points, super-penetrators and greatly improved short-range man-stoppers are all readily obtainable.

Few guns are perfect combat tools straight from the box, apart, perhaps, from the Heckler & Koch P7M13 (it is dangerous to attempt to improve its trigger pull) and the Glock 17. Though I am not a fan of extensive customization − particularly those 'Christmas Tree' compensators favoured by top IPSC competitors − I was still keen to transform my High-Power into a properly combat-worthy gun.

As the sights on the standard military version were totally unacceptable, I selected the Sport Model with a massive high front sight blade and an adjustable back sight. After removing the superfluous magazine safety, I asked a gunsmith to substitute a fixed back sight and reduce the height of the front-sight blade until I had an 'aim point − hit point' system. The safety lever on the High-Power is uncomfortably short; not only can the thumb be injured while attempting rapid manipulation, but it is easy to miss the safety completely...with potentially fatal results. My favourite pistolsmith made a superb new safety, with a greatly extended thumbpiece, but fitting it required re-cutting the upper part of the grip. The bevelling of the magazine well is not important on the High Power, but the thinness of the walls is not conducive to alteration without unnecessarily complicated gunsmithing.

Trigger improvements can be done in two ways. It is easy to refine the contact surfaces between the sear and the hammer (a speciality of the German company, Peters Stahl) though this can cause problems if the hardness of the contact surfaces is unwittingly destroyed; if the edge of either part breaks away, the gun will fire fully automatically. I preferred the alternative, undeniably more complicated solution in which the spindle of the sear lever is moved a short distance backward and a new sear made with a longer forward projection. This has the mechanical advantage that a weaker trigger-pull — 1.2 kg (2.6lb) on my gun — is permissible without compromising safety. Unfortunately, the High Power trigger system promotes considerable backlash (or over-travel) after the sear has released the hammer. As a result, an efficient stop-screw was placed ahead of the trigger, taking care to ensure that the trigger was blocked shortly after release rather than before it.

Externally, my gun looks much like the factory version, but the comparatively minor modifications make an enormous difference to its shooting qualities. Since finishing the customization, I have fired an average of a hundred rounds through it per week and participated in many IPSC or police shooting competitions. The barrel has been replaced once, the sear twice, and the hammer once, while the slide re-cently fractured. The frame is still original, however, and the life of the other parts was materially extended by the modifications.

The High Power is certainly not an easy gun to master, many shooters finding the Colt Government Model easier to use, but I have never found a gun as suited to my hand and my shooting techniques (right or wrong!). And if you remember that, with some minor changes, you can use cheaper sixteen-shot Beretta magazines with the HP, there seems little reason to hesitate over buying the FN-Browning. With a little care, and careful choice, it is possible to carry the High Power in a belt-, waistband- or shoulder-holster.

The gun is fast, accurate, reliable and a perfect embodiment of the adage that '99 per cent of guns are better than the man behind them'.

Index

3 1191 00288 9624

DOWNERS GROVE PUBLIC LIBRARY

DOWNERS GROVE PUBLIC LIBRARY